WOMEN BEHIND BARS

The Crisis of Women in the U.S. Prison System

D0950400

Silja J.A. Talvi

SEAL PRESS

This book is dedicated to all the girls and
women who never made it out.

Women Behind Bars
The Crisis of Women in the U.S. Prison System

Copyright © 2007 Silja J.A. Talvi

Published by Seal Press
A Member of the Perseus Books Group
1400 65th Street, Suite 250
Emeryville, CA 94608

ISBN-13: 978-1-58005-195-8
ISBN-10: 1-58005-195-2

Library of Congress Cataloging-in-Publication Data has been applied for.

Cover and Interior design by Tabitha Lahr
Printed in the U.S.A.

Contents

Preface

This book about female incarceration has been a genuine labor of love for me, one that required a deep level of immersion and investigation into the often surreal and bleak realities of life behind bars for girls and women.

My intent with this book is to bring incarcerated women's voices to the fore, to let their stories communicate their own experiences, traumas, struggles, and triumphs. Interviews with people close to or regularly in contact with female prisoners were also of importance to me, ranging from prison reform advocates to wardens, prison social workers, and correctional officers.

Consequently, this is a book that relies less on the perspectives of "experts" and academics in the fields of criminology and sociology than many other previous books regarding female incarceration, the authors of which have tended to focus their interviews in one women's prison or jail, or have written their work without visiting any kind of detention facility. This does not mean that I am unfamiliar with or disrespectful of academic theories and writings—on the contrary, I study and learn from them on a regular basis—but simply that I did not want to produce yet another book that relies primarily on the writings and studies of inhabitants of the "free world," as prisoners put it. Where appropriate, I do weave in expert findings and insights, but it is absolutely my contention that there are no individuals more insightful and informed about the realities of female incarceration than prisoners themselves.

My in-person and phone interviews with roughly one hundred incarcerated girls and women spanned two years, during which time I also received letters from approximately three hundred women behind bars. In addition, I interviewed more than a dozen women who had been released from jail or prison.

Of these women who responded to me by letter, I stayed in regular contact with fifty women locked up in state and federal prisons in Arizona, California, Colorado, Delaware, Florida, Georgia, Kentucky, Louisiana, Michigan, New Jersey, New Mexico, Oklahoma, Tennessee, Texas, Virginia, Washington, and Wisconsin. Phone interviews were also part of the process, although most women were understandably reluctant to reveal critical details in this manner, because all prisoner phone calls are subject to unannounced monitoring and recording.

For my research, I was granted permission to visit and tour the women's section of the nation's biggest federal prison complex, in Coleman, Florida, as well as the two prisons that constitute the world's largest women's prison complex, in Chowchilla, California. In addition, I visited the women's county jails in Los Angeles and San Francisco, as well as the Seattle/King County detention facility for juveniles. Other in-person prison visits included the Corrections Corporation of America–owned and –operated women's prison in Grants, New Mexico; the Perryville women's complex in Arizona; and the Washington Corrections Center for Women. I attended a two-day conference on prison issues, held at the New School for Social Research in New York; a juvenile detention conference in Bellevue, Washington; an American Correctional Association conference in Phoenix, Arizona; the last of four hearings of the Commission on Safety and Abuse in America's Prisons at Loyola Marymount University in Los Angeles; an in-person interview with Marc Mauer, executive director of The Sentencing Project in Washington, D.C., as part of a *SourceCode* documentary on the privatization of prisons; and a gender-responsive strategy meeting put on by the California Department of Corrections and Rehabilitation in Fresno. I also spent a fair amount of time talking with and learning from low-income women on Seattle streets who were willing to talk about their encounters with law enforcement and incarceration, as well as having conversations with several women participating in a unique transitional housing program, A New Way of Life, in Watts, California.

Nationally, only one prison denied me access, citing unspecified "security" concerns: the federal women's prison in Dublin, California. Whether intentionally or unintentionally, the Tennessee Department of Corrections also thwarted my effort to interview women in a Memphis women's prison by not granting me security clearance, despite having advance notice of my announced and scheduled trip.

Internationally, I was gratified to be able to visit three women's prisons, including the European Union's biggest women's prison, Holloway, in London, England; the sole female prison in Hämeenlinna, Finland; and a provincial Canadian prison in British Columbia.

It is my hope that, by providing stories from a wide variety of settings and women's personal backgrounds, you, the reader, can gain a deeper understanding of why the plight of female prisoners should be a matter of serious and urgent concern for our society as a whole. As it now stands, most of these women rightly feel as though they are a nearly invisible group that has been dehumanized, forgotten, and locked away from the public eye, and whose identities have simply been reduced to the nature of their offenses and the prison numbers they have been assigned.

Introduction: The Invisible Struggle

"This place just teaches us to be better criminals. It's like a criminal-training school."
—A fourteen-year-old girl in Seattle's King County Juvenile Detention Center,
incarcerated for the second time in her life.

These were the words of a shy, observant young girl who had been silent for the majority of the time I had been conducting a learning workshop at the aforementioned juvenile detention center. Although I made it clear to the girls that I was there to write about aspects of their lives, I also made it clear that I was there to learn from them, and that I was willing to share aspects of my own life if they cared to ask about them.

Building trust in adolescents requires a different approach. Simply walking into a room and asking for answers to a list of questions just doesn't work. In truth, it rarely works to elicit real responses from grown folks, but with preteens and teens, it's particularly important to let the process be a two-way street.

This was the first time in my presence that any of these girls had simply come out and said it, exactly like that: For them, juvenile detention was a criminal-training school. After she uttered these words, many of the other girls in the room nodded in silent agreement.

What had begun as a fierce facade of toughness in that cold, concrete "pod" housing unit in juvenile detention when I walked in a half-hour earlier had transformed into an emotionally raw environment of utterly vulnerable honesty. One girl soon revealed that she was pregnant, and hadn't found out until she was locked up. Another revealed that she couldn't wait to go back to "slinging" (dealing drugs) so as to finally be able to support her family again. Another girl spoke of just how ugly and undesirable she felt being locked up, having to exist in a six-by-eight-foot cell with a thin mattress. The girls made do with low-quality menstrual pads and wore drab, unisex clothing. They ate unhealthy institutional food and were not allowed to wear any makeup, get their hair done, or even shave their legs.

With the exception of one girl I met during an ensuing visit to the King County juvenile detention center, not a single other one of these girls ever said that she had learned anything truly healthy or worthwhile that would help her move toward a better future as a result of being incarcerated.

The sole exception was a seventeen-year-old girl who had already been locked up, starting at age eleven, no less than twenty times. In this institution, she was a "regular"—absolutely everyone knew her name, and this had become a perverse matter of pride for her.

Juvenile detention had already become this young girl's primary home. She talked openly about "belonging" to this environment, of looking down on girls who cried or expressed themselves emotionally while there, and of her strength in being able to take it "like a man."

"If you can't, you don't belong here," she said, jutting out her chin and puffing out her chest.

Many of the girls shifted uncomfortably in their seats, but no one said a word.

I gave her the moment and let her enjoy her sense of superiority over the other girls in the group. And then I started to ask her the kinds of questions that her case workers seemed to not have bothered with before.

"Are you actually learning anything good from being in here?"

"No."

"Do you have any future plans?

"No."

"Are you sure this place was the best way for you to get help for your family issues?"

"No."

"Are you so comfortable here that you would rather be here than in the real world?

"Right now, yes," she responded honestly.

"Do you know what the word 'institutionalized' means?" I asked.

There was an awkward pause.

This wasn't the kind of role I usually assumed in interviewing prisoners. But there was something about her comfort level with her predicament—something about what she had been taught about her place in the world, and about why she had ended up in a place like this—that actually bothered me. No one wanted to be straightforward with her about the idea that feeling acclimated to juvenile detention wasn't necessarily the best thing for her future.

I briefly explained what "institutionalized" meant. I didn't talk down to her; I just explained that people can get so comfortable in institutions like detention centers and jails that these places begin to be the only ones where these people feel they can live. And that it can be hard to move on from that comfort level to the challenges of the "free world."

She lowered her defiant gaze.

"Yeah, I guess, I guess . . . that's what I am," she finally said.

Another pause.

"Maybe it's not so great," she muttered.

It seems highly unlikely—although far from impossible—that this girl will actually have a real, fighting chance at making a healthy transition into civilian life when she turns eighteen. In fact, given the amount of time she's already spent cycling through the juvenile detention system, it is very likely that she will end up in jail or prison very soon. The "comfort" of which she speaks has now become an ingrained pattern in her life. There is a very real part of her that feels more comfortable in a highly structured, restrictive prison environment than in what may feel to her like a far less predictable and more dangerous "real world."

Regrettably, female incarceration—including repeated periods of incarceration, known in criminal justice jargon as "recidivism"—is a more common phenomenon in the United States than ever before. This is particularly true of girls and women from broken homes or economically disadvantaged communities (rural and urban alike), as well as females born into marginalized communities of color, where a heavy police presence and racial profiling are facts of life.

It is truly disturbing to consider that one of every thirty-two Americans is under some form of correctional supervision.[1] Although Americans represent only 5 percent of the world population, one-quarter of the entire world's inmates are contained in U.S. jails and prisons, something that baffles other democratic societies that have typically used prisons as a last resort, especially for nonviolent offenders. The United States has more people in prison than any other nation, followed by China, which has 1.5 million.[2]

Just about five years after this book is published, the United States will have 1.7 million people in state and federal prisons, up from 1.53 million in 2006.[3]

Assessing the consequences of our country's soaring imprisonment rates has less to do with the question of guilt versus innocence than it does with the question of who among us truly deserves to go to prison and face the restrictive—and sometimes brutally repressive—conditions found there.

By mid-2006, the total number of women and men in prison *and* jail rose to over 2.24 million, representing a 3 percent increase over the previous year. We're now adding more than one thousand prisoners to our prison and jail systems every single week.[4]

While the overall incarceration rates were covered by some mainstream media outlets, far less attention was paid to the fact that a historically high number of more than two hundred thousand women are now doing time, in addition to another 94,400 on parole and 958,000 on probation.[5] In fact, the number of incarcerated adult women has jumped by a shocking 757 percent since 1977, at nearly twice the growth rate of male prisoners.[6]

More than ninety-six thousand juveniles are in custody—up to 20 percent of them in major cities are girls—and these young people are usually held in the kinds of facilities that seem to make their lives only more troubled.[7] As was the case in 2006, six of ten in our state and federal prisons are people of color.[8] (Actually, that number is likely to be higher, as Bureau of Justice Statistics doesn't keep comprehensive, national statistics on Native American or Latino prisoners.) Black women are four times more likely these days to be incarcerated than white women.[9]

"The number of women in prisons and jails has reached a sad new milestone," explains Kara Gotsch, director of advocacy for The Sentencing Project in Washington, D.C. "Since 1980, [especially] as women became entangled in the 'war on drugs,' the number in prison increased at nearly double the rate of incarceration for men. The impact of their incarceration devastates thousands of children, who lose their primary caregiver when Mom goes to prison."

Statistics like these are invaluable for journalists like me, when we have to "prove" that what we're talking about isn't based just on anecdotal information or the observation of a recurring trend. When it comes to prisons, statistics have become their own version of a double-edged sword.

Why? Because with numbers as big as the ones related to prison, those statistics easily obscure the individual stories and struggles of those caught in the sticky, far-reaching net of American mass incarceration. For *Women Behind Bars,* I focused on women's prisons and jails, as well as three international women's prisons. My sole visit to a juvenile detention facility was in Seattle/King County, with the assistance of a remarkable local nonprofit organization, Powerful Voices. Through talking with the girls, who are locked up increasingly for crimes ranging from truancy to drug dealing, I also hoped to gain more insight into their lives. I told the girls what I wanted to know about them, and most of them opened up to me, a complete stranger, with a searing, brutal honesty that surprised me.

During another one of those sessions, I found out that one of the fifteen-year-olds was pregnant, although most of the other girls didn't know that yet. She held her stomach tenderly from time to time. Some of the girls were loud and boisterous, competing for attention and trying to show precisely how "fierce" they were. (Coming from thirteen- and fourteen-year-old girls, that's an easy enough bluff to see through.) One girl, just a few months shy of turning eighteen, admitted to the group that this was her twelfth time being locked up in some kind of institution. Her first time had been in another state, where she had been thrown into a mixed juvenile/adult psychiatric facility as a twelve-year-old, with understandably traumatic consequences.

In each of these sessions, I asked all of the girls to participate in a few writing exercises about their fears and dreams. One of these writing exercises had to do with the first night they were incarcerated in juvenile detention. This caused a fair amount of consternation.

"Do you mean this time or the first time?" one girl bellowed. As it turned out, most of the girls had been in juvie more than once. The cycle of incarceration and reincarceration had already begun for them.

When we finally settled that they were to write about their first time being locked up, everyone got to work, munching on microwave popcorn and drinking Tang as they went along.

"It was scary, dirty, and just not a place for me," wrote one fourteen-year-old. "I felt sad and lonely."

Later, I asked her where she saw herself in five years. She laughed. I got her to talk a bit about why she found this question so ridiculous, and this is what she finally said: "I don't even know me five minutes from now."

Eventually, here's what she disclosed to me on a piece of paper: "How am I supposed to know that tomorrow is even promised? If I make it to five years from now, I hope that I'll have a job, a boyfriend, and [that] I'm doing good. But that's never promised."

I told her, as she walked out, that she was right. Nothing's promised to us in this world. But I believed that she could actually defy her odds and live a fulfilling life in the "free world."

"When will it change?" a thirty-five-year-old Texan prisoner, Cara Nicole Barker-Royall, pleaded with me in one of her letters. "When will the system treat us like humans? Yes, I'm a convicted felon, but the judge did not sentence me to inadequate healthcare and pain. But that [has become] my sentence. To them, I am only a number."

Cara Nicole Barker-Royall is a lifelong victim of physical and emotional abuse. She is now serving an eight-year plea-bargain sentence for a robbery and kidnapping that an abusive man, in fact, appears to have actually staged and committed without her willing participation. (He and his co-conspirator walked away from even being charged with any crime because they blamed everything on her, and the prosecutors were satisfied with the end result.) Like so many other women in the prison, Barker-Royall refused to "snitch" on him because she had been raised with an old sense of street code and honor—"no snitching allowed." The fact that this man had already been abusive to her in the past didn't change that.

In a subsequent letter, Barker-Royall thanked me for using the word "survivor," rather than "victim," to describe her ability to identify negative influences in her life and then move forward in a more positive way. Even her continual pain from multiple medical issues—she nearly died on an operating table while incarcerated—and the fact that she lives out her prison days in an unheated converted horse barn in Gatesville, Texas, do not break her spirit.

Women like Barker-Royall will nearly always admit to their real crimes. (In her case, she readily confessed to a plethora of crimes that she really had committed—some of which she was never charged with—leading up to the incident that landed her in prison this most recent time.)

I can count on one hand how many women have written to me or met me in a prison yard and claimed "innocence" all the way around; most women are more than ready to tell me what they did to get into prison. Those women who proclaim innocence do actually have compelling stories and a plethora of supporting evidence that I have already begun to pursue. Many male inmates, on the other hand, tend to tell me that they were "framed" or were not responsible for the crimes they were imprisoned for, and they are far less convincing, because they do not offer to document their innocence (although there are, of course, many innocent men locked up as well, in addition to the men who do not deny their crimes but contact me to speak out about abusive prison conditions or unfair sentencing). Women are more likely to contact me and tell their stories, because they want the rest of us to begin to consider the essence of their humanity. They want to be seen and heard, and they feel like they are completely forgotten, even invisible, in the eyes of society at large.

It is my contention that we, as "free world" inhabitants, must begin to think about our vast number of incarcerated persons—women and men alike—as a complicated mix of individuals, most of whom will be released back into society during our respective lifetimes. By dismissing them wholesale as "criminals" and "subhumans," we do them, and ourselves, a great disservice. Indeed, I believe that our very humanity suffers for it.

To be clear: I focus on girls and women on this book not because men are undeserving of a similar amount of compassion and consideration, but because I believe that incarcerated females are the most misunderstood population in the vast U.S. incarceration system. Consider that in the next five years alone, female prisoners are projected to increase by 16 percent, compared with a 12 percent increase for men.[10]

Ask yourself this right now: Why is this the case? Do you buy into the popular notion that women are simply becoming more violent, more criminally minded? In the ensuing chapters, I'll break down the realities and the true operating factors behind these growing numbers, and I ask only that you keep an open mind. This situation isn't getting better, it's getting far worse.

In writing this book, I aim to shed light on what has contributed to this historic phenomenon of the mass incarceration of women (and men) in the United States. While there are numerous similar underlying causes, there are also some very, very notable differences—both in the causal factors and in the day-to-day realities and struggles of incarcerated women—that should no longer go ignored or be lumped in with the experiences of men.

Women behind bars are not, by any stretch of the imagination, a monolithic group. Many of them are not much different from the rest of us. Often, a series of poor judgments, lack of resources, lifestyle choices, drug habits, and/or self-destructive reactions to trauma in their lives has brought them to the place where they find themselves now, incarcerated and assigned a prison number that follows them everywhere they go.

Like every other prisoner, Barker-Royall had to memorize her number—1253606—as soon as she set foot in her Texas prison. But, as she rightly insists, the totality of her personhood, life experience, and unfulfilled hopes and desires is far, far more complex than the seven-digit number that will identify, regulate, and control her existence for years to come.

I wrote this book to bring the stories and experiences of incarcerated girls and women to as broad an audience as possible. I also wrote this book for the tens of thousands of girls and women who have not been given a legitimate chance to repair their lives. And I wrote this book for the women who are fighting for that second chance right now.

Barker-Royall shared with me this poem about what it feels like to try to live a life beyond the assignation of a prison number. I am glad to have her permission to share it with you.

Not **Just** a Number

I scream, I shout!
But my voice is silenced
behind these razor fences . . .
I'm scared to let down
my defenses.
My eyes are brown and wide
rimmed red from the thousands
of tears I've cried.

One mistake only leads to
another.

And I'm no longer a wife
or a mother—
Just a number . . .
You look through me
as if I don't exist.
The fear, the pain, the loneliness
I continually resist.
Behind these brown eyes
I hide the person I really am—
the way I feel,
that's the only way I can
deal.

With the fear that cruises
through my heart—
that keeps me apart
from all that's real . . .
This life behind the razor
is so surreal!
I am human!
Not just a number!

Will they put a barcode
across my head?
File away my remains
I dread?
Will anyone miss me
when I'm dead?
I am a woman!
I have a heart that beats!
But this crime,
my mistakes—
continually defeats, defeats,
defeats!
I am real!
Not just another story—
Not only these few words
you see.
I breathe!
I am slowly dying

Becoming all I can be!
I am not just a number,
but a woman,
a real person,
someone's mother!

Not just a number . . .
Not just a number . . .
Not just a number . . .

Chapter 1: Here's Your One-Way Ticket to Prison

"I accept full responsibility for my actions. I know where heroin addiction has led me. . . . I have no violence, weapons, or sex offenses on my record. I am doing a twenty-year term with two strikes under the California three strikes law for removing a screen off a window. . . . The court system [has] not once ever offered me any help [for my addiction]."

—Gricel Paz, Central California Women's Facility in Chowchilla

"No matter the damage to our tattered souls, we still have the spark inside us, the indomitable spirit to continue on, to never give up. We may be tattered and torn, but we still love and laugh, we burn bright. I believe every person is redeemable, there are no disposable people. A society which practices that [will] eventually implode."

—Delecia Hammock, serving thirty-two years for killing an abusive husband, writing from Tennessee Prison for Women in Nashville

A journalist once wrote the following about her prearranged overnight stay at a women's jail:

> The first step for the newly arrested is called "Reception" although it was unlike any reception I have ever attended. The handcuffs now dispensed with, we were assembled in a large room: our handbags emptied on a counter and the contents catalogued, we were photographed and fingerprinted. Ordered to strip, we were searched for narcotics: "Bend over, spread cheeks." Our heads were examined for lice. . . .
>
> From the recesses of the building we heard a disturbing muffled, rhythmic wail. Was it the sound of mechanical equipment, an air-conditioner gone slightly out of kilter? I asked a guard. "Oh, that's just Viola, she's in Adjustment for her nerves."
>
> "It doesn't seem to be doing her nerves much good."
>
> "Her trouble is she's mental, always bothering the other inmates. So we keep her in Adjustment."[1]

This journalist's account could well have been taken in any major urban women's jail in the United States today. But these observations were written in 1970, in a chapter entitled "Women in Cages," from Jessica Mitford's *Kind & Unusual Punishment: The Prison Business.* Mitford, one of the most talented muckrakers of the twentieth century, was writing about her experiences and perceptions of female incarceration at a Washington, D.C., jail.

At the close of the chapter, Mitford asked the poignant question of whether our city streets were actually safer because these women were locked behind bars, without access to psychological counseling, treatment for addiction, or vocational training. Moreover, she wondered, "Are these women 'improved' or 'reformed' by the experience?"

Nearly forty years later, many aspects of Mitford's observations during her overnight stay have remained the same, and the key questions about whether women are truly changed by incarceration are just as relevant today. Today, the number of girls and women doing time is unprecedented in U.S. history. In 1977, there were just slightly more than eleven thousand incarcerated females. By 2004, the number of women under state or federal jurisdication prison had increased by a breathtaking 757 percent, to more than 111,000,[2] and the percentage of women in prison has increased every year, at roughly *double the rate of men,* since 2000, according to the Institute on Women & Criminal Justice's report "Hard Hit: The Growth in the Imprisonment of Women."[3]

"To paraphrase the old saying, when the male prison population caught cold, women came down with pneumonia," wrote the authors of "Hard Hit."

Males are still, by far, the majority of people getting arrested and locked up; women comprise slightly more than 7 percent of people in prison and jail.[4] To many people working in criminology, that percentage is still so small as to warrant little, if any, attention or analysis. At many of the prison-related conferences that I have attended over the years, inmates are referred to by the male pronoun almost exclusively.

Readers of this book might ask the logical question of why an entire book should be focused on female incarceration. Why not write about men as well? Also a reasonable inquiry is whether this book's emphasis on women denies not only the prevalence of male incarceration, but also men's experiences and suffering before, during, and after imprisonment.

These questions are entirely valid, and they deserve a response. The truth of the matter is that I have actually written *more* about incarcerated men than about women in prison over a decade of criminal justice–related investigative reporting. I have seen and studied the unique issues that men face in jail and prison, including the brutal physical and sexual violence to which nondominant men are often subjected. I have explored the myriad manifestations of racism in the criminal justice system, insofar as African American men are more likely to be incarcerated at some point in their lives than to go to college.[5] And I have written about the tremendous impact of mandatory minimum sentencing and three strikes laws on the lives of men from low-income communities who have not even committed serious crimes that would seem to justify their lifelong incarceration.[6]

Ultimately, my research and writing on the criminal justice system have led me to the conclusion that although mass incarceration is a problem for juveniles and adults alike, the realities of female imprisonment are far more complex and underreported than most Americans seem to realize. Once I began to pay particularly close attention to the ways in which girls and women in the criminal justice system were portrayed in the media, it became clear that they were almost *never* portrayed as three-dimensional human beings, foibles, struggles, triumphs and all—although their more sensational crimes certainly get a inordinate share of exposure.

"When the United States embarked on a policy that might well be described as mass incarceration," explains criminologist Meda Chesney-Lind, "few considered the impact that this correctional course change would have on women. Women offenders have been largely invisible or 'forgotten' by a criminology that emerged to complement, explain, and occasionally critique state efforts to control and discipline unruly and dangerous men."

Chesney-Lind points out, "Little or no thought was given to the possibility of a female prisoner until she appeared at the door of the institution. It was as though crime and punishment existed in a world in which gender equaled male."[7]

To be clear, this is not a book about why women matter more than men in prison. Rather, it is about the realities and complexities of females who are locked up. Prisoners are already a largely invisible population in this country. When we think about inmates, we tend to picture men—and violent or sexually predatory men at that. Female prisoners don't even breach our national consciousness, except in the case of scandalous crimes, usually involving the murder of their children, their spouses, or sexual acts with younger boys. But the reality is that the female jail and prison populations combined have grown at a far faster rate than the equivalent male population in every state in the nation: 106 percent for women, versus 71 percent for men, between 1990 and 1999.[8]

I believe that one of the most profound indicators of a criminal justice system gone awry is the fact that we are incarcerating the most vulnerable members of our society en masse. In essence, prosecutors and judges are sending the people with the fewest resources and the least ability to afford decent legal representation to the slammer, often for very lengthy periods of time. Federal parole has long since been abolished, and plea bargains (especially for low-level drug offenders) are more common than not. Many women have told me that they did not even fully grasp the crime(s) to which they pled guilty. Often, the women didn't realize how long their sentences would be until they got to prison because of their stress during the proceedings, the fact that they were given heavy doses of pharmaceuticals when they were locked up, and/or the fact that their own attorneys did not explain adequately what was happening to them. In these kinds of situations, defendants are likely to be low-income, unemployed, or underemployed people; individuals with limited literacy and education levels; juveniles; alcohol and drug addicts; people with backgrounds of sexual, emotional, or physical abuse; and the mentally ill.

More often than not, incarcerated girls and women fall into more than one of these categories—and to a far greater degree than their male counterparts, as explored in the subsequent chapters of this book. The trend toward the incarceration of these vulnerable populations of girls and women is particularly noteworthy because females have traditionally been the easiest population to stabilize with social services, counseling, and other forms of support. This doesn't have anything to do with any kind of essential or intrinsic aspect of being female. Although we should always be careful about generalizing about any population group, social service providers, drug and alcohol counselors, and prison counselors indicate that women tend to express themselves more openly, allowing social service providers and therapists to better identify what the women need in order to get to a more stable place in their lives. Girls and women also tend to be less worried about their image in the eyes of the community around them, and they don't worry quite as much about the idea of losing face once they admit to needing help.

Whether in the case of juveniles or adults, our nation's single-minded pursuit of punishment—over preventative or intervention-focused social services, education, treatment, and recovery—is at a truly disturbing and unprecedented point in our societal history. Namely, more than 2.2 million Americans are incarcerated, and at least seven million are now under some kind of correctional supervision.[9] In themselves, these figures signify a criminal justice system spiraling out of control, especially when we take into account that *13.5 million* Americans are incarcerated at some point over the course of one year.[10]

Statistics like these give us only one part of the overall picture, but they serve a valuable purpose in helping us to understand just how serious the practice and the business of punishment have gotten.

Official statistics put the proportion of female inmates at less than one in ten prisoners in the United States.[11]

But when we crunch the numbers in a slightly different way, the fact emerges that nearly 17 percent of people imprisoned or under correctional supervision are women. Here's how it breaks down: At the end of 2006, there were 203,100 women in jails and state and federal prisons. (The female jail/prison population grew 3.4 percent between 2004 and 2005 alone, compared with the growth in the male rate of 1.3 percent.) Add to that nearly one million women on probation, plus over 94,000 women on parole, for an estimated 1.3 million females [11] under some form of correctional supervision. [12]

As for the total number of encounters with the criminal justice system, nearly two million adult women were arrested in 2005, in addition to nearly 382,000 girls under the age of eighteen. [13] None of these figures include female refugees and immigrants in detention, many of whom are locked up for indefinite periods of time in dire and repressive conditions, which we know little about because of the secrecy surrounding people detained by the Department of Homeland Security's Immigration and Customs Enforcement.

The incarceration of women of color has been especially dramatic, particularly when arrest and sentencing pertain to nonviolent, drug-related offenses and the prevalence of so-called conspiracy charges (see Chapter 2, "Women in Wartime"). Numerically, there are more Euro-American women in prisons and jails (95,300) than Black women (68,800) or Latinas (32,400), but African American women are almost four times as likely as Euro-American women, and more than twice as likely as Latinas, to be in prison. Collectively, African American women and Latinas represent more than 60 percent of women locked up in state and federal prisons. [14]

When I visited FCC Coleman in central Florida in the fall of 2006, nearly *every* woman with whom I spoke was either black or Latina, and had been sentenced for a drug conspiracy charge. Their lengthy sentences were even more troubling when I examined the evidence and court proceedings in their cases, which pointed to minimal or even nonexistent involvement in drug dealing. The thread that ran through all of these women's sentences was the idea that they couldn't or wouldn't snitch on boyfriends, husbands, friends, or casual acquaintances.

Even when conspiracy charges are not involved, and drug possession or sales is the cause of arrest and prosecution, class and/or racial dynamics are hugely significant factors in the length of a woman's sentence.

"More women, and especially black women, are behind bars as much because of hard punishment [as because of] their actual crimes," explains Earl Ofari Hutchinson, a prominent writer on black American issues. "Stiffer punishment for crack cocaine use also has landed more black women in prison, and for longer sentences than white women (and men). Then there's the feminization of poverty and racial stereotyping. More than one out of three black women jailed did not complete high school, were unemployed, or had incomes below the poverty level at the time of their arrest. . . . While black men are typed as violent, drug-dealing 'gangstas,' black women are typed as sexually loose, conniving, untrustworthy welfare queens. Many of the mostly middle-class judges and jurors believe that black women offenders are menaces to society too."[15]

The situation for girls mirrors that of their adult counterparts, often representing the first step toward the likelihood of adult incarceration. The crimes that girls are arrested and detained for (such as running away from home and prostitution) tend to differ from boys' crimes. Mental illness is a common thread in these girls' lives, often brought on by sexual and physical abuse in their homes or seriously dysfunctional parents with their own sets of disorders, including alcoholism and drug addiction.[16]

When I helped to cull and edit the material for Powerful Voices' "Living Diary" from "high risk" and incarcerated juveniles in Seattle, I was already familiar with all of the facts and statistics surrounding these populations. But the material and confessions that poured out of the teenage girls ended up being so disturbing that I found myself experiencing secondhand trauma just from reading their words. Girls wrote of being raped by their brothers, uncles, and boyfriends; of getting pregnant at ages as young as thirteen; and of surviving on the streets by prostituting themselves and "slinging" drugs. Girls talked of being locked up in juvenile detention five, ten, even twenty times over, and growing so comfortable with imprisonment that prison began to feel like the most normal and safe place they knew.[17] One teenager wrote the following in a piece she titled "I Keep My Clothes":

When I was younger I lived with my grandparents. Like many other women, I was molested, I've been raped dozens of times. At twelve, I went to live with my mom. I'd only met her a few times, had been told horrible things about her, but I can't even force myself to dislike her.

At first it was hard, no one thought we were gonna be staying with her, but while we were, my grandma passed. . . . The last year we were homeless. But no one knows. My friends don't know about it. I keep my clothes in a suitcase in a friend's tool shed, go there and change my clothes in the morning when the train starts running. Sometimes I ask friends if I can stay the night, sometimes I get a room or hang out where I'm at, act like I'm stranded. 'Cause I'm not living on the streets again.

A 2003 study by the Girls' Justice Initiative demonstrated that juvenile services consistently fail girls and their needs, especially as those needs relate to mental disorders and histories of sexual abuse and other forms of trauma.[18] Worse yet, some two hundred thousand juveniles annually don't even get to access what limited services *are* available in detention centers. Instead, forty states allow for them to be adjudicated in adult court and to serve time in adult jails and prisons.[19] Not unlike their adult counterparts, three out of four of the teens handled in adult courts are youth of color, as are teens dealt with in the juvenile system.[20] A recent research study conducted by the Centers for Disease Control and

Prevention found that a juvenile's experience of being processed as an adult makes it 34 percent more likely that they will be arrested again and generally increases the likelihood that the young person will commit a violent crime in the future, regardless of the nature of the crime for which they were first sentenced.[21]

On the whole, factors leading to female criminal behavior and incarceration are woefully misunderstood and are most certainly inadequately and poorly reported on. Girls and women are *not* growing more violent year by year, despite articles with sensational titles such as "No More Sugar and Spice," a March 30, 2006, piece that appeared in *The Washington Times* about a supposed explosion of violent girl gangs, or a CNN segment called "Girls Gone Wild," about an ostensible increase in fights between girls, which relied on cell phone–recorded footage of girls fighting each other.

All of that may make for scintillating media fodder, but these "reports" do not reflect reality. With rare exceptions, criminologists agree that girls *haven't* gotten more violent—in fact, evidence points to a decrease in teen violence—but that these perceptions are informed by reporting standards that "didn't exist years ago, such as zero-tolerance policies in schools." Fights between girls are these days are more likely to end in an arrest, a significant change from the days when adolescent behavior was dealt with in different ways, outside of the criminal justice system.[22]

We also know that 91 percent of all convicted violent offenders are male, and that 93 percent of all people convicted of murder are male.[23] The proportion of women in prison for violent crimes has actually *declined* since 1979, when violent offenses accounted for nearly one-half of incarceration in state prisons, compared with one-third of the women's prison population today. Violent crime should never be taken lightly, but it should be noted that the rate of murder and manslaughter among female offenders decreased by 12 percent from 1995 to 2004. The majority of women's violent crimes involve simple or aggravated assault.[24]

Stereotypes about female "criminals" are exacerbated by persistent, sensation-alistic media representations and promulgated by antiquated notions of scandal-ous "fallen women" who have transgressed their designated gender roles. Women behind bars are often regarded as damaged human beings and mothers who have failed their children and their families.

On that note, this work differs in one significant way from much of the exist-ing writing on female incarceration. Specifically, I do not focus on the experiences of mothers or pregnant women in prison, or on the experiences of their children. Readers should not interpret this omission as accidental. It is widely documented that the majority of women in prison are mothers, and that they must often de-liver their children in shackles and then have their infants taken away shortly after birth, an experience that some women describe as one of the most traumatic of their adult lives.

It should be a matter of great concern that almost two and a half million children have a parent in prison. Most mothers in prison devote much of their time to trying to sustain some kind of contact with their children, even when they have lost custody. Painful emotional struggles surrounding such efforts, ranging from the remote locations of most female institutions to the depressing limitations of mother–child visits (to say nothing of the exorbitant cost of col-lect phone calls from prison), are all crucial facets of women's incarceration that should inform any discussion of criminal justice and prison reform for women. With the exception of Chapter 6, "Criminalizing Motherhood," I do not ex-plore this broader topic, because it has already been covered in recent years with great depth, analysis, and compassion, most significantly in Nell Bernstein's *All Alone in the World: Children of the Incarcerated* (The New Press, 2005) and Renny Golden's *War on the Family: Mothers in Prison and the Families They Leave Behind* (Routledge, 2005).

For *Women Behind Bars,* I set out to write about other integral facets of female incarceration, with particular emphasis on the war on drugs as an underlying reason for the dramatic increase in the number of imprisoned girls and women. I also set out to explore the various kinds of sexual, mental, and health-care abuses that occur with disturbing frequency in female facilities. Among several other subtopics, I sought to uncover much lesser-known aspects of female imprisonment, including the practice of transferring women to other states, the growing trend of attempts to force religious conversion on women in prison, and the experiences of lesbians behind bars.

A significant schism exists in the present day regarding the criminal justice system's handling of women of different ethnicities and social classes. I believe that many of the related disparities in arrest, prosecution, and sentencing have their roots in social attitudes and policies that were set in motion beginning in the late 1700s.

In his book *Punishment, Prisons, and Patriarchy,* Mark E. Kann notes that the prevailing attitude about female criminality in early U.S. history had *everything* to do with the idea that women who defied their gendered roles (for example, by engaging in prostitution, vagrancy, or public drunkenness, or by having extramarital affairs) were more disgraceful and disturbed than men who committed even the most serious crimes.

"The reason for her 'rapid and precipitous moral fall' was that a woman who lost her moral footing had no other basis for restraining her passions, whereas men still had reason," Kann writes. "That was why both a seduced girl and a rape victim were fallen women; having lost their chastity, they also lost their moral footing. . . . Reformers considered fallen women more blameworthy than male criminals.

"Like black offenders," he continues, "female criminals were not deemed capable of reform and redemption. . . . The fact that they were mostly poor, minority, or immigrant women strengthened the perception of their incorrigibility."[25]

This approach to female criminality and imprisonment has echoes in the perceptions and criminal justice policies of the present day. A woman who is hit with a lengthy prison sentence, for anything ranging from prostitution to possession of a few rocks of crack, is *still* viewed with disdain and a lack of compassion, even by her own family or community. Of course, most of these arrests and sentences rarely make the news, especially when the perpetrators of these "crimes" are women of color and/or women from lower economic backgrounds.

But when the likes of Martha Stewart, Paris Hilton, or Lil' Kim are sentenced to jail or prison, the media and public response is tremendous and always inspires a lively debate.

When a woman with celebrity status faces the possibility of imprisonment, gossip columnists begin to speculate on what her incarceration experience might be like, sometimes suggesting quite ominously that they might well be the targets of sexual or physical abuse at the hands of hardened female predators. The conditions of their confinement are explained—often inaccurately—and petitions are circulated to try to win their release.

Some of this coverage is understandable, considering the fact that ours is a celebrity-driven culture. *Of course* it's big news when members of celebrity royalty are about to get sent down the river. But it's fascinating to study how radically different the language used to describe celebrity women is from that used to discuss "ordinary" imprisoned women. Whereas noncelebrity women are depicted with terms like "crack ho" and "gold digger" on cable stations ranging from VH1 to BET—or as ruthless, heartless criminals on television shows like *Snapped* and *Women Who Kill*—the celebrity women are covered in special segments, including CNN's "Ladies Who Serve Time."[26] This particular show featured a discussion of how female celebrities, including Zsa Zsa Gabor, Leona Hemsley, and Martha Stewart, have effectively discarded their "convict" status, noting that most of them have "dropped their reputations as former inmates."

The fact that these women have both the resources and the luxury to do so doesn't enter the discussion at any point, nor does any meta-analysis of the scope of women's incarceration. There was a glimmer of hope that this might happen when Stewart was incarcerated for five months and started to talk with other women doing time at FCI Alderson. Many of these women had been sentenced to multiyear or multidecade terms for their nonviolent, drug-related offenses, and Stewart promised to take a stance on the unfairness of drug laws once she was released. Not surprisingly, she never followed through.

"Instead of indulging in the details of Jones's post-sentencing couture, those of us who share the privilege of ignorance about daily life inside prison walls could have been asking hard-hitting questions about the rap diva's new home," Sarah Stillman wrote, quite poignantly, in an essay for *The Huffington Post* about the imprisonment of Lil' Kim (a.k.a. Kimberly Jones). "Why do young women of color with significantly less dough than Jones comprise America's fastest-growing prison population? Why do incarcerated women in Jones's home state of New York test positive for HIV at sixty times the national rate? What role does each of us play in promoting this current catastrophe of a criminal 'justice' system?"[27]

Remarkably, only *The New York Times* journalist Judith Miller (of "Plamegate" fame) bothered to share some of her observations about her experiences in jail. "The first day is terrifying," she told the *New York Post*. "Humiliating. They take everything away. Can't even have an aspirin. . . . It's about control. Women journalists like us fight for control. Control over stories, control of our days. And the first thing they take away is the ability to control your own life."[28]

Miller also addressed the fact that women in jail are deprived of all possible displays of their femininity, and resort to "amazing skills" by using crushed M&M's for lipstick, coloring pencils for eyeliner, and toothbrushes to apply mascara.

Just as Miller described, girls in juvenile detention and women in jail are deprived of ways to make themselves feel better about their circumstances by expressing themselves in their outward appearance. Not only are females in juvenile detention and jail typically deprived of makeup, they are given clothing identical to that of jailed boys and men, something I witnessed in Los Angeles, San Francisco, and Seattle (although San Francisco County Jail allowed women and men alike to purchase makeup from the canteen). The undergarments are different, of course, but the girls and women in all of these detention facilities complained to me that their clothing was laundered together with the men's clothes—and poorly at that—so that the women would often smell men's sweat on their clothing.

Although makeup and jail-issue clothing might seem like petty concerns to people in the "free world," these are the kinds of things that would make the experience of incarceration more tolerable. Although not all women like to wear makeup, it's fair to say that most women don't like looking drab or being robbed of their external individuality. This was more upsetting to the girls and women than almost any other aspect of their incarceration, on par with their lack of privacy when using the toilet or showering; the poor unnutritious and sometimes sickening quality of food; an overall lack of even the most basic personal grooming items, such as lotion and shaving razors, or shampoo, deodorant, and soap *not* designed for men's bodies (or, for that matter, not designed solely for the skin and hair texture of Euro-Americans). Close behind were complaints about the rampant overcrowding of facilities, to the extent that four to eight women have to sleep in a two-person cell, and that dayrooms and rooms once used for educational or recreational purposes are used to hold inmates. This situation is only slightly better for women in state prisons, because some facilities allow women to wear clothes of their own (within certain guidelines), or they provide clothing that is slightly more feminine in appearance. Even then, some prisons have strict regulations that deemphasize femininity and standardize a masculine appearance.

In her recounting of her jail experience in Alexandria, Virginia, Miller was, knowingly or unknowingly, identifying some of the key systemic problems in the realm of female incarceration. The conditions in girls' and women's detention facilities are a complete afterthought compared to those in men's facilities. The specific emotional and physical needs that females present once they are incarcerated are completely off the radar of most state and federal correctional departments, although some jails and prisons have now begun to experiment with what is being called "gender-responsive programming."

In response to criticisms that the state's women's prisons were poorly equipped to deal with the range of issues and needs of an ever-increasing female population (numbering twelve thousand at the time of this writing), the California State Legislature established the Gender Responsive Strategies Commission (GRSC) during the 2005–2006 legislative session. The GRSC is empowered to make recommendations to the California Department of Corrections and Rehabilitation (CDCR), although those recommendations are not binding.

The GRSC has held meetings across California (one of which I attended in Fresno in July 2006). The commission has conducted open meetings and encouraged the participation of a wide array of members, including advocates, former offenders, academicians, wardens, and other correctional employees. So far, the GRSC's steering committee has come up with numerous suggestions relating to the creation of "honor wards" for prisoners free of infractions for a long period of time; special treatment for the elderly in prison (including passes to allow them to move to the front of the food line); improvements in women's clothing; and recognition by some senior-ranking officers that a response escalation to the use of force may not be as necessary with a female population.

The latter has echoed throughout the few gender-responsive plans and committees springing up in other states. At the maximum-security Lowell Correctional Institution, in Florida, the concept has taken root upon the realization that nearly all of their female prisoners come from abusive backgrounds, and that half are arrested with a male counterpart. Laura Bedard, the Florida Department of Corrections' deputy secretary, has undertaken the gender-responsive effort by firing guards accused of illegal conduct and has initiated training to educate correctional employees about the common threads in female prisoners' life histories. The training has included the recognition that women do not respond well to "barking orders or yelling."[29]

In California, some of the GRSC's suggestions have begun to be implemented, in bits and pieces, at some of the women's facilities. The California Institution for Women opened a new mother–baby unit in 2007, and the CDCR now hosts occasional, free-of-charge bus rides from central locations in Southern California so that children can visit their mothers.

The GRSC has also helped to expand awareness about the need for woman-centered alcohol/drug rehabilitation services, housing, and other social services for roughly thirteen thousand women paroled annually. Such community resources are still very scarce, largely because so much of the state budget has been diverted to the expansion of the CDCR's prison maintenance and construction budget. On the front end, precious little has been done to stem the flood of thousands of men and women into state facilities. The number of inmates increases year by year, and a legislative proposal endorsed by the GRSC to divert 4,500 nonviolent female offenders into small-scale, community-based "miniprisons" was quashed in 2006.

"We no longer have a gym," Sara Olson wrote to me from the California Correctional Center for Women (CCWF). "Two hundred women cycle in and out of [the former gym], with new inmates coming in daily. . . . We now house over 4,100 [women at CCWF], sometimes almost 4,200 women, daily."

Overcrowding is unlikely to be alleviated soon—particularly as the single largest prison construction program was proposed by Governor Arnold Schwarzenegger in 2007, at a cost of $8.3 billion and the addition of fifty-three thousand beds, ostensibly to alleviate the pressure on the CDCR to recover from a governor-declared "state of emergency," and an inmate health system now under federal court–appointed receivership. The expansion has not gone over well with many critics of the CDCR's massive sprawl. Even former governor George Deukmejian, certainly no enemy of prison expansion during his tenure, has called the state's prison system "dysfunctional."[30] The bipartisan Little Hoover Commission, an independent state-oversight agency, released a report in early 2007 warning that California's prison system was in a "tailspin that threatens public safety and raises the risk of fiscal disaster."[31]

In a *Seattle Post-Intelligencer* article regarding the soaring number of women in jails and prisons in Washington state, reporter M. L. Lyke succinctly describes these problems facing incarcerated females: "These shifts [in incarceration trends] raise concerns about the way male-dominated institutions deal with a burgeoning female population. Women menstruate. They get pregnant. They stress over losing their children to Child Protective Services. Many come into the system physically and sexually abused. Most come in addicted to drugs."[32]

At the heart of these deprivations and denials of women's needs is the fact that women's jails and prisons have always been based on physical structures and regulations originally designed for men, for male bodies, and in response to the way men are expected to behave behind bars.

As a result, incarcerated girls and women face a peculiar intersection of expectations regarding their appearance, behavior, and method of incarceration. On the whole, women are guarded, locked down, and subject to harsh retaliation for infractions as if they were men in prison. Such retribution includes prevalent and lengthy stays in control units (see Chapter 5, "Trying to Stay Sane"), which I believe is a cruel and unusual method of punishment where *both* genders are concerned. Prison guards carry and use stun guns and pepper spray, and conduct forcible cell extractions. But the kinds of infractions that can result in solitary confinement, write-ups, extra work duty, and even extensions of prison sentences are often far from being very serious or violent. This seems to speak to the theory that women are expected to understand a top-down hierarchy and to simultaneously obey orders as if they have been conditioned along the same lines as many men. (This would also explain why so may correctional employees expressed their frustrations to me over the fact that women asked "Why?" in response to a command that didn't make sense to them.)

Despite the fact that women are usually treated as if they are men, prison guards respond to "unladylike" behavior with a certain degree of harshness. The language that I have heard used countless times to describe female inmates has included references to them as "girls" and "lost souls."

Kathryn Watterson, who wrote one of the most comprehensive texts to date on women in prison, picked up on this strange, dichotomous phenomenon of expectations of masculine behavior coupled with a condescending infantilization of female inmates.

"Even though women are locked in their cells at night, roughly treated, and locked in solitary as punishment for infractions, they still are told to act like ladies," Watterson wrote in *Women in Prison: Inside the Concrete Womb*. "The patriarchal goal still seems to be that fallen or erring women should conduct themselves in a ladylike manner, even though nothing about life in prison affords a woman prisoner the gentleness, grace, or respect theoretically afforded a lady.[33]

"People confined in these institutions are forced into childlike status. . . . The role of the prison system to the prisoner becomes that of parent and child," Watterson added. "Forced dependency is illogical, especially when we expect people to come out of prison as independent, law-abiding, responsible citizens."[34]

Writing from the women's prison in Nashville, Delecia Hammock puts it this way: "We are still perceived under that patriarchal stigma of 'sugar-n-spice and everything nice,' and if you're not, then you're the lowest of the low."

One of the prisons that I visited, Arizona State Prison Complex—Perryville, touted a "parallel universe" concept where women were ostensibly being prepared for their release by living in a less restrictive environment. Even there, the emphasis was on the fact that they could cook their own meals and work from sunup to sundown doing menial labor—in a way that seemed to be training them to be released into low-wage work. (With the exception of a few women's prisons, including the Washington Correctional Center for Women, most jobs available to women exist along traditional lines of gender conformity: sewing, cooking, cleaning, handicrafts, gardening, and the like.)

Several years before my visit to Perryville, I came across an internal prison newsletter that attempted to explain the unique challenges faced by the guards who had to supervise female prisoners and the facility.

"[T]he biggest difference between the inmate sexes is that females respond more emotionally to situations," the article explained. "Although some female inmates show some pride in their work and like to be social, most are still capable of playing games. . . . Female inmates present less of a threat to harm staff physically, but [correctional officers] agree the female population can be manipulative."

"In a physical confrontation, the strongest female at ASPC—Perryville couldn't take advantage of my weakest male officer," opined Sergeant Warten Snipes. "But female inmates will use their female wiles against male officers and use their gender against them!"[35]

From the Mark H. Luttrell Correctional Center, a prisoner by the name of Patricia Wilcox has managed to send me dozens of copies of minutes taken at "inmate council meetings" with the warden of the prison. The minutes are shocking, revealing that women are made to grovel for the simplest of requests, such as pleas to not be served raw scrambled eggs or raw meat and potatoes. The women ask for fresh fruit, and are told that juice qualifies as such. Food for diabetics is denied, as are bug repellents and clean new sheets and blankets. The women also plead for a few additional bars of antibacterial soap, pads, and tampons, which are promptly denied. The lists of requests and denials along these lines go on and on, as do the endless forms of degradation in women's jails and prisons across the country.

"Rehab is a thing of the past," seventy-year-old Eddie June Martin wrote to me from her prison cell in Gatesville, Texas. "We have no programs anymore except [for] GED schooling. Talk about being second-class citizens. Sometimes I feel I'm in a third-world country."

Martin's assessment is not far from the truth. The criminal "justice" system is in obvious and dire need of an overhaul. All the while, U.S. detention facilities, jails, and prisons are a long way from treating girls and women as human beings worthy of respect and dignity.

The situation is now clearly beyond needing simple reform or cosmetic change. Something has to give, and give soon.

Chapter 2: Women in Wartime

"If there were only some way for people to understand that there is an entire nation of families locked away, many for one mistake, and they think that it can never happen to them or one of their own."

—Elizabeth Cronan, who is serving twenty-eight years for her first offense for conspiracy to manufacture methamphetamine, and who was arrested with less than two grams in her possession

"I beseech you all to think about these women—to encourage the American people to ask for reforms, both in sentencing guidelines, in length of incarceration for nonviolent first-time offenders, and for those involved in drug-taking. They would be much better served in a true rehabilitation center than in prison, where there is no real help . . . no way to be prepared for life 'out there,' where each person will ultimately find herself, many with no skills and no preparation for living."

—an open letter from Martha Stewart while serving a five-month prison sentence in Alderson, West Virginia, December 22, 2004

Oklahoman Tina Thomas has been caught up in the American war on drugs. In many respects, she fits the common profile of a woman doing time for a drug-related offense. Her crimes have ranged from possession to check forgery and theft, including an arrest for trying to steal a $64 comforter from Wal-Mart.

Eventually sentenced to a two-year state prison term, Thomas admits that she committed her crimes to feed the "eight-hundred-pound gorilla I carried on my back that I just hadn't been able to shake."

Like so many other women in prison, Thomas has her own individual story. She is also part of an alarming statistical trend and modern-day American incarceration phenomenon.

For starters, Thomas is one of half a million people (roughly one-fourth of the total prison population) locked up on drug-related charges, not counting those doing time for crimes *related* to drug or alcohol problems. (As discussed in Chapter 3, "The Danger Within," these issues are usually tied to backgrounds of abuse and unresolved trauma.) Thomas is also an inmate in a state that locks up women at one of the highest per capita rates—129 per 100,000 residents, a figure that comes in right behind Texas, the federal system, and California. Oklahoma's imprisonment of women rose a stunning *1,237 percent* from 1997 to 2004.[1]

Drug addiction is what led Thomas down the river to prison, she admits freely. So what's really going on with Americans and drug use? Are we just smoking, snorting, shooting, popping, and inhaling more than ever before?

There are no easy answers to these questions, but addiction is just one aspect of drug use. The truth is that people in this country have a long history of altering their consciousness, and enjoying themselves doing it. No matter how the government wants to spin that, the truth is that people have gotten intoxicated in one form or another since the beginning of time. But it is also true that the demand for drugs in the United States tops that of any other country in the world. No matter how many border guards, customs officials, busts, or searches and seizures we put in place, the flow of drugs into and throughout the country continues, unabated. Illicit drugs are also easier to find, and in greater quantities, than ever before.

Are we just a nation of addicts? It certainly seems like it, given the range of things people are addicted to: gambling, sex, pornography, video games, and so forth.

There is no war on gambling or sex addiction, and people usually don't go to prison for those things. But Thomas and many other women have had the misfortune of being sucked into what the federal government openly calls the "war on drugs." We have our own "drug czar," who sits atop the massive Office of National Drug Control Policy (ONDCP). President Nixon started up this war in 1969, and Reagan kicked it into a higher gear. It's been a full-throttle battle ever since then, even through the Clinton years. By 1980, for instance, the number of drug-related arrests stood at 581,000. Just ten years later, that number had nearly doubled to 1,090,000. In 2005, the FBI reported that law enforcement officers made more arrests for drug-abuse violations (1.8 million) than for any other offense.[2]

One of the most surprising facts about these figures is the drug of choice where police arrests are concerned: marijuana. Part of that has to do with the fact that cannabis is classified as a Schedule I drug, which means that it is considered one of the most dangerous drugs imaginable, a drug that has no "medicinal" benefit. If police bust a bunch of pot smokers, well, they're putting a dent in the sale and use of one of the most "dangerous" drugs on the black market.

Cocaine, on the other hand, a leading cause of overdose deaths, is classified as a Schedule II. And so is PCP.[3] Go figure. In 2005, nearly 43 percent of *all* drug arrests were for cannabis possession (37.7) or "sales and manufacture" (4.9).[4]

Millions of arrests, billions of dollars—it all amounts to lots of misery and money down the drain. In 2008, the ONDCP drug-war budget will reach a record *$12.9 billion,* with $8 billion of this funding being funneled into law enforcement. Bear in mind that these are the *official* numbers. Many criminal justice experts point out that the figure doesn't incorporate the costs of incarcerating people sentenced for drug offenses. The real expenditure, including the costs of imprisonment, put the real figure close to $22 billion.[5]

But we're not getting much of a bang for these big bucks. Unintentional drug overdose rates are still high, doubling between 1999 and 2004, and have become the second-most common form of accidental death after car crashes.[6] While funding for antidrug missions in Columbia and Afghanistan increases by tens of millions every year, federal allocations to the Center for Substance Abuse Prevention and the Center for Substance Abuse Treatment are being cut by $32 million in 2008.[7] A 2006 Government Accountability Office (GAO) report revealed that our $1.4 billion antidrug media blitz wasn't working as it had been intended to. The GAO wasn't the first organization to do so: In 2003, the White House Office of Management and Budget disclosed that it found the advertising lacking any demonstrable success.[8]

The antidrug campaign isn't working, and the drugs keep flowing, but the people who need help aren't getting it. In the rest of the Western world, assistance with drug and alcohol problems, whether in the form of "harm reduction techniques" (discussed in Chapter 12, "Hope and Healing") or inpatient rehabilitation programs, is widely accessible. Heavy drug use or full-blown addiction are viewed predominantly as public health issues, not behaviors subject to prosecution, except in cases involving other criminal activity. In the United States, however, rehabilitation and counseling are very hard to access without money. The waiting lists for subsidized or free rehabiliation programs can run from a few months to a couple of years—even in progressive cities like San Francisco or Seattle.

Delays or denials of care are antithetical to the imperative that a community step in and help people when they are suffering, especially when a person comes forth to *ask* for help. When a woman comes to terms with the fact that she needs help for herself and for the sake of her family, delays in assistance can be tragic. By the time help finally arrives, a woman can very well have sunk even deeper into addiction or homelessness, lost custody of her children, and be in far worse emotional and physical condition than she was before.

People have asked me over the years why I think so much about women and drugs in the first place. I've heard people tell me that women don't have nearly as much of an issue with drugs as men do, and/or that a woman doesn't get into drug use unless a man introduces something to her. The former statement is patently untrue, but the latter scenario has happened to many women I have talked to, particularly meth and heroin users.

What we do know is that most women, as well as men, have used some form of intoxicant (legal and/or illegal) during their lives, and that half of all women ages fifteen to forty-four admit to having used illegal drugs specifically.[9] An estimated twenty-two million Americans are currently dependent on alcohol, drugs, or both,[10] although the real number is likely to be much higher, particularly as the figure does not take into account the 71.5 million people age twelve and up who use tobacco, the majority of whom are likely to be addicted to nicotine.[11] Anyone who has ever smoked cigarettes habitually can relate to what even heroin and other hard-drug users have told me on numerous occasions—that nicotine is the most addictive drug they have ever taken, and the hardest substance to quit. (Small wonder that the tobacco ban in many prisons across the nation has started a fierce black market, where cigarettes are usually more expensive than marijuana or heroin, costing between $5 and $10 per cigarette.)

Whether they are caught or not, more than nine million women each year use illicit drugs, and another 3.7 million use prescription drugs without medical authorization.[12] [One such woman, Danielle Pascu, twenty-nine, got hooked on prescription drugs after the birth of her daugher, which she first obtained legally and then by falsifying her prescriptions.] Pascu had no criminal record, had never used drugs before, and was generally unaware of the risks involved. She was grateful for the Vicodin that got her through the lingering pain from a cesarean section and untreated postpartum depression. It didn't take Pascu long to develop a full-blown habit, and to get caught as a result. These days, Pascu is serving nearly three years in the sunbaked and dilapidated Arizona State Prison Complex—Perryville, where at first she was sent to the prison's converted death row (a new facility was built for the women awaiting their execution). When I visited this area of the prison, I witnessed a lack of air-conditioning, rundown tiny cells, and rampant spider bites making women's lives utterly miserable.

At this point, drug violations and property offenses account for a majority (59 percent) of females in state prisons. By comparison, men in *both* of these offense categories add up to 39.5 percent.[13] Put together, women and men convicted of drug offenses constitute nearly 60 percent of people in federal prison.[14]

Tina Thomas knows that she has a quadruple strike to overcome: She's a black female with a former cocaine addiction, in a state that prefers to lock people up for substance abuse and will deprive her of most forms of public assistance when she gets out. She now faces a lifetime ban on federal benefits, including contracts, licenses, and grants. As a drug offender, Thomas won't ever be able to get Temporary Assistance for Needy Families (TANF) if she should need it. Food assistance, higher-education funding, and even income tax deductions for pursuing a college degree are all yanked away from most felony drug offenders. It is utterly illogical and absurd that nearly every other category of ex-offender—including sex offenders, murderers, arsonists, and perpetrators of domestic violence—is eligible for these benefits. And, as if that isn't already bad enough, Thomas will find that even getting a job will be difficult, because she must report herself as an ex-felon.

Many times, I've also been asked whether African Americans might just be using and selling drugs *more* than any other group of people. (Mass media certainly hasn't done anything to contradict this idea.) My response is always met with disbelief until I can actually prove it, using the government's own health statistics. It's true: African Americans constitute only 15 percent of drug users nationwide.[15]

When we look at FBI data, at first glance it looks like Euro-Americans are bearing the brunt of drug-related arrests. Numerically speaking, that *is* true, because they are still the majority population in the United States. But a closer look at the statistical data reveals something else. African Americans are actually arrested at *three times* the rate of their demographic representation in the United States.[16] There isn't a lot of truth-telling going on about all of this. All in all, the most common images of drug users and sellers in media and entertainment are still those of men and women of color.

Marc Mauer, executive director of the Washington, D.C.–based Sentencing Project, asks the very pertinent question of whether police are arresting crack and cocaine users *in general,* or specifically going into communities of color and lower-income neighborhoods, where *some* people are using drugs and engaging in the street trade.

This kind of targeting in neighborhoods can have deadly consequences, as in the case of Kathryn Johnston, a ninety-two-year-old black woman who was shot in her Atlanta home in November 2006. The incident was originally framed by the involved white police officers as an unfortunate but necessary shooting of a woman who pulled a gun when plainclothed police broke down the door of her home. Johnston, who lived in a high-crime, low-income neighborhood, was shot at least six times and was later discovered to have marijuana in her home. But by April 2007, three of the officers involved had been indicted for the killing, opening up a sweeping investigation into widespread corruption in the police department. As it turned out, the "no-knock" raid (now a common practice in the United States as a result of the drug war) had been a complete mistake; it was conducted without a solid lead and most certainly without a warrant or reason. Worse yet, the officers had actually *planted* the marijuana after the incident to try to make the murder seem justifiable.

"Conducting drug arrests in minority neighborhoods does have advantages for law enforcement," writes Mauer. "First, it is far easier to make arrests in such areas, since drug dealing is more likely to take place in open-air drug markets. In contrast, drug dealing in suburban neighborhoods almost invariably takes place behind closed doors and is therefore not readily identifiable to passing police."[17]

Mauer makes a crucial point. Many substance users are men and women with professional careers, ranging from whiskey drinkers to pill-poppers, from marijuana smokers to powder cocaine "aficionados"—to say nothing of nicotine, the most popular, physically dangerous and, arguably, most addictive drug. People with middle- to upper-class incomes tend to use their drugs behind doors in nice houses, in well-to-do neighborhoods. They slip under the drug war radar, just as college students do. A quarter of full-time undergraduate students meet the criteria for substance abuse or dependence, something that the National Center on Addiction and Substance Abuse calls "wasting the best and the brightest."[18]

Yet none of this is anything that the ONDCP cares to have a real conversation about. It's just another one of those inconvenient truths.

We also distort our own history when we say that people who drink or use drugs will always end up in bad shape, or as addicts. There are endless examples of people today who fit the category of recreational substance users *without* habits, and people who use drugs to help them think creatively, or even process and grasp the world around them in a different way. These days, this sounds crazy, even heretical, to any antidrug crusader. For this reason, it's particularly worthwhile to go back in history to find examples of talented women who used drugs on a regular basis, with self-control and with a purpose. Just to pick two examples: One of the most notable poets of the Victorian era, Elizabeth Barrett Browning, used opium and morphine. Florence Nightingale relied on opium to help her manage stressors associated with her work in Crimea—something that might well be diagnosed today as post-traumatic stress disorder.[19]

These two women were *not* exceptional as drug users in their day. Heroin, cocaine, and opiates were once enjoyed quite legally as both high-society pleasures and medications by middle- and upper-class Americans.[20] Marijuana was also once completely legal, then taxed, and then only made illegal much later in the twentieth century. Much of the criminalization of these substances took place in the context of racialized hysteria about Asian, Latino, and black men using marijuana, opiates, and cocaine to tempt white women into a life of degradation and immorality. These images persist to this day, although they are far less obvious.[21]

None of this is to downplay the seriousness of addiction or to discount the prevalence of self-destructive behavior among Americans, in the past or the present. In this sense, our country *is* in a crisis. It doesn't take more than a quick survey of our social landscape to see how dysfunctional families, increasing personal debt, poverty, lack of health insurance, and harried work schedules all contribute to the kinds of stressors that make it more likely for Americans to turn to alcohol, nicotine, legal and illegal drugs to cope with their stress. But if people develop serious problems and start shooting up with dirty needles, mixing barbituates with alcohol, using hard liquor or cocaine to get through the day, or snorting crushed Oxy-Contins (often thinking that they are safe because they are "prescribed drugs"), we start to see the worst that drugs can do.

Addicts don't have to be locked up to be miserable, but prison doesn't help most people get better. (However, some women *have* told me that prison was the only place where they could access free drug counseling and rehabilitation, or that a short stint in jail was their first opportunity to feel sobriety in several years.)

People who have never had the misfortune of being imprisoned—or had a friend, partner, or family member doing time—tend to stereotype prisoners serving time on drug charges as antisocial, dangerous addicts lacking vocational skills or educational attainment. To some extent, this is true; studies bear out the fact that addiction plus lack of housing, education, and job training add up to a likely recipe for imprisonment. At least half of female drug offenders in prison have *less* than a high school degree,[22] and at least one-third of women in some stage of being processed through the criminal justice system are homeless.[23]

Despite the common perception that crack is a "black thing," Euro-Americans and Latinos add up to 66 percent of crack users nationally.[24] This is not to downplay the fact that crack *has* spread through many low-income, African American neighborhoods like wildfire, ruining the lives of countless men, women, and families in the process. Seattle is one of those cities where crack users *are* disproportionately African American, something that I have certainly been witness to. That said, there is no justifiable explanation for the fact that African Americans account for *more than 80 percent of people* sentenced under federal crack cocaine rules, which mandate a mininum five-year sentence for five grams or more of crack cocaine possession. In order to receive the same minimum sentence for powder cocaine, a person has to be caught with five hundred grams, a nonsensical 100:1 ratio that has yet to be rectified by Congress, despite repeated recommendations from the U.S. Sentencing Commission that they amend this gross disparity in the mandatory minimum related to crack should be amended.[25]

The pretext for the law that set up the five-year minimum penalty for five grams of crack cocaine (the equivalent of about two sugar packets) began with the first major shift in federal drug policy, when the 1984 Sentencing Reform Act

(SRA) was implemented during the Reagan era. The legislators who drafted the act sought to *reduce* existing race, gender, and class disparities in sentencing. Such disparities in prison terms varied wildly from one person to another, and were often based on a judge's personal prejudices. The SRA also put an end to parole—something that nearly all federal prisoners with whom I have spoken don't understand. They see the concept of parole as a real chance to transition back to the community and to prove their ability to do right by their families and communities.

When the SRA was passed, Congress created the United States Sentencing Commission (USSC) to monitor sentencing changes and establish mandatory minimum sentences for both drug crimes.

Two years later, by 1986, the hysteria had reached its peak. More than one thousand media stories about crack appeared in the national press in that year; NBC News ran four hundred separate reports on crack cocaine alone. *Time* called crack cocaine the "issue of the year," while *Newsweek* called it the biggest news story since Vietnam and Watergate. CBS News aired a documentary entitled *Forty-Eight Hours on Crack Street.* Almost all of these reports focused on crack use by African Americans and, to a lesser extent, Latinos.[26]

Politicians and reporters picked up the most sensational aspects of the crack epidemic and ran with them. A real, pressing drug problem was quickly turned into a national frenzy as writers and legislators predicted the spread of cracked-out black male killers and breeding female zombies who would birth scary, crack-addicted babies. These children were ostensibly going to grow up to be disturbed, angry adults with severe mental deficiencies, draining public resources in the process. As we now know, this did not happen, although family structures and incarceration rates certainly *did* devastate many inner cities and poor people who did not have access to resources to combat addictions when they developed.

The federal government never attempted to strategize about intervention. Instead, they allocated billions for prison construction and law enforcement. Without hesitation—and with a drug-war mentality already in place—the White House jumped on the antidrug bandwagon with fanaticism, and set about generating a giant caravan of rhetoric and legislation. The Anti-Drug Abuse Act passed in 1986 and introduced the 100:1 crack-to-powder cocaine ratio. The act was little more than a rash congressional reaction to pressure from the White House and ever-present media sensationalism. The decision was made swiftly and without real debate. Most of the discussion seemed to revolve around professional basketball star Len Bias, who had died a few weeks earlier. Although Bias had actually died of an alcohol and powder cocaine overdose, Congress proceeded as though crack cocaine had killed him and was a sign of things to come. By then, it was too late.

Law enforcement went after drug users of all stripes with stings, undercover agents, and overall aggression. For all intents and purposes, the "war on drugs" meant exactly that, complete with casualties and "collateral damage." Although the media did not report on it, crack cocaine actually spread quickly into *all* communities, even as the battle for drug turf was fought most fiercely in low-income black and latino neighborhoods.

The first person who tried to introduce me to crack (a term I had never heard until that moment, in 1984) was a young, middle-class, Euro-American teen from a different school; she had previously had a meth problem. In the entire time I attended my high school, at the height of the crack drug wars taking place inside the inner city, I did not meet one young student of color who used crack, although students of color were the majority at my school. Other drugs were certainly in plentiful supply, but crack was looked down upon as a drug of desperation. Good intentions might well have been at the center of sentencing reform, but the results have proven to be devastating, to the point that the USSC urged the *revision* of the crack cocaine sentencing disparity in 2004.

The minimum five-year sentence is still in place, although a significant U.S. Supreme Court case in 2006, *U.S. v. Booker*, ruled that mandatory federal sentencing guidelines were *unconstitutional*, and that judges should sentence offenders as they saw fit, using the preexisting sentencing grid only as a guideline. The ruling was significant, but has been ineffective thus far. In March 2006, the U.S. Sentencing Commission found that most judges were sentencing people according to the old guidelines. Most alarming was the finding that the average sentence had actually gone *up* to fifty-eight months.[27]

What does all of this have to do with women? A great deal. Mandatory minimums in general, and the crack cocaine law specifically, started to drag countless women into the drug-war vortex. The SRA permitted little in terms of "downward departures" in sentencing, which would have allowed for consideration of a woman's circumstances, domestic abuse, drug addiction, caretaking of children or parents, employment, and so on. Worse yet, detectives, agents, and prosecutors began to throw in federal conspiracy charges, which had previously reserved for people involved in high-level organized crime activities, fraud, and gambling outfits, as well as large-scale prostitution rings and the import of slave laborers.

With the passage of the Anti-Drug Abuse Act, women began to be arrested and charged with impunity, and were threatened increasingly with conspiracy charges if they didn't "roll" or "snitch" on their boyfriends, husbands, family members, or acquaintances. Women were interrogated, harangued, and warned that if they did not cooperate in the manner expected of them, they would face serious repercussions. Most threatening of all—aside from separation from their children—was the real threat that they could and would be charged as though they were the "drug kingpins" themselves, subject to ten- to fifty-year sentences (and beyond) in prisons far away from their families.

Most women "caught in the net" have little or no information to offer. Women are often completely unaware of what their boyfriends, sons, or husbands have gotten into. Some women and their partners are recreational users, and sometimes the men themselves are completely innocent of drug dealing—but detectives want to be able to make their quotas and earn praise from their department and the media, as in the Tulia case discussed later in this chapter. In other cases, women are aware of *some* drug activity by their partners but do not participate in deals. Still other women participate to a limited extent, knowingly or unknowingly picking up or delivering a package, passing on a phone message, signing for a postal delivery, or housing someone with drug involvement. The ACLU and other organizations now refer to this phenomenon as the "girlfriend problem."

Anecdotally, in talking with current and former prisoners, as well as correctional employees, I have come to understand that women are very rarely willing to snitch on their loved ones or their male partners, whether out of loyalty or fear. The same has unfortunately not been true with many men charged with drug conspiracy crimes. Stories abound about the extreme lengths that some drug dealers have gone to in order to put the blame on other men or, failing that, on their girlfriends, wives, former partners, or relatives—anything and anyone to get out of a long prison sentence.

Most of the many women in state or federal prisons whom I have interviewed are first-time, nonviolent offenders sentenced on drug conspiracy charges. It bears mention that these women are serving far longer sentences than most first-time-offender rapists, child molesters, or even murderers convicted of second degree murder or aggravated manslaughter. Here are just three examples:

Tracy Coven, forty-six, is in her second year of a twenty- to forty-year conspiracy sentence in Michigan for the delivery of cocaine and marijuana, as well as a felony firearm possession, although her fingerprints were not found on any of the bags or guns discovered in her home. Coven was charged as a drug kingpin after she went to trial and would not snitch on the man who was most likely to have stashed the drugs and guns. "I can truly say that I played no role in this offense: no sale, no buy," she says. "I took the weight for everything because I didn't have any information to give. Even if I did, this person belonged to a very violent gang in Detroit. Me, my family, and my friend's lives would have been in danger." Coven subsequently found out that the unnamed man in this case snitched on other men in return for a ten-year federal sentence, although it was his second felony drug case. He will be released ten to thirty years before Coven gets out of prison.

Deborah Campbell, fifty-two, is incarcerated at FCI Alderson in West Virginia. She was recently transferred across the country from a federal prison in California, where she lived in the Lake Elsinore area. On the word of a government informant, Campbell was sentenced to twenty years (fourteen of which she has already served), despite the fact that she was a first-time, nonviolent offender who was arrested with no drugs whatsoever in her possession. That informant was given probation in exchange for testimony about Campbell and her ex-husband.

Campbell doesn't deny her drug involvement, but asked the court to consider her circumstances. She met her husband when she was twenty-eight, and had two children by him, despite an escalation in his drug use and abusive behavior. He introduced Campbell to meth and his lifestyle, but when his behavior continued to worsen, Campbell kicked him out of the house. She stayed to take care of her two daughters. When the money ran out, Campbell decided to take up what she had seen her husband doing: dealing meth. Her plan was to make ends meet and then quit the work. Shortly thereafter, she was arrested and sentenced to federal prison, without being able to raise her children. Her twenty-one-year-old daughter is now in drug rehab in California.

Stephanie Nodd, forty, is imprisoned at FCC Coleman in Florida, serving her sixteenth year. A mother of five from Mobile, Alabama, Nodd was slapped with a thirty-year sentence in a kingpin conspiracy charge, although this offense was nonviolent and her first. Nodd was also convicted on the word of a government informant. She admits that she was hanging out with "bad company" in her early twenties, but the real kingpin in this case, according to Nodd, got fifteen years for cooperating with the government. Nodd tries to keep up hope, but, in her own words, she has suffered "a lifetime of pain." Her mother, who raised three of Nodd's five children, died while Nodd was incarcerated. Nodd was not allowed to attend the funeral.

Back in Oklahoma, forty-four-year-old Tina Thomas says that she never expected to join the ranks of the incarcerated. Thomas is near the end of her six-year sentence, assuming that the state grants her early release with one-third of her time served. All of this might sound familiar, perhaps even unexceptional, until this aspect of her life is revealed: Thomas holds a medical doctorate from the University of Illinois. She was a practicing neurologist and a professor in a teaching hospital. No matter where she went, Thomas stood out, both as a woman in a very male-dominated field and as a dreadlocked African American lesbian. The combination of her identity and her appearance was something that most of her peers had never encountered before.

What is even more remarkable about Thomas is that she had overcome the kind of childhood trauma that might have completely derailed her adult life. It might have been precisely that background that first propelled her to become an overachiever and attain a high level of professional success, but then came back to haunt her just as she had gotten to where she wanted to go. The dark secret of her life was that she had been forced to perform fellatio on her uncle when she was just four years old. Thomas explains that this unresolved trauma became "the template for a lifetime of distrust, fear, uncertainty, and a spirit of self-negation."

In the late 1990s, Thomas was introduced to cocaine. "In my thinking, [given] all that I had had to overcome to get to that point, I handled life pretty well," she explains. "I had jumped more hurdles than ninety percent of my colleagues. I could handle a little cocaine; what would it do to me?"

Unfortunately, Thomas's recreational use of cocaine and then crack morphed into full-blown addiction. Her partner and friends tried to stage an intervention, but after a short stint in rehab, Thomas was back to her habit. She lost a job in Toledo, Ohio, after which the Ohio State Medical Board began to investigate. As a result, her medical license was permanently revoked in 1998, so that she can never practice medicine in the United States again, no matter how many years of sobriety she has behind her. Says Thomas, "Not a day goes by that I don't fret about the future I am likely to face as an ex-con, albeit clean and sober, who is highly trained but unable to use that training."

There are some eight hundred women at the Taft women's prison, outside of Tulsa, where Thomas has been incarcerated for the past few years. She estimates that two-thirds of the women at the prison are doing time for drug-related offenses, yet only seventy-five prisoners at a time are allowed to participate in the only real drug rehabilitation program, which in itself relies on a questionable approach: a military-style course, originally designed for male prisoners, named the Regimented Training Program.

"The remaining inmates go through a course called Substance Abuse Education," Thomas tells me. "This is a one-and-a-half-hour class that meets on Saturday afternoons and is first and foremost a good ol' down-home church service. SAE is 'taught' by three or four married couples—teams of evangelical Christians with no particular credentials in counseling, substance abuse treatment, or mental health training. We enter the auditorium to gospel music, we have a prayer, then one of these volunteers will read from a fact-sheet blurb on whatever drug is being covered that day. There is [always] a Bible story correlate and tie-in. . . . Then the church service begins, replete with sermonizing, laying-on-of-hands healings, rebuking of the devil, and occasionally speaking in tongues."

This approach to "drug treatment" in prison is problematic from a number of perspectives, not the least of which is the obvious violation of the constitutional imperative for the separation of church and state. The SAE is a required twelve-week program that is watched over by guards on prison grounds—all of which is funded by the state. (For more on the incorporation of religious programs into prisons, see Chapter 9, "Living in the God Pod.")

"I believe that the decision had a lot to do with my race and my particular drug of choice," Thomas explains. "I don't think this collection of Midwesterners could reconcile a renegade, crack-addicted neurologist who had relapsed. Second and third chances might be afforded to my alcoholic white male colleagues . . . but crack? Too ghetto! Too black!"

Again, Thomas's story is unique to her life experience but not entirely unheard of. In Seattle, I met one woman (who didn't want her real name to be used, for obvious reasons) who was going to medical school by day and dealing drugs by night. "Nobody in my school knows what I do to make ends meet," she told me. "I live a double life."

Many impoverished women on the streets are living a double life in order to make money to support their families, their drug habits, or both. Small-scale drug dealing is one of the ways women do so; the other common way is by selling their bodies to men who cruise the streets, looking for cheap sex.

Despite cinematic portrayals that depict smart-talking, jaded hookers or highly cautious, all-wits-about-her prostitutes à la *Pretty Woman,* street prostitution is one of the most dangerous occupations imaginable for women in this country. This is particularly true if a woman is the "new face" on the block, or when her judgment is seriously impaired by her alcohol or drug use. The most common method of acquiring STDs is, of course, through unprotected sex. Although HIV infection is rarely the subject of news stories these days, women in this country are still getting infected, and African American females are infected at the highest rate of all women. Drug use accounts for 70 percent of HIV cases,[28] and unprotected sex increases the odds tremendously.

Streetwalkers face overwhelming odds of being arrested, as well as the ever-present risk of being assaulted, raped, or killed by johns, misogynists, even police officers. Teenagers and young women—as well as women hooked on drugs—are particularly at risk for the latter, although sexual violence, kidnapping, torture, and murder are a constant threat to absolutely anyone who engages in sex work without having people to call on for immediate assistance. Safer circumstances, although not foolproof against incidents of violation or violence, include exotic dancing/lap dance establishments, brothels, massage parlors, and private "dates" in upscale hotels with check-in calls to outside parties.

Some advocates of the decriminalization or legalization of prostitution argue that women who participate in the trade are not actually likely to be drug users, and that most women choose their occupations freely and without coercion. I, too, support the decriminalization of prostitution in the United States because I have visited other countries where prostitution is not demonized or punished (with largely positive results) unless a sex worker is engaging in such behavior as having sex without condoms.

But I do *not* agree that women who work the streets are largely free of substance addiction, or that they are choosing their professions freely. Yes, there are professional sex workers who live safe lives, are highly paid, and enjoy their occupations, and I have met enough of these women to know that this is the case. But my experience in talking with (and researching the lives of) street prostitutes has taught me that many are, in fact, using drugs to get through their days, and to make money when there few other viable economic choices. Moreover, women who work the streets have often been "turned out" by pimps, drug dealers, or even their family members.

One of the most powerful documentaries in recent memory that addresses precisely this reality for street prostitutes is *Turning a Corner,* directed by media activist Salome Chasnoff.[29] The film focuses on African American women in Chicago who left street prostitution behind. Roughly a dozen women open up to tell stories that are brutally honest and utterly harrowing. Nearly every woman reveals an agonizing childhood filled with physical and sexual abuse, alcohol and drug use by the people around them, and even parents who pushed them directly into sex work. One of the women, who spent twenty-six years working as a prostitute in a poor neighborhood in Chicago, explains that her mother, who took her to a "trick house," first introduced her to the trade. Her mother got her drunk and indulged the request of an older man who wanted to look at and photograph a naked young girl. Shortly thereafter, she met a pimp who got her working the streets. Her childhood ended right then and there.

Former prostitutes in *Turning a Corner* talk of barely surviving sexual violence: rapes, kidnappings at gunpoint, a sex worker who was found in an alley with her eyes gouged out, women raped and shot by a serial killer. One of the women who survived a gunshot from a serial murderer went to the police with her story, although prostitutes generally avoid going to the police after any kind of attack, fearing that they will be disbelieved or arrested. (One woman in the film tells of being raped and beaten, and when she finally recovered in the hospital, the police arrested her for prostitution, while the john wasn't even investigated or searched for.) Not surprisingly, the victim of the serial killer finds that she is ignored and dismissed as a drug addict and a hooker. It takes the woman's own detective work—finding other sex workers attacked by the man—to get the police to pay finally attention.

Norm Stamper, former Seattle chief of police, has been one among an increasing number in the ranks of law enforcement to argue for the decriminalization of prostitution.[30] In his groundbreaking book, *Breaking Rank: A Top Cop's Exposé of the Dark Side of American Policing,* Stamper puts forth the position that the criminalization of prostitution is an abject failure because it has pushed women underground to ply their trade, all the while dehumanizing sex workers as immoral and sinful beings unworthy of societal concern.

In *Breaking Rank,* Stamper writes that he heard many police officers refer to the murders of prostitutes and/or African Americans as "misdemeanor murders." More telling is the terminology used to describe this attitude toward the murder victims: "NHI, no humans involved."[31]

"Dehumanizing or demonizing sex workers makes it easier to ignore them when they go missing or are found dead," he writes. "I wonder how these officers of the law would respond to the murders of forty teachers? Forty homemakers? Forty ER nurses?"[32]

One of the most recent and horrific examples is that of the Green River Killer. Although the task force was touted for their exhaustive work—something that *eventually* was true—detectives ignored early evidence that Gary Ridgway was involved, at least in part because the eyewitnesses were prostitutes.

Before he was caught, Ridgway raped, choked, killed, and discarded forty-eight women, including many teenagers as young as fifteen. Ridgway was a married man and a father; a white guy from Auburn, Washington, who held the same job for thirty years—and who got away with killing one female after another for more than twenty years. Detective work, diligence, and a decision on the part of the King County prosecutor to spare Ridgway the death sentence in exchange for information were hailed as a job well done. Ridgway will never kill again.

But the question remains: Why was he allowed to murder women, again and again, when so much evidence had already pointed in his direction two decades earlier? The answer, in great part, lies in Ridgway's own admission of whom he preyed upon. "I picked prostitutes as my victims because I hate most prostitutes and I did not want to pay them for sex," Ridgway said in his confessional statement. "I also picked prostitutes as victims because they were easy to pick up without being noticed. I knew they would not be reported missing right away and might never be reported missing. I picked prostitutes because I thought I could kill as many of them as I wanted without getting caught."[33]

At least one-third of Ridgway's female victims were girls and women of color, and the vast majority were under the age of twenty-two. Ridgway, an extreme incarnation of a brutal misogynist, considered killing female prostitutes a "career." He felt proud of what he did and thought he was damn good at it. Ridgway even believed that he was helping the police out, as he admitted in one interview with investigators: "I thought I was doing you guys a favor, killing prostitutes."[34]

Like most street prostitutes, these were girls and young women with families. Some had drug and alcohol problems, yet many stayed close to their partners and parents, who understood the economic struggles inherent in all of their lives, despite the common perception that sex workers are shunned by their relatives. Would Ridgway have been stopped in his tracks fifteen or twenty years ago if his female victims had had different socioeconomic and ethnic backgrounds?

If they had not used drugs? If they had not participated in the street economy and had thus been more innocent in the eyes of the law?

Consider that in April 1983, the boyfriend of sixteen-year-old Kimi-Kai Pitsor told police that she had gotten into an older green Ford pickup truck. He went to the police and described the driver. Ridgway's girlfriend at the time owned an older light-green Ford. (Four years later, Pitsor's boyfriend picked Ridgway's photo out of a book of suspects.) In May 1983, Marie Malvar, eighteen, disappeared after getting into Ridgway's truck. Malvar's boyfriend actually took police to Ridgway's house four days later and then identified the pickup he saw Malvar climb into. When two detectives questioned Ridgway, he actually admitted to picking up prostitutes but denied any contact with Malvar. His arms were covered with scratches from the fight that Malvar put up to try to save her own life, but Ridgway wore long sleeves, and the police didn't bother to look on his person or in his house for any evidence of a struggle. (Later, Ridgway poured battery acid on his arms to disguise the marks.) Despite the eyewitness identification, neighborly, upstanding Ridgway was left alone.

Ridgway continued to have many close calls with police, evading officers and detectives all the while. In 1984, Rebecca Garde Guay actually came forward to police to say that she had been assaulted two years prior by a man who tried to kill her by placing her in a chokehold. Not only did Guay know Ridgway's place of employment (he had shown her an identification card), but she also picked him out of a book of photos. What's worse, Ridgway had the sheer gall to admit to having "dated" Guay and even choking her. But by then, Guay no longer wanted to pursue charges.[35] She became the only known survivor of the Green River Killer, although I interviewed one former prostitute (name withheld) who had worked the strip where Ridgway usually picked up his victims, and she recalled his trying to cajole her into his car. She sensed danger and declined. One of her friends disappeared that same day, and her remains were not found until much later.

Perhaps Guay was afraid of being hunted down, or perhaps she just knew that she wouldn't be believed, which was probably true. Although Ridgway admitted to forty-eight murders, detectives believe that he may have killed as many as sixty women and girls.

"In most cases when I killed these women, I did not know their names," Ridgway stated during one interview after he was captured. "Most of the time I killed them the first time I met them, and I do not have a good memory of their faces. I killed so many women, I have a hard time keeping them straight."[36]

As a society, we still tend to see both drug users and sex workers as infestations to be kept under control. Words like "eradication" are used in tandem with both "drugs" and "street prostitution" by law enforcement on a regular basis.

Prostitution and drug-related arrests are unquestionably influenced by the color of a person's skin, which neighborhood they live in, and how they are dressed. Those who have been targeted in this way have no doubt about the prevalence of profiling, but can rarely prove it, much less raise the issue with the police themselves. Every now and then, a study appears that actually *does* point to serious discrepancies in who gets harassed or arrested in any given city, whether for DWB (driving while black or brown), WWB (walking while black or brown), or HOWB (hanging out while black or brown).

One such study in Seattle in 2004 found that while the majority of the users of "serious" illicit drugs—cocaine, heroin, methamphetamines, and ecstasy—were Euro-American (with the exception of crack, which is used more by African Americans in this city), more than 64 percent of arrested persons were African American, 14 percent were Latino, and 17 percent were Euro-American.[37] The black population in Seattle is below the national average, at 8.2 percent, as are

"Hispanics of any race," at 6.3 percent. Euro-Americans constitute the majority population of the city, at 69 percent.[38]

Prior to his position as Seattle chief of police, while he was the San Diego deputy chief, Stamper initiated a series of interviews with men on the force about their attitudes toward people of color, particularly African Americans and Latinos.

"Thirty-one personnel (including my lieutenant and two of his sergeants) admitted to using racial and ethnic slurs," Stamper writes in *Breaking Rank*. "African Americans were niggers, boys, splibs, toads, coons, garboons, groids (from 'negroid'), Sambos, Buckwheats, Rastuses, jigaboos, jungle bunnies, and spooks. Latinos were greasers, wets, wetbacks, beans, beaners, bean bandits, chickenos, spics. . . . Most cops said they used the terms among themselves, less often with the public, and then 'only jokingly' . . . or when they were '*really* pissed' at someone."[39]

One of the officers even admitted that he had made several busts for what he called 'BBN' . . . 'Busy being a nigger.'"[40]

African Americans are not the only ethnic group targeted for harassment or arrest, depending on which region of the country is being examined. However, depending on the state, both Native Americans and Latinos are, unfortunately, often lumped in with Euro-Americans in the criminal justice system, and/or counted as "Other," along with Asian Americans, Pacific Islanders, and people of mixed ethnicity. As such, the arrest and imprisonment rates of ethnic groups besides African Americans are far harder to track. Often, anecdotal evidence and rough estimates are all that we have. Other ethnic groups are also targeted across the nation.

I lived in New Mexico from 2002 to 2003 and returned in 2005 to visit the Grants women's prison. Traveling in New Mexico, I witnessed how Native Americans were arrested with alarming frequency for crimes that tended to revolve around public drunkenness, drug use, or more serious crimes that usually involved substance use of some kind. New Mexico has a greater concentration of Indian nations than almost any other part of the country, yet Native Americans are rarely counted as their own ethnic category, much less by their respective tribal/cultural affiliations. Instead, they are lumped in with either Euro-Americans or Latinos, based largely on appearance and skin color. This is also the case all over the Southwest and many parts of the West Coast, including Washington state, where Pacific Islanders have been imprisoned at high rates. From official statistics, we do know that the highest per capita incarceration rates for Latinos are found in states that are not usually associated with their Latino populations: Pennsylvania, Idaho, and Connecticut. In addition to blacks and Latinos, Southeast Asians and Pacific Islanders are often targeted for arrests in Southern California.

Montana is another state not usually associated with incarceration *or* the targeted arrests of people of color. But Montana's criminal justice system appears to go after Native Americans (who account for 6 percent of the population in an overwhelmingly Euro-American state) with particular zeal. Native men represent 20 percent of prisoners, and Native women represent *one-quarter* of all female prisoners in the state.[41] Similarly, Hawaii's prisons are bursting with indigenous low-income Hawaiians and Asian Americans in general, who are now shipped out of state because the island state's prisons are operating above and beyond maximum capacity. (See Chapter 10, "Shipping Women's Bodies.")

One need only watch the popular A&E television show *Dog: The Bounty Hunter* (with the tagline "In Dog We Trust") for blatant visual evidence of how true this is. Although Dog is celebrated by some in Hawaii as a public hero (he is a former drug user and inmate who usually talks to women and men sympathetically about their addictions after catching them), the sight of his all-white team, rolling around in SUVs, going after people of color who are drug addicts (usually they are addicted to the smokable meth derivative known as ice), is a disturbing reminder of how alcohol and drug abuse in this colonized island nation has truly wreaked havoc on people's lives. Women are no exception and actually tend to be "hunted" far more often than men on this show. In August 2006, the *Dog* crew gives the audience an earful of their special brand of criminal justice gender theory. Women are harder to "hunt," explains Dog's wife, Beth. "That's like a woman's main job: outsmarting men."

As the crew chases down one drugged-out woman after another, Dog and company explain the inherent dangers of dealing with women: Those who are about to be caught feel like it's "high noon" and will put up more of a fight. The "girls," as we learn, "are absolutely more aggressive [than the men]," although of course there's no real evidence, visual or otherwise, to back up this claim. The women *do* come across as having been wrecked by drug use and by their poverty and related depression. The women flee the criminal justice system and skip out on court hearings and bail but don't appear to be any danger to the people coming after them—they either give up or try to run away. It's Tim, Dog's brother, who best sums up the crew's prevailing sentiment: "I think all women are crazy," he says without hesitation.[42]

Incarceration, rather than treatment or structural/cultural analysis of *why* drug use is so common in Hawaii, has been the unfortunate "solution" to the suffering of its poorest citizens. The strategy may be more noticeable in Hawaii because there is a finite amount of space in which to build prisons, but it is part and parcel of a nationwide approach to drug use and abuse.

It's one thing to consider the incarceration rates of people of color and poor people as an unfortunate consequence of the scourge of drug abuse, underemployment and unemployment of youth and adults, as well as profiling by police. Viewed in the context of a sociohistorical framework, the massive rates of overincarceration in the federal, state, and local juvenile and adult criminal justice systems take on the characteristics of a pressing national crisis. Although mainstream civil rights organizations have been woefully slow in addressing the situation as such, others are already making valid comparisons to the struggle for civil rights that took place several decades ago.

"The drug war is a proxy for racism," ACLU Drug Law Reform Project attorney Andy Ko told me in 2002. "Most modern politicians wouldn't dream of explicitly advocating that society persecute or enslave poor people or members of minority communities. But that is exactly what is happening as a result of the 'get tough on crime' drug-war policies of the past few decades."

One-time political conservative Arianna Huffington has expressed similar sentiments. "[O]ur politicians have consistently failed to take action on what has become yet another third rail of American politics, a subject to be avoided at all costs by elected officials who fear being incinerated on contact for being soft on crime," she wrote in a commentary entitled "The War on Drugs Is Really a War on Minorities."[43]

Women with economic, social, and emotional problems are often ill equipped to deal with a court of law, particularly if they are being tried on felony charges for the first time. Women are eager to get out of the typically unpleasant conditions in overcrowded jails, rife with angry and distressed people, communicable diseases, and the sight and sound of women detoxing from their alcohol or drug addictions without medical assistance. Inmates also face the possibility of sexual harassment and violence at the hands of jail employees who choose to take advantage of a woman's pretrial stress and overall powerlessness.

Because they cannot afford bail, indigent and low-income women are often represented by rushed or inept public defenders. Poor women usually do not know how to navigate the criminal justice system unless they have educated themselves, usually in prison law libraries, if they exist. As such, they are typically unfamiliar with their legal rights, including the veracity of oral agreements versus written agreements on the part of prosecutors and defense attorneys who promise short sentences in exchange for guilty pleas.

This promise is something that I hear about frequently from prisoners who originally agreed to bypass a trial because an attorney promised them a short sentence for a quick plea. Only later do these women realize what they have actually agreed to, and that they had no actual guarantee of what was offered to them. Women's judgment is also clouded because of the shape they are in when they are brought in on drug charges and then often placed on heavy tranquilizers or psychotropic medications while awaiting their trials. Prisoners refer to this as wearing "chemical handcuffs," as domestic violence survivor Jane Benson explains. Most women that I've spoken to admit that they did not even know *which* drugs they were placed on, only that they were told to take the pills.

It's no wonder that plea bargains are so common in drug cases, and women are no exception. To use Oklahoma as just one example, drug-related arrests of women in the state are 116 percent above the national average. (Oklahoma also spends less than half the national average on drug treatment.) Of the women arrested each year in the state, *99 percent accept plea bargains.*[44]

Sometimes, there is little choice but to do so, especially when corrupt enforcers of the law use their positions to railroad individuals—even entire communities, as was the case in Tulia, Texas.

In the early morning hours of July 23, 1999, Officer Tom Coleman led a massive sweep of this small, rural town in the Texas panhandle, awakening forty-six women and men from their slumber. As the hapless citizens were dragged out of their houses, they were paraded in front of television cameras; meanwhile Coleman lorded his victory as an undercover drug agent working for the Swisher County Sheriff's Department. The Tulia case didn't start to make any waves until information started to trickle out that all of the early-morning arrests were conducted without drug evidence, audio or video surveillance, corroborating witnesses, or comprehensive note-taking of any kind on Coleman's part.

As if to confirm the guilt of those accused, over half of the defendants wound up pleading guilty in exchange for probation or somewhat shorter prison sentences. For some, that happened. For many others—including those who took their cases to trial—lengthy prison sentences were in store. In this mostly white Texan town, one particular aspect of the drug sweep was the fact that thirty-nine of the forty-six people arrested were African American, comprising nearly 15 percent of the town's black citizens. The majority of the seven Euro-Americans arrested were involved in interracial relationships.[45]

The racial overtones of the situation led a host of organizations and agencies to start looking into what had happened, including the NAACP Legal Defense Fund, an organization that would eventually play a primary role in overturning most of the sentences. The U.S. Justice Department (DOJ) and the state attorney general's office also began their own investigations, although the DOJ failed to call for a single oversight hearing or produce a single report on the situation. Among those arrested in Tulia were many young adults with no criminal histories, an elderly diabetic hog farmer, and several single mothers who had never left their own small town. Prison guard Mattie White, whom I met in 2002, was still in a state of shock over the fact that three of her relatives had been indicted for their ostensible roles in the "drug ring," including one niece, two nephews, and a son-in-law.[46]

As the postconviction appeals mounted, it came out that Coleman had an extensive background of making racist comments toward and about Latinos and African Americans, including his common use of "nigger." He had also been accused of the sexual harassment of women, official misconduct, and skipping out of town to avoid paying financial debts. Coleman should have never been believed to the extent that he was allowed to round up nearly fifty people in a tight-knit small town where families depend on each other for survival, and where the average African American makes between $9,000 and $11,000 per year.

Finally, the truth started coming out in startling detail. Coleman had failed to produce any tangible evidence of the drugs, or any proof of incriminating phone calls, messages, drug deals, or payoffs in what turned out to be an imaginary drug ring. He had made absolutely every part of the story up in his head, and spun it as gospel truth.

After four long years of incarceration for thirteen of the Tulia defendants, Dallas judge Ron Chapman announced in April 2003 that Coleman was "not a credible witness." He recommended immediate retrials for all of the men and women who had been swept up and incarcerated after that morning's drug sting. Within hours, the state's prosecution had agreed to throw out all the convictions, admitting that the entire debacle had been a "travesty of justice." Prosecutors said they would not retry the defendants. I had been following the case closely for years and penned a column on the subject entitled "Finally, Justice in Tulia," a title that I now regret.[47]

I, like many others, was glad to see most of the "Tulia 46" go free and eventually be exonerated of the charges. I was also hoping for a righteous result when Coleman was charged with perjury, facing a maximum sentence of ten years—a fraction of the time that many of the thirteen defendants received. But I had to eventually ask myself this question: What kind of "justice" system is willing to send small-town women and men old men away for *decades* without any evidence, save the vitriol of one man's word? What kind of justice can truly compensate the Tulia 46, who had to face public arrest and humiliation? What kind of justice is there for the parents, children, family members, and friends who spent years hoping for some kind of miracle?

What happened in Tulia may have been an extreme example of what happens in the American war on drugs, but it was far from being an isolated case. "Tulia is just the tip of the iceberg," attorney Vanita Gupta, of the NAACP Legal Defense Fund, said after the verdict. "We do feel victorious . . . but we also know that the problem is much deeper than what happened here."

And Coleman? Seven years of probation, no time served.

Chapter 3: Abuse Behind the Wall

"A prison guard indicted in a contraband-for-sex conspiracy opened fire at a Tallahassee correctional facility Wednesday when federal agents came to arrest him, and the ensuing gun battle left him and a federal agent dead."
—Peter Whoriskey and Dan Eggen, *The Washington Post*, June 22, 2006

"It's not unusual for male guards to walk through [Administrative Segregation] and ask you to show your tits or masturbate while they watch you to receive extra food or blankets."
—Rhonda Spain, Fluvanna Correctional Center for Women in Troy, Virginia

Female prisoners and officers alike have been complaining about sexual abuse by male guards at the Federal Correctional Institution (FCI) in Tallahassee since 1995, when the prison started to house female inmates.

Word travels quickly between inmates, particularly when transfers occur as frequently as they do in the Federal Bureau of Prisons (BOP). For years, similar stories circulated about women being impregnated by guards at FCI Tallahassee, some resulting in abortions, and others in unexplained childbirths, within the prison. Prisoners knew what was going on, but very few of them were willing to report what they had seen or experienced.

The women's fears were hardly irrational. Even when a prisoner reported being coerced into sex or being raped while locked up at FCI Tallahassee, she was likely to face the wrath of prison guards who cut visitation and phone privileges, take away prized possessions, and threaten women and their families with bodily harm. On the rare occasions when these crimes *were* prosecuted, the perpetrators were getting away with slaps on their wrists.

In 1998, for instance, Officer K. P. Price had sex with a woman incarcerated at FCI Tallahassee. When the woman suspected that she was pregnant six months later, the officer brought her a pregnancy test, and the results were positive. The woman had an abortion, but it took nearly a year for Price to be charged with any kind of crime. He pled guilty, but served no prison time.[1] In May 2001, Officer Michael Sneed was charged with having sexual intercourse with a prisoner at the same facility. He pled guilty but received only a three-year probation term.

Later that year, a nonviolent offender, Bobbi Bolton, was sent to FCI Tallahassee on a ten-month sentence for a probation violation. Guard Jeffrey Linton began to make increasingly suggestive sexual comments to her. Bolton brushed them off until Linton made his way into her cell one night and raped her without wearing a condom. One week later, he raped her again, but this time Bolton saved evidence of his semen on her clothing and sent it to her attorney in Texas. The result of her complaint against Linton was predictable: She was punished with solitary confinement in July 2002 and wasn't let out until October, when her sentence was up. Despite the physical evidence, Linton got away with a misdemeanor charge, the same way Price had—he ended up with a two-year probation period.[2]

And so it went. Another guard who pled guilty to sex with a prisoner got probation and home detention for three months in 2003; yet another was caught bringing in contraband and having sex with a woman in a bathroom, and then tried to turn off a surveillance camera set up by federal agents. Scared of retaliation, the woman dropped the charges, and the officer walked off with a five-year probation term.[3]

None of these men went to prison for their crimes. In fact, until 2006, prison rape had yet to even be classified as a felony within the BOP. But at least the Department of Justice (DOJ) had finally started to pay some attention, not only to what was happening at FCI Tallahassee, but to other women's prisons as well.

In 2005, the Office of the Inspector General and the DOJ released a report documenting widespread sexual abuse by prison employees nationwide, noting that only 37 percent had faced some kind of legal action. Of those, three-fourths walked away with no more than probation. It took all of this evidence for the BOP to finally criminalize sexual contact as a felony in 2006, so that guards could actually face up to five years in prison.[4]

In itself, five years for prison rape is hardly tantamount to serious punishment for the crime of sexual assault perpetrated against a person held in captivity. International law dictates the rape of a person in captivity to be an act of torture, and all forms of sexual abuse are considered clear violations of the prohibition against cruel, inhumane, or degrading treatment of prisoners.[5] "All persons deprived of their liberty shall be treated with humanity and with respect for the inherent dignity of the human person," reads Article 10 of the International Covenant on Civil and Political Rights, a crucial international agreement ratified (but ignored with ignominious frequency) by the United States.

In the rest of the Western world, women prisoners are guarded only or primarily by other women because of existing international standards.[6] This was also true in the United States until the passage of the 1964 Civil Rights Act and the 1972 Equal Employment Opportunity Act, both of which integrated the workforce but also moved men into more direct contact with female prisoners. "Men had always worked as officers in women's prisons, though their assignments were often restricted," writes Dana Britton in *At Work in the Iron Cage*. "Most commonly, men worked perimeter posts, such as gates and guard towers (rather than living areas), and served as the disciplinary threat of last resort for women prisoners."[7]

In theory, gender parity in all occupations makes sense. But in practice, it opens the door to a host of problems—especially where women prisoners are concerned. Today it's estimated that at least 40 percent of guards in women's prisons are men.[8] In some female prisons, the majority of employees are men, as is the case in California, where men represent 66 percent of correctional officers. At the Central California Women's Facility specifically, less than 1 percent of lieutenants are women; only 19 percent of sergeants are women; and females represent just 31 percent of correctional officers.[9]

Trine Christensen a primary Amnesty International researcher for the last decade's most comprehensive state-by-state survey relating to the treatment of women in prison. She talked to me, shortly after the 2001 release of "Abuse of Women in Custody," about the possible ways of addressing this issue in the United States while ensuring gender parity in the workplace.

"I understand the issue of men wanting to work in women's prisons too, but there are ways to prevent sexual abuse," Christensen told me. "Always have men accompanied by women; never allow them to do crossgender pat-downs; never allow them unsupervised access to women's living quarters.

"Obviously, many of the people working [in prisons] are professional, and they won't do anything wrong," added Christensen, "but the fact is that when you have situations like this . . . having unsupervised males in female facilities and giving them full access to females at night, or in intimate situations [such as when women] use showers or the bathroom—[these are] situations that are conducive to sexual abuse."

In these kinds of settings, outright violations of women's privacy—as well as visual or verbal sexualization by some guards—amounts to a regular part of life for female inmates in jails and prisons across the country. Today, one in four women reports having been sexually abused while in jail or prison. (Men experience sexual violence—particularly at the hands of other male prisoners—at an estimated rate of one in five. This crisis is even less likely to be discussed in public and is made far worse by the prevalence of "don't drop the soap" jokes and insulting notions that the experience of male-on-male rape is somehow humorous.)[10]

In 2005, more than six thousand inmates filed reports of sexual violence, another figure that is actually likely to be much higher because of the common fear of retaliation within prisons. The Bureau of Justice Statistics have also noted that sexual abuse and violence rates are higher at state-run juvenile facilities—*ten times higher* than the rates of sexual abuse reported at adult facilities.[11]

Today, there are some ninety-five thousand juveniles in custody in the United States. The percentage of girls in custody in any given state typically ranges from 10 to 20 percent, and females constitute as much as 30 percent of total juvenile arrests, particularly in urban areas. These girls usually come from low-income environments and enter the juvenile justice system with serious, persistent histories of sexual, physical, and/or emotional abuse. In most states, girls of color are disproportionately represented (just as women of color are in the prison system). In New York, for instance, 73 percent of girls locked up are African American or Latina, whereas in King and Pierce Counties (the greater Seattle/Tacoma region), African American, Asian American, and particularly Native American girls are detained at rates far disproportionate to their overall demographic representation in the region.[12]

Juvenile detention facilities are notorious for being even more closed to outside scrutiny than adult facilities are, at least in part because the identities of arrested minors are typically protected by law—except in highly sensationalized cases, or when a juvenile is tried in court as an adult. As such, very few incidents relating to the abuse of juveniles in custody actually make the news. But when they do, they are indicative of a systemwide failure to protect young people. In September 2006, for instance, Human Rights Watch and the American Civil Liberties Union released a report revealing the depth of abuse and neglect suffered by girls confined in New York juvenile facilities. In addition to reports of violent restraint and punishment resulting in abrasions, cuts, bruises, and even broken bones, girls were subjected to humiliating strip searches and verbal harassment, as their overseers would broadcast their opinions on the girls' sexual histories, including whether the girls had experienced sexual abuse or gotten sexually transmitted diseases. Members of the staff were documented as having molested and engaged in sexual intercourse with girls on several occasions.[13]

Major investigations and lawsuits in recent years, in states including Alabama, Texas, and Colorado, have also exposed the prevalence of sexual abuse and rape within juvenile detention facilities. As a 2004 lawsuit against the Colorado Department of Corrections revealed, the few girls incarcerated with hundreds of boys in a single facility called the Youth Offender System (YOS) were subject to constant sexual coercion, harassment, and rape by adult staff, resulting in several pregnancies. After the pregnancies, guards went to the extent of forcing the girls to take birth control pills. The girls were also threatened with violence against them *and their family members* if they spoke out about the abuse. Staff members were found to have "openly discussed which guards were molesting which girls."[14]

Tabitha Fleming, now a mother and journalist, spent three years at the same juvenile detention facility in Colorado, beginning in 1998. She was seventeen when she was sentenced for providing a handgun to a minor, although she says that the actual crime itself was theft. Regardless, she was sent to YOS, finding that she was one of only seven female juveniles there. While imprisoned, Fleming fell in love with another teenager, became pregnant, and delivered her daughter in the facility. "It was the biggest-kept secret," she says of the child and the relationship, which actually turned into a marriage once the two were released, and has stayed intact since then.

"I was ridiculed, singled out, told by staff that I didn't care about myself and that I was being a 'whore,'" Fleming recalls. "The abuse was worse from the [boys] that we interacted with on a daily basis. The only time we [girls] were separated was in our own housing unit. . . . All of the females in the facility were in some form of sexual relationship, with other inmates and with staff members."

Compounding the prevalence of sexual abuse in detention facilities is the fact that roughly half of female prisoners report physical or sexual abuse in their backgrounds before they were ever imprisoned. According to one national study, 57 percent of women in state prisons, as well as 40 percent of female federal prisoners, report such prior abuse.[15] The Bureau of Justice Statistics arrived at similar percentages, but with more detail.[16]

- One-third of the women in state prisons, one-quarter in local jails, and one-fifth in federal prisons said they had been raped before their incarceration, compared with 3 percent of incarcerated men.
- Incarcerated women reported higher levels of abuse as children than women in the "free world." One-third of female state prison and jail inmates said that they had been abused as children, compared with 12–17 percent in the general population, although those figures are likely to be much higher in actuality,

given that many women who have been abused are not comfortable sharing
their stories.

- *Nearly 90 percent* of incarcerated women who had spent most of their childhood
in foster care or juvenile institutions reported physical or sexual abuse.

- Of female state prisoners who had grown up with a parent or guardian who
drank or used illicit substances, *80 percent* revealed that those adults had
abused them.

- Among the prisoners who reported past abuse, *more than half* of the women
said they had been abused by their primary partners on the outside. Among
abused women, 80 percent of women used illegal drugs regularly. Both of these
figures are roughly comparable to the experiences of abused male prisoners,
representing one of the only circumstances in which prison statistics match
for both genders.

When I sat down to talk with a dozen adult females locked up at the San Francisco County Jail, absolutely *every* woman told me about her history of emotional,
physical, and sexual abuse. Their life stories of persistent abuse were so horrifying
in their brutality that I found myself struggling for a way to process the details
they shared with me.[17] (To protect the identities of these women, most of whom
were pretrial defendants, I agreed to use their first names only.)

Many of the women with histories of childhood abuse had turned to drugs
early on in their lives to self-medicate their pain away temporarily; this often led
to prostitution to support their habits. One woman, Juanita, explained that she
grew up in an abusive home environment. She eventually drifted into drug abuse
and prostitution. While she was on the streets, a john who picked her up in his

car wound up driving her away from public sight; he then raped and stabbed her. Juanita was left for dead with the knife sticking out of the back of her neck—the man who tried to kill her, as it turned out, had murdered several prostitutes in San Francisco before he was caught. Without counseling or a way of obtaining any kind of normalcy in her life, the trauma from the rape and attempted murder sent Juanita into an even deeper spiral of drug addiction.

Another woman, Rose, who was awaiting trial on a drug possession charge, was already well into her fifties. Rose was born to a family of seven in Berkeley. Her father, as she recalled, taught her how to read but then began to molest her when she reached puberty. "He caused me to shut down," Rose remembered. "There was no more singing or dancing in my life."

By the time she reached fourteen years of age, Rose said that she had lost all sense of herself as a child. Impregnated by a man in her community, Rose had a stillbirth. An abortion followed the next time she got pregnant. Rose was married at sixteen and had more stillbirths.

Later in life, she gave birth to four healthy children and eventually confronted her father about the abuse. But the confrontation brought up so much pain for Rose that she wound up trying to take her life shortly thereafter. "That's something else I still got to figure out," she shrugged. This was as far as she was able to go in talking about her attempted suicide.

Rose started prostituting to support herself and her family. Then came crack cocaine, which she started using when she was thirty-three years old. Rose had one period of sobriety in the ensuing two decades that lasted five years. "I've been raped out there, had guns and knives pulled on me," she explained. "The first time a man pulled a gun on me, he put it to the base of my skull, and I was sure it was over."

But Rose survived her extreme circumstances with a fury raging inside her that didn't explode until another man kidnapped her, took her to a school yard, raped her, and told her that he was going to shoot her in the head. A struggle ensued, and Rose reached into her purse. She pulled out a knife and stabbed him with as much force as she could muster.

"What happened to him?" I asked.

Rose paused, with a far-off look in her eyes. I had the distinct sense that she was reliving the experience. We sat in silence for a minute.

"As far as I know, I left him dead in that school yard," she finally said.

The fact that Rose didn't tell the police about what happened isn't surprising. Even when women in the "free world" try to do the right thing and come clean about the extent of their abusive pasts and the subsequent violence in response to that abuse, there is absolutely no guarantee of any amount of sympathy in the eyes of the law.

Sadly, many abused women and girls who have fallen on hard times end up in custody. A one-size-fits-all approach to females engaged in what are defined subjectively as "illicit" activities and "crimes" (but which are clearly survival oriented, self-defensive, or self-destructive) is questionable at best. Criminalizing women who have turned to self-medication and/or prostitution seems not only unwarranted, but completely counterproductive if the ostensible desire is to set them on a better life path.

The criminal justice system's capacity for callous disregard of the individual needs of people in custody was perhaps most evident to me at the women's jail in Los Angeles County. There, one deputy in particular openly derided the women locked up for street prostitution, saying that they "smelled bad" and had no sense of shame about what they were doing. But my experiences talking with women who have engaged in so-called low level sex work (as well as the outreach workers who try to work with them to lower the risk of sexually transmitted diseases, HIV infection, and sexual violence) have taught me that most prostitutes come from both severely economically disadvantaged and abusive environments. More often than not, these women struggle throughout their lives with shame and self-destructive impulses, often abusing alcohol or drugs to get through their days and nights, living in a blur of intoxication, violence, and suffering.

Experiences of extreme violence and sexual abuse in women prisoners' lives are far worse and far more commonplace than most Americans realize. Indeed, mentally ill women who have been abused are among the most vulnerable members of our society. Among mentally ill women in prison, 59 percent report sexual abuse histories, compared with 15 percent of mentally ill men. In jails nationwide, 63 percent of mentally ill women have been sexually abused, in contrast to 17 percent of male inmates with mental illness.[18] Although the American Psychiatric Association has recommended developing specific treatment programs to help female inmates address their high levels of trauma, such programs are rare.[19]

Because of the abundant sexual violence in men's jails and prisons—abuse usually occurs at the hands of other inmates, rather than guards or other prison employees—we should ask the logical question of whether women in prison sexually assault each other. Although I have not yet come across a young girl sexually assaulted by another girl in juvenile detention, I have come across plenty of stories about girls in juvenile detention being abused by boys and men. I have also interviewed roughly half a dozen women prisoners who experienced pressure to enter a sexual relationship with either a female prison guard or a dominant inmate. (Such prisoners are usually known as "studs" or "aggressive butches.") Most lesbian relationships in prison, however, do not fit this mold. Rather, they take the form of supportive camaraderie and intimacy, helping women to survive the prison experience. In my experience talking with women prisoners, this is true regardless of whether they identify on the "outside" as heterosexual, bisexual, or gay. (See Chapter 8, "Women Loving Women.")

When it occurs, female-on-female assault should certainly be taken as seriously as any other type of assault, although it must still be emphasized that the vast majority of sexual contact and overt sexual violence in women's prisons happens when male correctional employees decide to exploit the gender and power differential inherent in a female custodial setting.

The sexually intrusive or abusive nature of these experiences in prison has a devastating impact on a woman's likelihood of achieving a healthy and successful reentry into society. Upon arriving in a custodial facility, or after any kind of out-of-prison transport for medical needs, girls and women are usually strip-searched, a process that includes cavity searches (in which women must bend over and expose their vaginal and rectal areas), and then a squat-and-cough search for contraband. Many prisons also conduct mandatory strip searches or pat-downs before and after visitation with friends or family members. Women suspected of bringing in contraband can be placed in "potty" rooms forbidden to exit for days on end, and their feces are stored and searched for contraband.

If a prisoner begins to experience a serious emotional crisis and expresses suicidal feelings, she can be placed in a bare suicide-watch room after being stripped naked or barely covered with "suicide blankets" or "suicide gowns." Male or female guards stare through her window every fifteen minutes or monitor her through a surveillance camera.

As I have witnessed in every custodial facility I have ever visited, toilets and showers in jails and prisons offer minimal privacy. Much of a woman's body remains exposed to guards directly, or indirectly through surveillance cameras. The same lack of privacy exists within men's facilities, but an important distinction regarding the emotional landscape of men and women needs to be made on this issue. Although this fact shouldn't need explication, women in the United States and throughout the world continue to have far, far less sexual and physical power in society, despite obvious gains in economic, sexual, political, and personal freedoms made over the past several decades. It is still a sad truth that sexual violence against girls and women is prevalent in our society, to the extent that females logically perceive unwanted sexual comments and intrusions into their privacy as possible or *likely* threats to their safety, particularly when they are being held captive in some fashion. In contrast, men are typically not subject to the same kinds of intrusions from girls and women, so they have far less to fear from females, whether in the "free world" or while incarcerated.

On the face of it, privacy in bathrooms may not register as an obvious form of violation or sexual intrusion. Certainly, being watched showering or using the toilet doesn't seem nearly as invasive as groping or rape. But for many women in prison, being watched doing things that they are able to do in the "free world" without being observed is a very traumatic experience. By contrast, males grow accustomed to urinating and undressing near each other in bathrooms and gyms from an early age onward. Although men in prison also tell me that they want to be able to use the toilet in privacy, they do not typically experience the presence of guards as a form of sexual intimidation while doing so.

Female prisoners in what's called the "general population" have a difficult time with all of the above. The women locked away in twenty-two- to twenty-three-hour-per-day "control units" face the most intensive surveillance and the most direct invasion of their privacy. Prison administrators and guards justify this level of monitoring of inmates on the grounds that people sent to these units are most problematic and dangerous, or are the hardest to control in any other setting. There is truth to that for some of the prisoners, although many of them tend to be struggling with serious mental illness (see Chapter 5, "Trying to Stay Sane"). These sections of women's prisons or jails typically mandate a strip search anytime a woman leaves or reenters her cell—even if the destination in question is the shower just a few feet away from her cell. In these units, absolutely no form of privacy is allowed, whether a woman is changing her clothes, changing a sanitary pad, or using the toilet. Any attempt to cover up cell windows is cause for a write-up and can even result in a forcible cell extraction, loss of accrued credits towards reduced prison time for good behavior, or an extended stay in the control unit.

Rhonda Spain, doing time in the Fluvanna Correctional Center for Women (FCCW) in Troy, Virginia, told me about her experiences in Administrative Segregation (Ad Seg), temporary housing for women who have asked for protective custody, or who are awaiting a decision on punishment for violating prison rules. The primary control unit in that prison is called the Structured Living Unit (SLU), and both units are housed in the same building.

"The sergeant and officers in that building [try daily] to provoke the inmates to get a charge. It's a trap to give you more time. The sergeant is rude [and] manhandles the women," Spain told me. "I've seen him hit, slap, [and] feel up inmates."

Spain echoes the concern that mentally ill inmates are particularly easy prey for abusive prison employees, as they have a diminished capacity to defend themselves or articulate their experiences to supervisors. Spain added that at FCCW she has seen officers getting "lots of sexual favors [after] mixing up [prisoners'] medications," presumably to tranquilize the women or put them in a drug-induced stupor.

Women suffering from drug addiction are also particularly vulnerable to the advances of male guards who promise banned substances in exchange for sexual favors. The widespread availability of illicit drugs in prison attests to the fact that drug smuggling on the part of correctional employees is commonplace, although officials will usually blame the families and friends of inmates for bringing in contraband during visitation or through the mail. But it just doesn't add up, because most incoming mail is almost always opened and searched, and strip searches are de rigueur at most jails and prisons. Many correctional officers who personally refuse to participate in such behavior have admitted to me that they truly despise the actions of colleagues who exploit women and traffic drugs into prison.

At the Central California Women's Facility and Valley State Prison for Women, heroin has become the most commonly available illegal drug besides tobacco.[20] In one of the cruelest ironies of the war on drugs, many prisoners have told me that the predominant availability of one particular drug can even lead some prisoners to grow addicted to a drug that they have never abused before. Obviously, unprescribed, pain-alleviating drugs are prohibited in jails and prisons. Even women recovering from surgeries, suffering from cancer, or living with chronic pain are rarely given anything stronger than ibuprofen or acetaminophen. (Psychiatric medicines, on the other hand, are dispensed with largesse.)

These days, most prisons have disallowed cigarette smoking as well. Because of the nature of nicotine addiction, tobacco has become the most prized substance in jails and prisons, and many inmates rack up huge tobacco "debts" that they are unable to pay unless they resort to a barter system, providing favors to prisoners or correctional employees. By some estimates, a single cigarette can cost between $7 and $10, roughly twice the price of a marijuana joint.[21] In the New Mexico women's prison in Grants, one woman, who asked to remain anonymous, put it this way: "The girls are just learning how to hustle in here. They're flashing male correctional officers to get tobacco to sell and hustle."

The actual range and amount of sexual activity and abuse in women's prisons are impossible to quantify, and outsiders can hardly be the judges of what kinds of sexual advances and abuses might just anger one woman but severely traumatize another. But one thing is definite: The frequency of sexual harassment and abuse in a prison environment is a constant reminder of how little power the women have over their lives once they are sentenced to do time.

When women leave jail or prison, with even more traumatic experiences heaped upon their negative life experiences, there is rarely a way for them to avoid the traps of low self-esteem, shame, and internalized (or externalized) rage. On top of existing struggles with their emotional states, women reentering society manifest any number of serious problems: continuing mental and/or physical illness and the likelihood of an interruption of their treatment or medicines; ostracism by their families or communities; loss of custody of their children; readjustment to changed surroundings and technologies; limited education or career opportunities; denials of public assistance (if drug charges are involved); a lack of safe or stable housing; and the temptations of the neighborhoods in which their drug use or criminal activity took place. It is hardly a stretch, therefore, to understand why the majority of girls and women are eventually reincarcerated—sometimes just a few days or weeks after their release.

Amy Ralston, who spent twelve years in the federal prison system on a drug conspiracy charge, is one of the few women who did not end up returning to prison. Ralston was incarcerated at FCI Dublin, a large federal women's institution in the San Francisco Bay Area. While there, she noticed that male guards were "always preying [on] the emotions of the women who were desperately lonely, because many husbands divorce their wives (or leave their girlfriends) when they go to prison, unlike women, who tend to stick by their [partners]."

Some of these "relationships" between inmates and guards started out with flirtation and then escalated to well-honed sexual coercion. Many women got to a point where they were willing to ignore the obvious fact that they were being taken advantage of in exchange for items that they could buy easily and cheaply outside prison gates.

"[Male guards] brought in all kinds of things at Dublin," Ralston explained. "Alcohol, lipstick, drugs, and undergarments. It often starts out very innocent, like when an officer purposely leave some of [their sack] lunch sitting out, stating they are full, that they don't want or need all the fresh grapes, and the inmate hasn't tasted a fresh grape in over seven years. People can't comprehend how important and amazing a handful of grapes can become to someone who hasn't had fresh fruit, other than an occasional orange or apple, in what seems like an eternity."

Ralston saw all of this and more. "[Some] of the most horrifying memories I have from being incarcerated are the memories associated with fetuses being aborted in the showers," she recalled. "One day, I turned a corner and saw a commotion similar to a murder scene. Yellow tape marked off an area that no one could cross, and there were several federal correctional officers present that I knew to be from [internal affairs]. I asked an inmate what had happened and was told that another inmate had found an aborted fetus in the shower."

A "nightmare" ensued for the women when prisoners' names began to be called on the compound loudspeaker. "Whoever was called was told to report to the lieutenant's office. This is never good, and in this particular instance, it generally meant that the person called was going to have to submit to a gynecological examination. This too was a horrible violation, and many innocent women had to worry about being falsely accused of an abortion, which is exactly what happened. One Rastafarian woman was sent to segregation because a [person working in the medical department] said she appeared to have signs consistent with a woman who had aborted. Once an actual MD examined her, she was cleared. She had merely had a period, that's all."

Ralston is not sure, to this day, if the woman who aborted the fetus was ever identified. At the time, she couldn't stop thinking about how horrible it would have been to have been impregnated by a prison employee, and then forced to make the decision to carry the unwanted baby to term or, as Ralston put it, "having to assault [her] womb and body like that and not being able to tell anyone, for fear of being exposed."

During her years of imprisonment at the California Institution for Women in Corona, Jane Dorotik has witnessed a variety of forms of sexual coercion and outright abuse of her fellow prisoners by the men charged with overseeing them. The alcohol and drug abuse by prisoners, Dorotik wrote to me, was not limited to the captive population. "I know of correctional officers who literally reek of booze all day long, often stumbling, slurring through their work hours. . . . Then they are 'on leave' for several weeks. They return to work, and the cycle starts all over."

Verbal harassment from male guards is humiliating, but Dorotik explained that this is a regular part of prison life for women, to which everyone has to grow accustomed on some level: "[Some of the guards] denigrate these women and then laugh about it: 'Keep moving, you're attracting flies'; 'Get your ass back in here and stop slutting around'; 'Now what do you want? To put your mouth on my cigar?' But to speak out against any of this guarantees retaliation in the ugliest of ways."

When the Amnesty International report on sexual abuse in prisons was released in 2001, six states still had no law prohibiting sexual relations between prisoners and correctional staff. Just two years prior, the count had stood at fourteen. By 2007, only Vermont has not passed a law criminalizing sexual contact between prison employees and prisoners, although several states allow "consent" to serve as a legal defense for prison staff accused of sexual abuse.[22]

Since the passage of the federal Prison Rape Elimination Act (PREA) in 2003, most jail and prison environments have improved by making it harder for guards to take advantage of prisoners. The efficacy of these policies nearly always depends on the warden, sheriff, or superintendent in charge of a facility, and whether the prison has any committees that involve outside citizens, particularly family members of the incarcerated. All of these factors combine to create how the "culture" of a prison looks and feels; there is no such a thing as a monolithic jail or prison environment in this country.

Facilities where notable improvements have taken place include the Washington Correctional Center for Women (WCCW), although the prison was the source of many lawsuits relating to rape, sexual assault, and pregnancy throughout the 1990s. Today, things are significantly different. Reports of abuse are now taken very seriously; locked boxes for confidential reporting are located throughout the WCCW grounds. Brochures for male and female Washington state prisons inform inmates of their absolute right to serve their time without sexual assault, providing a confidential hotline number that both prisoners and their family members can use to report abuses. Confidential reporting, however, does not alleviate feelings of shame and trauma or lingering concerns that retaliation will be a consequence.

Susan Luna, who served a 125-month sentence for forgery and theft, told me that she was raped by a sergeant while at WCCW but never told anyone because, as she put it, "I was truly afraid of the outcome and how I would be treated after the investigation."

Luna's perception—and that of other female prisoners subject to sexual abuse—does not exist in a vacuum. Retaliation against women has proven intractable in some prison state systems. One of the most notorious is the Michigan Department of Corrections (MDOC), still under continual fire for sexual violence and retaliatory actions against female prisoners dating back to 1993. At least one woman committed suicide after reporting sexual assault and getting no assistance. Another tried to commit suicide by swallowing a bottle of Haldol under similar circumstances.[23]

When Human Rights Watch (HRW) published their aptly titled report "All Too Familiar" (1996), they included extensive documentation of rampant sexual abuse of women within the MDOC.[24] Two years later, after a joint civil rights lawsuit had already been filed by the justice department and attorneys representing female prisoners, HRW published another report, "Nowhere to Hide," that detailed the forms of retaliation against women who had dared to speak out against sexual assault. What happened next was hard for even HRW to believe: The Michigan state prison system filed a subpoena to try to force the New York–based organization to reveal confidential information about their research, including the names of women who had reported the abuse. With the assistance of the ACLU, HRW successfully fought the subpoena.[25]

A decade after the first HRW report, some things *have* changed, including the August 2000 decision that male guards would no longer be allowed to hold positions in Michigan's women's housing units. Male correctional officers sued the MDOC on Title VII grounds, which prohibit gender discrimination in the workplace. Initially, a lower court agreed with the plaintiffs, and the practice was brought to a halt. But the Sixth Circuit Court reversed the decision in 2004.[26] By all accounts, MDOC prisons are still dangerous places for women to be incarcerated.

At the age of twenty-four, Ne'Cole Anderson Brown was locked up for the first time, sentenced to two years for check fraud at the Scott Correctional Women's Facility in Michigan. Brown went to prison in 1996 expecting that she would serve her time and then "get out and go on with my life." Instead, she found herself targeted by a prison guard, who began to molest her in January 1997. At first, he would take her to a storage closet and grope her, and later he began to penetrate her.

Brown began to disassociate during the sexual assaults, eventually withdrawing from everyone around her. No one on the staff intervened, although other prisoners had already complained about the same guard. To her relief, Brown was transferred to a lower-security facility, but the abuse did not end there. Her abuser found out where she was and contacted fellow officers he knew at the prison; they forced her to talk to the officer over the phone. Later, the man showed up at the prison to assault her again, reminding her that he wielded power over her continued imprisonment or her eventual release.

Brown was eventually released and monitored with an ankle bracelet, which allowed the guard to stalk her at her mother's house. From there, he would take Brown into his car to have sex with him, reminding her again that he had the authority to have her sent back to prison.

Working two jobs, going to college, and trying to move on from her past, Brown was absolutely devastated by her situation. Things only got worse when she violated her parole in the simplest of ways: She went shopping, when the terms of her parole were that she could only be at home, work, or school. People are often sent back to prison for even the most minor infraction; this is one of the reasons why recidivism rates are so high.) Sent to the Western Wayne Correctional Center for a three-month stint, Brown realized, to her horror, that the officer had been transferred to the same prison. But this time, the officer overstepped his bounds and started asking personal questions about her family in front of other guards. The overt abuse stopped right then and there, and Brown found a lawyer with the help of a female officer, yet still feared retaliation. Her fears were soon confirmed when other prison guards began to taunt and harass her, cut off her incoming mail, interrupted attorney visits, and searched her without cause.

And then, finally, she was free. Despite her detailed deposition and willingness to take a lie detector test, no criminal charges were ever filed against the officer, although Brown was awarded a settlement in a civil suit. Married, with children, Brown has pulled her life together, at least on the surface. She works as both a paralegal and a phlebotomist but feels emotionally, irreparably scarred. "It's still a challenge," she told me. "I don't even sleep in the same bed with my husband sometimes. I get mad for no reason and isolate myself. I can't figure out how to fix it."

Regrettably, Brown's story is just one of many thousands. There is no shortage of sexual abuse reports stemming from women's jails or prisons nationwide. These situations represent just a few of the egregious cases that I have come across:

- In 2003, the New York Legal Aid Society filed a class-action lawsuit against the Department of Correctional Services for the systematic sexual abuse and rape of female prisoners. Three of the fifteen plaintiffs were impregnated by correctional employees and were then threatened and harassed after reporting the rapes.[27]

- In Española, New Mexico, ten female inmates accused municipal judge Charles Maestas of raping them after they appeared in his courtroom, telling them to have sex with him in exchange for reduced sentences. The abuse took place in his chambers, his home, his truck, and at the local jail. The women, who settled for nearly $900,000 in 2004, contended that the judge's abuses were facilitated knowingly by both jail guards and city officials, who also used their access to sexually molest the women again. One woman, who tried to retrieve her impounded car, refused to obey the judge's requirement that she leave with him for the weekend. In retaliation, her boyfriend was arrested. Maestas was convicted of five counts of rape and was sentenced to just three years in prison.[28]

- LeTisha Tapia, incarcerated in the privately run Val Verde County Jail in Texas, hung herself in July 2004 after reporting that a male inmate had raped her. The civil rights lawsuit filed in 2006 accused guards employed by the nation's second-largest private corrections company the GEO Group, of allowing male inmates to have access to the women and failing to protect female inmates or responding to their reports of abuse. Tapia had spent six months in the jail, awaiting transfer to a federal prison for a marijuana possession charge.[29]

- In Seattle/King County, three male jail guards were accused of sexually abusing and raping female inmates in 2005. Two of the guards have been sentenced to four- and six-month sentences in jail, and the other case ended with a mistrial. After interviewing ninety jail employees, consultants assigned to analyze the jail culture found a "sexualized atmosphere" and a prevalence of female inmates deprived of soap, toilet paper, underwear, sleepwear, and privacy in showers. In March 2007, the Department of Justice (DOJ) commenced an on-site investigation into conditions at the downtown Seattle jail.[30]

Clearly, a great deal of work remains to be done to stem the tide of sexual abuse and retaliatory action in jails and prisons. When PREA was passed, the legislation did not actually introduce any formal standards for how juvenile and immigrant detention centers, jails, or prisons should deal with sexual violence. In essence, all detention facilities can still go about doing things the way they decide is best. Organizations like Stop Prisoner Rape hope that the federal Prison Rape Elimination Committee, established after PREA's passage, will issue actual standards and procedures to reduce the prevalence of sexual assault, but the PREA process is already suffering from budget cuts.[31]

The Commission on Safety and Abuse in America's Prisons strongly recommends that detention facilities of all kinds protect at least some inmate privacy by switching to noninvasive drug-detection devices, computerized chairs that can detect weapons and replace pat searches, and radio frequency identification to track the movements of and durations of interactions between prisoners and staff.

The commission also calls for increased use of surveillance cameras in detention facilities, while acknowledging the "additional stress and loss of dignity that might accompany the use of such technology."[32]

"What we need to see are aggressive prosecutions, and the people who actually perpetrate these crimes brought to justice," Christensen told me after Amnesty International's 2001 report about abuses of women in custody came out. "It's a terrible sign to send to other correctional officers who work within these systems that you can do these things and go unpunished, or get a slap on the wrist, or get let out through the back door."

Back in Florida, the prison guards at FCI Tallahassee were no exception to the slap-on-the-wrist phenomenon, despite early statements by federal prosecutors that each of the men could face up to twenty-year prison terms.[33]

Investigators had built their case on prisoner testimony, surveillance, and the placement of at least one undercover agent. The indictment came down on June 20, 2006, accusing the prison guards of participating in a three-year period of conspiracy, sexual abuse, bribery, witness tampering, and mail fraud.[34] One of the real heroes of this story was a former Secret Service agent, William "Buddy" Sentner, of the DOJ's Office of the Inspector General, who took extra steps to reassure prisoners who had made accusations of abuse at FCI Tallahassee that something was being done.

When Inspector General Special Agent Sentner and other federal agents went to arrest the six men indicted of the conspiracy, they had no idea that Ralph Hill had smuggled a personal sidearm into the men's side of the prison. When he realized that the federal agents were about to arrest him, Hill opened fire. He wounded a BOP lieutenant and killed Sentner at the scene before being fatally shot in the hail of bullets that ensued. Sentner, forty-four, was survived by his wife, parents, and two siblings.

"A week before he was killed, Buddy came to see me in prison to let me know that they were finally going to arrest some of the guards that were involved in the kind of sexual abuse that I had witnessed," Yraida Guanipa told me when I visited her at FCC Coleman in September 2006. "He really believed what I had said about what was going on there, even though I knew my life was still at risk for doing that. And then he was gone.

The shooting at FCC Tallahassee made headlines, but then quickly faded away from press coverage. The fact that the four remaining guards ended up with ridiculously light sentences was barely mentioned in the national press: E. Lavon Spence received a year of home detention, plus three years of probation; Gregory Dixon, Alan Moore, and Alfred Barnes received one-year prison sentences; and Vincent Johnson was sentenced to a year of probation, at least in part because he shielded a federal agent in the shootout."

The female prisoners at FCI Tallahassee didn't fare quite as well. Right after the shooting, the women's side was locked down. Women prisoners were denied all visits and phone calls for several days. "This problem is still going on," long-time FCI Tallahassee inmate Peggy Gustafson disclosed to me during a hushed phone conversation in September. "Things have gotten worse here since the shooting—the food, the medical care, everything."[35]

"We lost a good man," Guanipa told me a few months after Sentner's murder. "The worst part might be that he died trying to make a difference, and we all worry that things will stay the same."

Chapter 4: Dangerous Medicine

"I am dying. I have been diagnosed with end-stage kidney disease. . . . In 2004, I was given two years to live. By the grace of God I am still alive. My [heartfelt] request is to spend what time I have left with my children and family."
—Tracy Sanchez, thirty-seven, Federal Medical Center in Fort Worth, Texas. Sanchez is a mother of five, denied compassionate release by the Bureau of Prisons.

"From what I've heard, cats and dogs are treated better than some of these people."
—California Assemblyman Carl Washington, at the end of a seven-hour legislative hearing on women's medical issues inside Valley State Prison for Women in Chowchilla, California, October 11, 2001

Shirley Southerland has known nothing but pain during her seventeen years of incarceration in the Gatesville, Texas, prison complex, where she is serving a life sentence for a murder conviction.

Unlike most women who have contacted me about their lengthy sentences for murder (which they readily admit to, especially in the context of an abusive relationship), Southerland was accused of killing a woman with whom she was barely acquainted. She was ultimately convicted with no physical evidence, on the word of a drug dealer and a jailhouse informant.[1]

But the pain that Southerland speaks of is not the psychic or emotional pain related to her ongoing struggle to prove her innocence and reverse the murder conviction. What she refers to is the relentless *physical* pain that she must live with every day. Southerland's story is representative of the abject cruelty to which so many women are subjected while incarcerated.

In 1990, Southerland was incarcerated at Mountain View Unit, one of the three women's units run by the Texas Department of Criminal Justice (TDCJ) in the town of Gatesville. Within one year, she developed a mysterious pain on the lower left side of her body, which seemed to get worse day by day. Sensing that something was very wrong, Southerland submitted the required paperwork, the "Sick Call Request," in the manner in which all nonemergency requests for medical attention must be placed in federal and state prisons across the country. Southerland's request was ignored, and she put in another request. She waited but still received no response. Southerland began to send the requests in one after another, until finally, after two months, one of her forms came back with what she described as a "crybaby face drawn in orange Crayola."

As it turned out, Southerland hadn't been exaggerating her pain in the least. Over the course of many months, a large tumor had been growing on one of her ovaries, to the point that she collapsed and had to be rushed to a nearby hospital for emergency surgery in July 1991. Doctors told her that she would have died in short order had the prison continued to ignore her cries for help. At least the excruciating pain was over, Southerland told herself, and the tumor had been removed in time. She was grateful to still be alive and went on dealing with the mundanity of prison life as best she could.

Four years later, after being moved to the Hobby Unit just outside the town of Marlin, Southerland was assigned the job of operating a printing press.[2] She picked up the job quickly and soon had the sense that something wasn't quite right with the machine itself. On five separate occasions, Southerland told her boss that the machine needed maintenance, but her comments were ignored. One day, when the paper fed into the press began to jam up, Southerland knew she had no choice but to try to fix the situation on her own. As a safety precaution, she turned off the machine and then cut off the electricity at the circuit breaker, for extra safety. She put her hand into the machine to retrieve the paper, and that was when she heard the terrible sound of a slipping chain. Gravity proved far faster than her reflexes; her pinky finger exploded when a chrome cylinder slammed down on her hand.[3]

Southerland sat for four hours, completely engulfed by pain, until she was transferred to a Waco hospital, where she given nothing but over-the-counter pain medication. (Prisoners in the TDCJ and other state prison systems rarely receive even the lowest level of prescription pain medication.) An emergency room doctor who showed up to examine her expressed his irritation that he couldn't go home, something she said bothered him particularly because, according to Southerland, he "disliked" prisoners. Perhaps as a way of demonstrating his distaste, the doctor amputated Southerland's finger above the first joint rather than attempting any kind of reparative surgery. The amputation was done so quickly and carelessly that a piece of bone popped up through her skin shortly thereafter.

"The pain was unreal," she told me. "I was told to get a bristle hairbrush and brush the bone to toughen it up."

Southerland was sent to another medical unit in Amarillo, where a doctor noticed the bone poking out of what remained of her finger and scheduled a second surgery. The stump of her finger had healed so poorly that there was no choice but to amputate it completely, to the knuckle. Southerland now had to wait for the remaining nub to heal, growing accustomed to a four-fingered hand. Unfortunately, the healing process was short lived. Elated about the fact that she was no longer engulfed by waves of agonizing pain and was beginning to have limited use of her right hand, Southerland was finally able to wash her own clothes in a sink. When she started to wring out her T-shirt, squeezing her hands together, she heard and felt something in her arm snap. Her knees buckled, and she collapsed to the floor from a new kind of pain that superceded everything she had suffered until that point.

Initially, doctors dismissed the pain in her arm as lingering trauma from the amputation—as the "phantom pain" that amputees often experience. But when the x-rays came back, doctors realized that Southerland had also broken her ulna (a bone on the pinky side of the forearm), something that was likely to have been a fracture at first, before pressure was applied and the bone snapped. The severity of the break required more surgery, during which a seven-inch plate was inserted in Southerland's arm. A cast was placed on her arm to prevent movement, and she was sent back to prison, clearly unable to work or do any kind of lifting.

The very day after the cast was removed, Southerland was inexplicably assigned to one of the most exhausting and labor-intensive jobs in the prison, as a new member of the officially named "Hoe Squad," in temperatures that could rise above 110 degrees in the heat of summer. Despite the fact that she had just recovered from a succession of serious surgeries, Southerland was assigned to work breaking up the hardened, sunbaked earth, without any accommodations made for the severity of her injuries.[4] Not surprisingly, the hard labor caused more damage to her arm—and more pain.

During a visit to the hospital just one month after she had been put on the "Hoe Squad," new x-rays verified what Southerland feared most. The bone had separated underneath the plate, necessitating another surgery. Southerland was told to await an available slot with a doctor specializing in this kind of surgery. In the meantime, doctors ordered that Southerland not be allowed to lift objects or to work, and that she wear a fracture brace all the time; they also gave her a prescription for stronger pain medication than what the prison usually allowed.

It was bad enough that Southerland had been assigned to hard labor without any regard for her recent physical trauma, but what ensued was even more outrageous than she could have ever imagined. Rather than be left at the hospital to await an opening for an operation, Southerland was shipped to Gatesville's Murray Unit. When she stepped off the bus, Southerland came face to face with a gruff female correctional captain ready to give her a housing placement in the prison. Knowing that she would otherwise be asked to carry her own belongings, Southerland spoke first, quickly explaining that she had a broken arm and medical orders to not carry anything. The recent amputation was certainly noticeable and, at the very least, suggested that something had indeed gone wrong. Unfortunately for Southerland, the high-ranking officer was not interested in following such medical orders, much less in expressing any kind of compassion. Instead, the situation seemed to bring out the captain's sadistic impulses, as she ordered Southerland to carry her heavy belongings all at once to the housing unit, which was roughly four hundred yards away from where she stood.[5]

"I could feel the plate of my arm moving. The pain was unbelievable," she recalled. "The captain said that she knew nothing about my medical issues and did not have time to look it up. I almost fainted from the pain more than once. By the time I reached the gym, I couldn't do it anymore. I told the officers, 'I can't carry nothing anywhere else.' I was threatened with a write-up for lying and disobeying a direct order if there were no instructions in my medical file."

Southerland's arm could take no more. She stood with her arm limp at her side, radiating pain. Eventually, a cart was brought for her to transport the rest of her property the remaining few yards. It was too little, too late. The damage had already been done.

Instead of the ninety-day medical rest that the doctors had mandated, she found out shortly after her arrival that her medical care was henceforth completely *discontinued,* her surgery and pain medication *denied.* Southerland was immediately put to work in the prison kitchen: "It took all the strength I had to endure the pain of trying to lift crates of heavy pans of food," she told me.

Southerland wasn't about to let the TDCJ ruin any chance she had of recovering. She wrote to the American Civil Liberties Union, and the organization took on her case. Their first step was to complain to the state prison that the treatment Southerland was being subjected to constituted cruel and unusual punishment. Soon, all of her family members had mobilized community members to contact the prison as well. The efforts paid off, as the prison didn't want this kind of attention to their practice of denying medical care to prisoners. Three months after she arrived at the Murray Unit, Southerland was back on a bus, this time to a hospital in Galveston, where she was admitted to the hospital immediately. (Most TDCJ prisoners must endure a three-month waiting period before doctors and prison officials agree on whether a stay at the hospital is warranted.)

"Both doctors who viewed my x-rays could not believe what they saw," Southerland recounted. "They asked, 'How can you stand the pain?'"

The doctors were incredulous of her ability to even function day to day, because the plate that had been surgically placed in her right arm was digging directly into the bone in a way that should have been utterly intolerable. The ensuing emergency surgery was so lengthy and severe that a cast was placed up to Southerland's armpit and replaced every five days to ensure that not even an iota of movement would occur. The doctors subsequently requested permission from the Murray Unit to start Southerland on intensive rehabilitation at the hospital. That request was promptly denied, and so Southerland was returned to the prison with the strictest of instructions from her physicians: "No lifting, no work."

What ensued was a surreal repeat of the outright callousness to which Southerland had now grown accustomed. Once again, she was made to carry her belongings to the housing unit and was put back to work in the kitchen *the very next day*. To this day, she has not been given respite from physical prison labor. Another invasive surgery is inevitable.

To add to an already devastating series of events, Southerland was diagnosed with Eagle-Barrett syndrome, a life-threatening disorder characterized by partial or complete absence of the stomach muscles, which she had to research on her own to understand what was in store for her as the condition worsened. Although she had complained of serious gastrointestinal pain, acid reflux, and throat discomfort as far back as 1999, she did not receive her diagnosis until 2004, when an outside doctor asked Southerland if the medical department at the prison had ever informed her of her condition. It turned out the prison medical staff *had* known what she was suffering from, but had not disclosed the information to her, whether out of negligence or an attempt to save money on the cost of treatment.

Because of the multiyear delay in her treatment, the lining of Southerland's esophagus has been eaten away. (As of February 2007, twenty-three centimeters had been dissipated by nonstop acidity.) With complete disregard for her suffering, the prison has denied her any kind of a special diet that would alleviate at least some of the daily anguish of living with this condition. To make matters worse, acid constantly rises into her mouth, to the point that the roots of her teeth are visibly exposed and her gums are literally worn away. From this point forward, her situation will inevitably only get worse, but the decision-makers at the prison obviously couldn't care less. In fact, they are seemingly more interested in accelerating her suffering than in alleviating it.

The troubling extent to which Southerland has been subjected to medical neglect and carelessness—as well as all-around refusals to make even the simplest of accommodations for her physical disabilities—is utterly unique to her experience. That said, there are echoes of Southerland's story in those of the thousands of incarcerated women who must grapple with degrees of indifference (and cruelty) when they attempt to access healthcare and treatment for a variety of illnesses and diseases.

Of course, there are the exceptions—the women and men working in jails and prisons as doctors, nurses, psychologists, and social workers, and even corrections officers—who go the extra mile to help women access the healthcare that they need. But over the years, I have heard more health-related horror stories than I could ever have imagined when I first set out to do this research. Sadly, a few women have died since I first interviewed them or wrote about their cases.

We do not just have to rely on the anecdotes that women in prison are willing to share, although many prisoners become so well versed in understanding medical terminology that they can accurately read their own medical charts and point out obvious discrepancies and mistakes in test results and blood work; dangerous prescription drug interactions; gaps in mandated treatment; and obvious attempts by medical staff to disguise the severity of their illnesses. In addition to this kind of anecdotal and evidentiary information, a plethora of class-action lawsuits and nonpartisan research studies points to the preponderance of inadequate healthcare in jails and prisons. I can say without any exaggeration that medical "care" represents one of the absolute worst aspects of life in women's jails and prison, on par with sexual violence and the abhorrent treatment of the mentally ill.

There is also no question that prison medicine should be viewed in its larger context—that of the wide reach of the American healthcare crisis, in which forty-six million Americans from all walks of life go without health insurance and many millions more are underinsured. However, it is too simple to lump prison healthcare in with the lot of all the nation's residents who are poorly served by our lack of a medical safety net. More specifically, we need to consider that illness and disease among prisoners are a particularly problematic component of the larger healthcare crisis, as this subpopulation of Americans has no choice but to accept whatever level of medical attention, medication, or surgery is doled out, whether in the form of total denial of care or in the form of experimental surgery that prisoners feel as though they have no choice but to accept if they want to live.[6]

Deficient healthcare and serious medical problems apply to both genders in prison. Men have far higher rates of mortality in prisons, yet the leading causes of death for both genders are identical. The most common form of death is from heart disease, followed by cancer, liver disease, AIDS, and suicide.[7]

Even if prisoners make it out into the "free world," they don't tend to fare well in the long run. A longitudinal study conducted in Washington state found that former prisoners were at far greater risk of death than people who had never been incarcerated, and that this risk was particularly high in the two weeks following a prisoner's release. The most common forms of death for both men and women leaving prison were drug overdose, cardiovascular disease, suicide, and homicide. Between the sexes, researchers found that the risk of death for female ex-prisoners was "significantly higher" than it was for their male counterparts.[8]

While there are obvious similarities between women's and men's medical issues in prison, women present far more serious and longstanding health problems when they first enter the system.[9] Sociologist and ethnographer Tammy Anderson emphasizes these differences in her examination of the availability of healthcare for women prisoners.

"Women's reproductive events of pregnancy, childbirth, and puerperium [the period between childbirth and the return of the uterus to its normal size] give women unique morbidity risks not experienced by men," Anderson writes. "Even when reproductive conditions are removed from consideration, significant sex differences persist. . . . Compared to men, women have higher illness rates for infective disease, respiratory and digestive system conditions, injuries, ear diseases, headaches, genitourinary disorders, and skin and musculoskeletal diseases."[10]

The lack of essential checkups and follow-ups for irregular Pap smears—to say nothing of necessary treatment when things *do* go wrong—is among the biggest complaints that women have about medical care in prison. Because the design of the prison system and attendant services have always centered around men's needs, gynecological care is treated as a "specialty service," according to attorney Cynthia Chandler of Justice Now, an Oakland, California–based advocacy organization specializing in compassionate release for terminally ill prisoners.[11] According to one study on healthcare at the California Institution for Women (CIW) in Corona, prisoners reported that they had never had a Pap smear (a recommended annual test for cervical cancer and other gynecological complications), because they could not afford the required $5 copay while earning twenty-eight to thirty cents an hour.[12]

Dozens of other nonfatal (but serious) illnesses are also more common among female prisoners when compared with the male inmate population, including gall bladder and thyroid conditions, colitis, anemia, migraine headaches, chronic urinary infections, and complications resulting from sexually transmitted diseases, as well as a wide range of poorly treated and often ignored psychological problems. The shoddy treatment of physical illnesses among imprisoned women signifies the likelihood of poor treatment for the mentally ill.

Take, for instance, a 2006 ACLU lawsuit filed on behalf of the seven hundred prisoners at Taycheedah Correctional Institution, the largest women's prison in Wisconsin. Almost half of the women at Taycheedah have at least one chronic illness, ranging from cardiac disease to diabetes, but most inmates complained that they were not being cared for consistently or effectively. One of the cases cited was that of a woman who suffered from endometriosis but wasn't allowed to see a gynecologist for the first seven years of her incarceration; she was forced to have a hysterectomy in 2003. The lawsuit also emphasized staff disregard for women's struggles with mental illness, to the point that women were harming themselves and manifesting full-blown psychoses after long periods of not receiving psychiatric attention. Over one-quarter of the prisoners at Taycheedah are mentally ill.[13] (For more on mental illness among women in prison, see Chapter 5, "Trying to Stay Sane.")

There is clearly no single reason why incarcerated women's health is so poor before, during, and after incarceration. The underlying reasons are usually attributable to a combination of these factors:

- Lack of preventative healthcare before and after incarceration
- Self-destructive behaviors vis-à-vis drug use, unprotected sex, and violence, which often lead to a woman's imprisonment
- Persistent medical neglect and lack of treatment after incarceration
- Misdiagnosis of diseases
- Copayments for medical care in most jails and prisons that many prisoners are unable to afford, resulting in lack of medical attention for anything but a dire emergency

- Botched or experimental surgeries, as well as a lack of postsurgery care and pain management
- Ineffective, nonstandarized prevention and intervention strategies regarding the spread of communicable diseases
- Inadequate supplies of soap or antibacterial gels, sanitary pads, and toilet paper, as well as the irregular collection of trash
- Callous disregard for or slow responses to women suffering from immediate, life-threatening medical crises
- Emphasis on cost-cutting by means of limiting access to quality medical care and balanced, healthy meals
- Overreliance on over-the-counter pain relievers, even for excruciating pain related to broken bones, back injuries, cancer, and postsurgical recovery
- Privatization of medical services, where outside corporate health providers are brought in to handle the entirety of physical, dental, and mental health services, often with little or no oversight
- The difficulty of filing and proving intentional medical negligence because of the passage of the Prison Litigation Reform Act
- Policies that force sick, elderly, pregnant, and disabled women to endure the same housing, work, and physical demands as the rest of the prison population
- Fattening, low-quality diets; a lack of special diets for women suffering from diabetes, food allergies, heart disease, or gastrointestinal disorders; and no provision for vitamins or herbal supplements to enhance nutrient intake
- Hiring and retention of poorly skilled medical staff in some facilities, and/or the relegation of frontline medical assessment to correctional officers who do not have proper training
- Sexual or physical abuse by medical and/or dental staff

These factors are interlinked, and magnify the severity of physical illnesses and diseases. A nutrient-poor, high-fat, cholesterol- and sugar-laden diet devoid of fresh fruits and vegetables,[14] combined with improper heating of ingredients and rushed mealtimes (as short as fifteen or twenty minutes), can result in everyday gastrointestinal distress and fatigue. Over years or decades of incarceration, women can easily develop problems that they have never experienced before, including obesity, clogged arteries, diabetes, and lowered resistance to contagious disease.

Attorney Ellen Barry, a 1998 recipient of a MacArthur Fellows Program "genius grant" and the founding director of the San Francisco–based Legal Services for Prisoners with Children (LSPC), has been deeply immersed in legal and advocacy work for female prisoners for more than a quarter-century. For the past several decades, Barry has spearheaded numerous lawsuits related to the abuse of women behind bars.

"Although many of these medical shortfalls affect men as well as women, there are a number of issues unique to female prisoners," Barry wrote in an article for the American Bar Association's *Criminal Justice* magazine. "[It has] been my experience that women prisoners are often regarded as complainers, maligners, or drug seekers who have more psychosomatic than actual illnesses. . . . Women prisoners are assumed to have fewer 'real' medical complaints than do male prisoners. In the prison setting, this can be a life-threatening assumption."[15]

From FCI Tallahassee, Peggy Gustafson told me of the humiliation that female prisoners endure when trying to access medical and dental services:

"For dental, we only have it three days a week, and only the first five [to arrive at the clinic] get in, so that's fifteen people per week with a population of over 1,200. As a result, we run when the doors [from our cells] open at

6:30 AM, hoping to be the fastest and not get caught running. (That's right, we are not allowed to run on the compound.)

Medical has so much wrong with it. Do I start with the women who die of cancer because the physician's assistants do not investigate their [medical] complaints? Or the pharmacist who prohibits certain medications because inmates report to her that some inmates are abusing them? Take my prescription for colitis [as an example]. For nine months, I had to go to the pill line three times a day because my prescription is to [be taken] as needed. The pharmacist crushed my pills, so they did not do what they did when I took them whole. I got an endoscopy done to diagnose my condition, so abuse of the medication on my part was moot."

One of many outrageous health-related cases that I came across involved a woman named Sherrie Chapman, who was imprisoned in CIW. As a child, Chapman experienced all manner of physical and sexual abuse. By the time she was a teenager, she was full of fury at the world around her and, unlike most teenage girls who experience childhood abuse, Chapman lashed out violently by murdering a man she barely knew. She was sentenced to life in prison.

In 1981, never having denied committing the crime, Chapman didn't have particularly high hopes for ever getting out of prison, but she certainly did not expect to be subjected to torturous medical care.

Three years into her sentence, Chapman started to feel pain in her breasts. She tried to not get alarmed. By the following year, there seemed to be more cause for concern, as Chapman noticed new lumps in both her left and right breasts. Because of the history of breast cancer in her family, Chapman immediately asked to see medical staff. They promptly dismissed her concerns by diagnosing her with fibrocystic breasts without a real examination or mammogram.

Each year, the number and the size of the lumps increased. During this time, prison medical staff labeled Chapman as a "drug seeker" when she begged for something stronger than Motrin to manage her pain.[16] A decade passed before medical staff finally agreed to give her a mammogram. By this time, the growths in her breasts were visibly protruding through Chapman's clothes. More than eight months later, a biopsy was finally taken, confirming Chapman's worst fear: She had invasive breast cancer. Chapman was rushed into surgery for a mastectomy of her right breast. Despite the pain and trauma of this disfiguring operation, CIW medical staff did not allow her to spend even one postsurgery night at the hospital.

Unfortunately, Chapman's struggle with her health and the prison medical care system didn't end there. Throughout 1996, Chapman complained of pain and vaginal blood clots, as well as the remaining masses that were growing in her left breast. In January 1997, surgeons removed Chapman's left breast as well, but the prison medical staff waited until later that year to look into her worsening uterine pain. By that point, Chapman's diagnosis was uterine cancer, necessitating an immediate hysterectomy. Within the space of a year, Chapman had to learn to live with a disfigured body that had taken away her femininity.

The resulting lawsuit, *Chapman v. Maddock,* asserted that her life-threatening physical condition was a direct result of the medical "care" at CIW. The lawsuit also alleged purposeful, negligent indifference to the medical needs of other women incarcerated in the California state prison system. Chapman was not willing to focus solely on her own suffering, because she had fought for the basic human rights of her fellow inmates throughout her incarceration at CIW.[17]

In 1999, the California Department of Corrections (CDC) denied my request to interview Chapman by phone, citing an existing (and ongoing) ban on prearranged phone or in-person media interviews with prisoners of any classification status. I wrote to Chapman, but she was already too weak to write back.[18] Chapman was losing weight rapidly and was in a tremendous amount of pain, but the medical staff was still refusing to provide her with anything stronger than over-the-counter palliatives.[19] Inexplicably, CIW was also withholding a prescription for Tamoxifen, a breast cancer treatment (and prevention) drug.[20]

I finally saw Chapman—although I was not able to interview her—when she testified at a legislative hearing held inside Valley State Prison for Women (VSPW) in Chowchilla, California, in October 2000. Among many women testifying about the many severe complications and deaths resulting from delayed and inadequate treatment of their illnesses (cancer, hepatitis C, HIV), Chapman came forth with her story. Her neck was bandaged because a growth had just been removed from her throat. The state legislators in attendance appeared visibly disturbed by her testimony.

"One-half of what I've heard today curdles my stomach," Assemblywoman Cathy Wright (R–Simi Valley) told representatives from the Centers for Disease Control (CDC).[21]

The claims of widespread negligence, delayed care, and sadistic responses by some correctional officers toward women suffering from acute illnesses with obvious symptoms could have been considered somewhat exaggerated, as then–CDC Health Care Services Division Director, Dr. Susann Steinberg, implied at the hearing. But *less than two weeks* after the hearing at VSPW, the first of eight deaths of nonhospitalized female prisoners began at the Central California Women's Facility; the others took place over two months.[22] Finally, there seemed to be verifiable, concrete evidence of what so many incarcerated women had been begging people on the outside to recognize, through letter-writing campaigns, testimonies at the hearing, and a class-action lawsuit, *Shumate v. Wilson*. That lawsuit was filed in 1995, settled in 1997, and dismissed just two months before the legislative hearing because the court determined that the CDC had met its obligations. (The settlement allowed the CDC to admit no culpability for wrongdoing and to consent to a court-monitored agreement to improve the quality and availability of medical care to female prisoners.)[23]

Among the eight deaths were women living with HIV—and who were quite possibly coinfected with HCV, according to several prisoners' testimonies about the symptoms they exhibited. One woman, Pamela Coffey, forty-six, was not believed to be infected with either disease. She died mysteriously and suddenly on December 2, 2000, in front of her cellmates. According to the prisoners who witnessed her death, Coffey had been pleading for help and attention from the medical staff, but several correctional officers had refused to take her to the ward. Although no overt foul play was suspected, the guards were alleged to have made fun of her desperate demeanor just half an hour before her death. An autopsy proved that Coffey had no narcotics in her system but could not determine the underlying cause of her death.[24]

Back at CIW, Chapman's health deteriorated even further as growths multiplied throughout her neck and shoulder areas. At one point, prison doctors told her that the lumps were just "swollen glands," although it was obvious that these were cancerous growths. By that point, Chapman knew that she was about to die, and LSPC started campaigning for her parole. In June 2002, she was denied and told to turn to self-help groups at CIW instead.[25]

Chapman succumbed to the cancer that ravaged her body on December 12, 2002, in a community hospital but still in the official custody of the CDC; a prison guard was posted outside her hospital room, even though Chapman could no longer even get out of bed.

Repairing the poor quality of medical care in prisons will continue to be one of the hardest challenges for correctional administrators and state legislators alike. There is no way around the fact that women brought to jail or prison represent some of the sickest people in our society, in terms of the scope and severity of their physical and/or mental illnesses. Incarceration heaps on a whole new set of potential problems, including communicable diseases and correctional employees who are either unskilled or unsympathetic to the plight of women struggling with health complications.

The following are among the most significant components of what amounts to an interlinked web of substandard medical care in jails and prisons:

HIV, HEPATITIS C, AND TUBERCULOSIS

HIV and hepatitis C are two of the most life-threatening diseases for prisoners.

Today, prisoners are eight to nine times more likely to be infected with HIV than the general population, as well as nine to ten times more likely to have hepatitis C (HCV), a potentially lethal disease with a low treatment success rate.[26] Compared with the male prisoner population, women are more likely to harbor HIV and/or HCV. African American women are the most likely of all subgroups of prisoners to be infected with HIV, a trend that mirrors the general population insofar as black women represent the fastest-growing group of Americans acquiring HIV, usually through sexual intercourse.[27]

Accordingly, U.S. jails and prisons are harboring the highest concentrations of HIV and HCV in the country; these facilities are somewhat akin to incubators of the diseases, particularly when prisoners are left to fend for themselves, are not tested (or given their results), and are given little or no information about the health consequences and transmission of both diseases.

From state to state, one-fifth to one-half of women's jail and prison populations are believed to harbor HCV,[28] which is spread only through infected blood
and can lead to chronic liver disease, cirrhosis, and liver cancer. If treatment has
been unsuccessful (or nonexistent), the disease usually progresses in the body—
although I have met a few women in prison who have tested positive for HCV and
HIV but have not developed symptoms, even a decade after their diagnoses. But
when the disease *does* take hold of a human body, the end results are gruesome.
Toward the last stages of HCV disease, the liver can no longer detoxify the body,
and virus-related difficulties with memory, speech, and concentration morph into
full-blown delirium. A person's eyeballs and skin tone take on a green–orange tinge,
signifying a high level of toxicity in the body. The abdomen begins to swell, and a
sufferer usually begins vomiting blood. Nothing can be done at this point to stave
off the inevitable, short of heavy medication to provide a modicum of pain relief.

At least eight thousand Americans die from HCV every year, and another five
thousand die from hepatitis B, which is sexually transmitted. Regrettably, there is
no vaccine—or foolproof cure—for HCV. (Vaccinations exist for both hepatitis A
and B.) In response to the HCV epidemic, state prison administrators have been
implementing widely divergent and typically ineffective strategies to deal with
what has rightly been termed the "silent epidemic."[29] New Jersey, for instance,
doesn't test prisoners for HCV until they begin to show symptoms of liver disease.
Pennsylvania tests all of its prisoners, but the Oklahoma prison system has gone
so far as to adopt a "don't ask, don't tell" policy as a way of avoiding costs affiliated
with HCV treatment. Other state correctional systems, including those in New
York and California, say they provide testing upon request and treatment only if a
prisoner can meet certain criteria.[30]

But prisoners and their advocates insist that too little is being done, and too
late. The bottom line, they charge, comes down to money, not the welfare of inmates or the health of the community at large. Jackie Walker, the AIDS information

coordinator for the ACLU's National Prison Project, says that prison officials regularly cite high costs as their reason for denying treatment. The truth of the matter is that hepatitis C treatment *is* expensive. Only two antiviral drugs are currently approved for widespread use in treating HCV: interferon and ribavirin. Standard treatment per person per year can run from $10,000 to $25,000, unlike HIV medications, which are often subsidized by states and pharmaceutical companies for low-income people, including prisoners. Because people are not treated for HCV while incarcerated, the disease usually progresses. Ironically, a prison is one of the best environments for treating people who engage in high-risk lifestyles, because the controlled environment actually ensures treatment compliance and progress monitoring.

Every year, 1.4 million female and male prisoners carry HCV back to their communities upon release. Another 98,000 to 145,000 women and men are released into the general population with HIV; 39,000 have an AIDS diagnosis. There is no precise way of tracking the number of women and men who get infected while they are in prison, but sex between male inmates is certainly a significant contributing factor, as is the fact that between 3 and 21 percent of prisoners (female and male alike) admit to engaging in IV drug use while they are incarcerated.[31] When prisoners are released but are not provided with transitional healthcare and medication management, their well-being declines rapidly. Interruptions in prescribed medication for opportunistic, infectious diseases are especially dangerous, because individuals can easily develop drug-resistant forms of both diseases.

After a yearlong process of intensive public hearings held across the country, the Commission on Safety and Abuse in America's Prisons concluded in 2006 that when HCV prevention and treatment are not made available to people in prison, the "public health system pays a much larger cost down the road, when those untreated prisoners are released and are more likely to require liver transplants."[32]

People working in the social service field with high-risk populations are best positioned to speak out about the public health implications of releasing former prisoners into the community with inadequate follow-through, yet prisons and parole officers rarely ask for their expertise or assistance in ensuring some kind of healthcare continuity, as well as other necessary services such as counseling, harm reduction, affordable medicine, case management, and support groups for chronically ill persons.

"Partnerships with community and public health providers broaden the pool of qualified caregivers who are committed to working in a correctional environment by allowing them to remain connected with community clinics and hospitals, teaching universities, and public health agencies," says the Commission on Safety and Abuse in America's Prisons.[33]

Progressive, harm reduction–minded social service providers understand that removing persistent stigmas associated with both diseases increases the efficacy of HIV and HCV prevention and treatment. Regrettably, very few prison education or support groups exist to minimize incorrect perceptions about how the diseases are spread, and how women can best support each other (and themselves) if they are infected. There are some exceptions, including the prisoner-initiated and -run support groups in women's prisons in California, as well as the inmate education programs and emphasis on compassionate medical staff in the San Francisco County Jail system. Because San Francisco was one of the "ground zeroes" in the rapid spread of the HIV epidemic, city government decided to respond early on with an approach that encouraged free or low-cost, anonymous or confidential testing for gay men, as well as for youth, women, and the elderly. As early as 1989, the San Francisco Sheriff's Department became the first jail system to provide condoms, dental dams, and safe-sex information to male and female inmates. Even today, it is one of only six to provide free condoms without any questions asked.[34]

MRSA AND TUBERCULOSIS

The American public might have some idea about the prevalence of HIV in prison and, to a lesser extent, about hepatitis C.

Very few people that I come across, however, are even aware of what MRSA is, much less how quickly it has spread throughout jail and prison populations across the country—especially in women's facilities. MRSA, pronounced in medical vernacular as "mersa," is an acronym for methicillin resistant staphylococcus aureus. While the staphylococcus bacteria (usually shortened to "staph") can be treated with a course of antibiotics, MRSA is a virulent and highly dangerous mutation of staph that is resistant to all but the most rare and expensive antibiotics.

MRSA thrives in close, crowded, poorly ventilated quarters, especially hospitals, prisons, jails, unsanitary public bathrooms, and homeless shelters. Unlike HIV and hepatitis C, which can be spread only through blood contact, MRSA can be spread easily through any number of methods, including athletic equipment, benches, toilets, various forms of sexual contact (including kissing), tattoo and IV drug needles, clothing and linens that have not been disinfected with bleach, open sores, and sharing of personal items such as towels, tweezers, and razors. Even prisoners who understand how MRSA is transmitted and who *want* to take the proper precautions often find that they cannot, as soap and antibacterial gel are doled out in very limited quantities.

Once infected with MRSA, a person either starts manifesting symptoms quickly or becomes what's known as a nonsymptomatic carrier. (The latter condition is actually more dangerous, in that the bacteria can be spread very rapidly while the infected person does not have any external evidence of the infection.) Common symptoms of MRSA include boils, pneumonia, oozing sores, and, if left untreated, the possibility of fatal toxic shock.

In my travels to women's jails and prisons, I've seen many inmates suffering from MRSA, most notably in New Mexico's women's prison in Grants. The prison, run by the Corrections Corporation of America, had a veritable epidemic on their hands, something that even some staff members admitted to me on the condition that I not publish their names. Many women called me over so that I could witness the jarring sight of large, oozing, open sores, usually on their upper legs. None of the women I spoke to were receiving medical treatment, and they complained that the prison had yet to emphasize providing enough soap and sanitary conditions to stem the spread of the bacteria.

The latter circumstance is something that jail and prison inmates in various states have written to me about, especially women incarcerated in Texas, Oklahoma, Virginia, Florida, Washington, and California. Other states known to have high rates of MRSA include Ohio and Pennsylvania, where female inmates have been hardest hit, leading to deaths in jails and the infection of several guards.[35] Another state that has seen outbreaks, Mississippi, was the focal point of a Centers for Disease Control (CDC) MRSA study. Of the infected prisoners, nearly 60 percent had infections on their legs, 16 percent had infections on their arms, and 4 percent had serious systemic infections requiring hospitalization.

"Most disturbing was the high number of asymptomatic carriers of MRSA, and the fact that 58 [percent] reported lancing their own boils or other prisoners' boils with fingernails or tweezers, and 89 [percent] shared potentially contaminated personal items such as linen, pillows, clothing, and tweezers," *Prison Legal News* reported in 2003.[36]

Practices like these signify a lack of public education campaigns (especially within prisons) that utilize fact-based information about contagious diseases, drug use (including homemade intoxicants), and the risks of unprotected sex. Such messages also need to include suggestions for commonsensical ways for prisoners to stay as healthy as they can through hygiene, balanced meals, harm-reduction techniques, and accessing counseling or medical attention when problems do arise. Such informational campaigns are rare in American jails or prisons (although I have encountered some notable exceptions in the San Francisco County Jail, as well as within some prisons run by the Washington Department of Corrections).

One prisoner at VSPW, Shelbi Harris, commented on prison conditions in the newsletter of the California Coalition for Women Prisoners, *The Fire Inside:* "We are exposed to infections and illnesses daily (such as staph infections), with no protection other than the preventative measures we take on, on our own. The CDCR should meet us halfway in preventative care by supplying hand soap, adequate access to laundry facilities, mandatory posting of preventative care signs, and [by following] their own rules and standards."[37]

Because of the size of prison populations and the length of women's stays, most research about incarcerated women focuses on state and federal prisons, where some teenagers and all women above the age of eighteen convicted of felonies are taken to serve out sentences of a minimum of one year.

Lesser charges result in jail incarceration, but the vast majority of the jail population, on any given day, is the pretrial population. People who can come up with bail money can wait for the day of their trial in the "free world," but most people arrested and charged with crimes in cities like Chicago, Seattle, San Francisco, New York, Houston, Montgomery, New Orleans, and Los Angeles, to name but a few, have to wait months—sometimes even more than a year—until their trial finally gets underway.

In the women's division of the Los Angeles County Jail, I walked into a segregation housing "pod," containing three separate units. One of them had been converted to a nonlockdown housing unit because of overflow of the inmate population as a whole. The middle unit held women in twenty-three-hour-per-day segregation for violations of jail policy, but the unit to my left confused me. It was so dark that the women moving around in there looked like shadow puppets.

I asked what classification of inmate was assigned to this unit, and the answer genuinely shocked me: "That's where we keep the people with contagious diseases, scabies, and lice," one of the two women at the controls in the middle of the pod told me. Women identified as having tuberculosis, staph, scabies, and so forth were quarantined from the general population; that was something I could understand. But why would they all be housed together? The concept seemed so asinine and regressive that it could have jumped off the pages of reports on conditions in sanitariums in the 1800s. Granted, there didn't look to be more than a dozen women locked up in there (although it was impossible to tell for sure), but the idea that people with various contagions would all be grouped together seemed like a recipe for disaster.

Equally problematic was the sight of the in-transit holding cell, with women who had returned from court hearings throughout Los Angeles County earlier in the day. These women had been booked into the jail previously and could have been returned promptly to their housing units, but staffing constraints mandated this holding period. That would have been one thing. But a more problematic aspect altogether was the fact that these women were crammed into one small housing unit.

Of equal import was that at least half a dozen adjacent cells sat empty and available in another part of the jail, roughly a couple dozen women, mostly African American and Latina, were crammed into one cell that was probably designed to hold eight inmates at most. There were no bars, only something that looked like a Plexiglas window with a small vent on the bottom half.

Several women crowded around it, trying to get gulps of fresh air—or the closest thing approximating it inside this jail. Historical drawings and photos of human bodies packed into cattle cars and slave ships flooded my mind almost immediately—I did not set out to make the comparison, but the images could have easily been transposed onto one another. Women were squeezed into every nook and cranny of the cell, which held one toilet in the back (as usual, there was no semblance of privacy) and a single pay phone. There were no towels, linens, mattresses, or antibacterial gel in the cell, which already had a grimy veneer.

If even *one* of those women entered that cell harboring TB or staph, there would be a high chance of at least one other inmate acquiring it under such circumstances. This is the kind of consideration that should be first and foremost in the minds of people trying to run an epidemic-free jail. But maybe that's just the point; it's *not* first and foremost. Although the staff did not discuss it when I visited, both the women's and men's jails in L.A. County have had several staph outbreaks, particularly in the last several years, as the overcrowding of all facilities has reached new highs. (Los Angeles has the biggest jail system in the United States, surpassing Rikers Island in New York and Cook County Jail in Chicago.)

When *The New York Times* reporter Brent Staples visited the Los Angeles County Jail system in 2004, he arrived just after the latest in a string of in-custody murders, and during a staph infection "that was ranging through the cellblocks." Inmates crowded at the bars, Staples wrote, to show him their lesions, not unlike what I had witnessed in the women's prison in New Mexico.

"Staph can be partly contained by giving inmates access to soap and hot water and making sure that the laundry is thoroughly washed and dried," Staples noted. "But jails that cannot organize themselves well enough to provide clean sheets stand little chance of success against heavyweight infectious diseases that have become endemic behind bars today."[38]

Even accessing hot water from the tap, as many prisoners have told me, is a rarity in itself. (As the accounts go, the water in cells comes in either hot or cold; cold water is more common than hot.) And L.A. County's problems with MRSA infection didn't just happen to coincide with Staples's visit. In 2003, the Los Angeles County Department of Health Services investigated a MRSA outbreak among inmates, citing at least one thousand cases to start with, and hundreds of new cases each month after the original investigation. Less than 10 percent of the infected inmates were believed to have entered the jail system with staph, which means that nine out of ten acquired staph within the jail setting.[39]

With the exception of these kinds of state-specific studies, the exact numbers of MRSA-infected prisoners are impossible to obtain. We know a little bit more about the prevalence of tuberculosis, including the fact that, each year, prisoners are released into the community with 12,000 active and 566,000 latent cases of tuberculosis.

Because tuberculosis has been around longer, the symptoms are easier to identify. Prison medical and correctional staff are more likely to respond right away to someone suspected of having TB because it is an airborne contagion; everyone is potentially at risk if they breathe the same air as the infected person. Unfortunately, it can still take a serious epidemic for jails and prisons to set about containing diseases as they should.

One of the most telling examples was that of the emergence of a major, drug-resistant strain of TB in New York City in 1989. Eighty percent of the cases were being traced directly to prisons and jails, particularly Rikers Island.

Just two years later, Rikers had become a flashpoint of concentrated TB infection. The CDC intervened and helped to set up a joint city/state/federal response project, including the creation of the Communicable Disease Unit at Rikers Island. Between 1992 and 1998, TB cases dropped nearly 60 percent throughout NYC, and drug-resistant forms of TB dropped by more than 90 percent.[40] The problem hadn't been solved—in fact, it could be argued that even a small amount of preventative effort could have averted the entire crisis—but a concerted public health approach did make a difference in the long run.

FOOD, HOUSING, AND WATER

The three essential components of what we humans need in order to survive—food, housing, and water—should be the inalienable right of every woman, man, and child on this earth.

But as we know all too well, far too many among us don't have clean water, decent food, or proper shelter to call our own. Prisons are no exception, despite what you may have heard about "three hot meals and a cot."

I am always surprised by the outright anger that some civilians express when I broach the subject that American society needs to recognize the civil and human rights of all people, including prisoners.

"At least they know they're going to be taken care of," many men and women have huffed in retort to my suggestion that inmates aren't supposed to give up their humanity as a condition of their incarceration. I've always found it particularly interesting that, rather than setting the bar a bit higher—say, taking into consideration that these basic human rights should be guaranteed to all people—many Americans prefer to be dissatisfied with the idea that anyone without resources can have access to basic amenities if they aren't paying for them.

But prisoners actually *are* paying for much of their incarceration, which is one of the reasons why women and men leave prisons with such high levels of LFOs, or legal financial obligations. State and federal governments pick up the rest of the tab—using our tax dollars. The very use of our money would seem to warrant concern about *how* that money is spent in the process of incarcerating people.

With all that money flowing, it's hard to understand why the key components of what keeps a person alive and healthy are of such poor quality. The tens of thousands of dollars being spent per prisoner per year may be going somewhere, but they certainly aren't going toward providing most prisoners with anything akin to decent housing, medical care, and nutrition.

I've interviewed women who sleep in unheated horse barns; on the floors of control units in seeping toilet water; in housing units infested with roaches, spiders, and vermin; in tiny rooms designed for two prisoners but packed with eight bodies; and on mattresses so hard, worn, and thin that there is no way for a woman to leave prison without a back problem. Almost every woman who has written to me from prison has described struggling to make it through the week with inadequate supplies of toilet paper and sanitary pads, or about the filthy clothing and linens that she has no choice but to use.

Federal prisoner Debi Campbell, sentenced to almost twenty years on a drug "conspiracy" charge (see Chapter 2, "Women in Wartime"), first wrote me from FCI Victorville in Adelanto, California. She spent more than six years living there in what she called a "human warehouse," a giant structure with cinder block stalls and concrete floors. The lights, she pointed out, never get turned off—it's something that the prisoners have no control over, so sleep becomes a difficult feat for even the most exhausted woman.

Cutbacks in prisoner meals have been well documented. After all, prison food is one of the easiest areas in which to trim a budget, particularly in order to fatten the paychecks and perks at the higher end of the corrections spectrum. Among the states that have openly made serious cutbacks in the quantity and quality of food served to prisoners have been Arizona, Iowa, Minnesota, Nevada, North Carolina, Texas, and Virginia—and these are just the states willing to go on the record about their cost- and calorie-cutting strategies.[41]

In the Washington state prison system, I've examined meals that consist of a plastic-wrapped "salad roll," a hard, compressed, hand-sized chunk of iceberg lettuce and a few carrot shavings. A powdered orange "drink mix" or milk powder is accompanied by a slab of an often unidentifiable meat, sometimes accompanied by overcooked potatoes or rice. Fruits and fresh vegetables are so rare, in nearly every prison, as to be cause for celebration when they are provided.

In the New Mexico women's prison, I saw some of the worst-looking food imaginable, which included a beige mash of what was supposed to be beans and rice, a single slice of lettuce, and an oddly colored tomato slice. I sat down next to a group of Native American women who were initially embarrassed about even being seen eating this food. I asked them whether this meal was typical of the ones they were served.

"We usually get sick from the food," they acknowledged, but also expressed amazement that there was even a slice of a tomato on the plate, no matter how inedible it looked.

"This is the first vegetable we've seen in months," one woman admitted and began to speculate that my visit to the prison might have been the reason for the "upgrade" in the meal, something that left me shaken to the core. If a slice of a diseased-looking tomato was the prison's idea of what to serve when a visitor was around, I couldn't even contemplate these women's typical daily diet.

At Valley State Prison for Women (VSPW) in central California, I noted a similarly poor quality of food served to the overflowing prison population. Lieutenant Callahan, giving me the tour of VSPW, said that women who complain about the quality of the food are "really just complaining about the quality of their fellow inmates' cooking."

It's true that most prison kitchens put inmates to work. But the key issue here is that many of the people assigned to the kitchen don't know how to cook for others, much less for hundreds or thousands of prisoners at a time. They are also given only a few ingredients from which to make three meals a day, something I pointed out to my tour guide when I asked him if the kitchen workers would be allowed to provide fresh fruits and vegetables.

"No, they wouldn't," he answered honestly. "There are no 'special' diets at VSPW."

Prisoner complaints about the quality of their meals may seem annoying to people who perceive a prison sentence as a punishment in *every* sense. But the practice of taking away someone's liberty as punishment for a minor or major crime was never supposed to entail forcing people to eat the kind of food that makes them have diarrhea nearly every day, or that is so greasy and laden with carbohydrates and starches that maintaining one's weight is almost impossible. The fact is that these kinds of diets make people sicker, and ultimately our society assumes the cost of the related healthcare in one way or another—that is, unless the prisoner drops dead quickly, which is something that many prisoners think is the point of it all.

"Texas prisons have already cut back on our food medications," Helen Ann Caples wrote me from Hobby Unit, outside the town of Marlin, Texas. "We only get six tampons a month . . . and a roll of toilet paper a week. The rest of the time *we are using rags as toilet paper* [emphasis mine]."

Caples filed a lawsuit in 2005 on behalf of her fellow prisoners, who were getting sick because of contaminated water being funneled into the prison. Her lawsuit was rejected in federal court, but Caples has continued to try to warn her fellow prisoners, as well as the general public, about the situation.

In 2003, the water was considered so dangerous—and the plumbing system so damaged—that the prison limited offenders to drinking no more than three six-ounce cups of water per day. Worse yet, prisoners were not allowed to flush toilets. "The toilets in our cells were backed up with urine and feces, while foul flies and gnats had started to surface due to the toilets' being unflushed," she testified in the court documents.[42]

Today, things aren't much better, Caples told me in an April 2007 letter: "The water here in Marlin is still contaminated. A lot of women have breast cancer, colon cancer, [and] fibrosis on uteruses."

In the nearby Lane Murray Unit, Texas state prisoner Lou Johnson expressed similar concerns. No cleaning rags are even available to the prisoners, Johnson told me, so prisoners resort to using their socks to try to keep their units clean. Officers often refuse to provide the women with disposable gloves to clean the pipe chases in the unit plumbing. "[It] is most often covered with fecal material," Johnson said, a fact that seems to delight a few of the male officers, who force the women to clean with their bare hands.

Johnson, like many other prisoners, also talks of being denied medical care, of being denied meals for small infractions (most often for talking in the food line), and even of being denied the opportunity to go to the bathroom. "I witnessed a middle-aged lady urinate on herself," Johnson recalled bitterly. [The class teacher] was unmerciful in her continued attack on this woman. She made her sit the remainder of class in her soiled clothes. This is cruel and unusual punishment."

Johnson is right. This kind of suffering is inexcusable, just as it is inexcusable to give prisoners no option but to eat the equivalent of dog food.

Or real dog food, as the case may be.

Writing from Hobby Unit, Shirley Southerland brought the "Vita-Pro" scandal to my attention. In 2001, Texas inmates were told that a new meat substitute would be added to their menu.

"When the kitchen staff began to cook with the Vita-Pro," Southerland told me, "the whole prison stank like a wet dead dog being burned with napalm. The smell would sicken you. For many indigent women, they had no choice but to eat this stuff. There were trays and pans of it mixed with other foods, like a sort of Hamburger Helper dish. Later, the kitchen served the Vita-Pro straight up. It stank and didn't look right to me or anyone else."

Southerland asked one of the women in the kitchen to cut out a label from the package. "It was partly in English and partly in Spanish, packaged in Mexico. I sent the label to a friend [who translated the label] and confirmed that it was meant for canine consumption."

The scandal was uncovered after an endless stream of prisoners complained of nausea, diarrhea, and stomach cramps. It turned out that James Collins, the former director of the Texas prison system, had illegally pushed through a $33 million, five-year backroom deal so that Vita-Pro would become the "meat staple" of the Texas state prison system. When the whole mess was exposed, Collins jumped ship to go work at Vita-Pro.[43] Although the company maintains that the prisons were given a human-grade, soy-based meat substitute, Southerland sticks by what the label in the kitchen indicated.

When I read Southerland's account of prisoners being fed as though they were dogs, I immediately thought of one of the signs that hung in the visiting room of the L.A. County women's jail. No jail visits, it announced, were allowed during "inmate feeding."

Perhaps our prisons and jails are more like zoos than we care to admit.

THE ELDERLY IN PRISON

Seventy-two thousand prisoners in the United States are fifty-five or older, and many of them present serious medical conditions.[44] Elder care is one of the reasons that prison healthcare costs the U.S. $3.3 million annually.[45]

When elderly prisoners are locked up for nonviolent crimes or are serving out unnecessarily punitive "three strikes" life sentences, it would seem logical that they should be considered for early release, particularly in cases of demonstrable rehabilitation during their periods of incarceration. High-security incarceration for most sick and elderly people simply doesn't make sense, whether from a fiscal or a humanitarian perspective. Undeniably, some prisoners over fifty-five do pose a genuine risk to society, but they are usually readily identifiable by extremely violent, persistent criminal histories, as well as ongoing evaluations by staff, psychologists, and parole board investigators. Yet most correctional systems aren't even at the point of considering release for a few older prisoners, much less the larger subpopulation of these inmates.

"Dignity Denied," a 2006 report by Legal Services for Prisoners with Children on the plight of incarcerated elderly women, was the first to extensively document the real human and financial cost of the aging prison population.

While older prisoners have the lowest rates of recidivism of any group of prisoners, most states are hesitant to release them if they haven't yet served out their lengthy terms. But as they age, prisoners of both genders begin to suffer from indignities and infirmities to such a degree that it is difficult to understand this rationale of continued incarceration at any cost.

According to "Dignity Denied," written and researched by Heidi Strupp and Donna Willmott, older women in prison are typically housed with women in small cells regardless of their age, disability, security classification, or the nature of their criminal offense. Women well into their fifties, sixties, seventies, and even eighties can be assigned top bunks and heavy manual labor, without any regard for their disabilities or limitations.

"More than half of respondents report that they fell at least once in the last year," Strupp and Willmott reported. "Two out of five respondents report being injured while performing a daily prison routine."

Older women face a plethora of difficulties in prison that are hard for people in the "free world" to grasp. They must drop to the ground during drills, are subject to random pat and strip searches, and have to stand in food and medical lines, without any designated priority status, in 100-plus-degree weather or freezing temperatures.

One of the many older female prisoners with whom I've corresponded is Myrtle Green, a seventy-five-year-old prisoner at CIW who is suffering from heart disease, diabetes, the residual effects of stroke, and many other health complications. Green has already spent seventeen years in prison on a twenty-five-to-life sentence for an "attempted murder," although no one was even injured in conjunction with this case. In essence, Green says that she was hit with the charge because her unscrupulous son-in-law had gotten involved in a scheme to kill someone. When he was caught, prosecutors demanded that he snitch on the higher-ups. Rather than reveal the real dealers up the ladder, Green says that he pointed the finger at her. Green says she pled guilty only after her son-in-law threatened to injure or kill her family.

Whether the story is completely accurate or not, the clear issues here are twofold: Whatever plot may have been hatched, this was a victimless crime based on the word of a known drug dealer, and Green is now an old woman in an overcrowded prison, suffering from serious, debilitating, and life-threatening health conditions. She has gone blind in her left eye from hypertension, has lost her sixty-four-year-old brother, and has barely been able to see her daughter and grandchildren, who live in Jackson, Mississippi, because of the cost of travel.

Seven women between their forties and their sixties had died in the space of a few months the last time Green contacted me, in late April 2007. "It seems death is the answer to our leaving [this prison]," she wrote in her letter.

All she has asked for is to be able to parole back to Mississippi, to spend the rest of her years with her family. Green's daughter, Myrelle, is fifty-three, and she told me that her mother did everything imaginable to provide for her when she was growing up: "I believe I've always had the best mother in the world."

The idea that her mother may not live long enough to be released is something that Myrelle cannot even begin to imagine. "We were never a family of money to be able to buy ourselves out of anything," she explained. "We've tried to let the 'justice system' work as it should for all, but for us, it has not been fair and just at all."

COMPASSIONATE RELEASE

In California, a "compassionate release" policy designed for inmates dying in prison became legal in October 1997, the only one of its kind in the United States. But since January 1998, when the law became effective, the numbers of compassionate releases have actually decreased year by year, according to Cynthia Chandler, an attorney for the Oakland, California–based organization Justice Now, whose office handles every compassionate release case in the state.

While the CDCR used to allow prisoners with terminal illnesses (and even those seriously ill prisoners who could not find adequate treatment for their conditions inside prison) out in time to spend their remaining few months with their loved ones, Chandler says that most prisoners are not being released at all—they are handcuffed and even shackled by their ankles to their deathbeds, with a guard posted outside their room. "Of the few that prison officials are willing to release," says Chandler, "the women are usually minutes or hours away from passing away."

There are so many cases of denials of compassionate releases, as well as those "mercy" releases granted in a most unmerciful fashion, that the stories could fill an entire book.

Judy Greenspan, a prisoner advocate and coauthor of the compassionate release legislation, finds the current overall lack of compassion toward severely ill prisoners particularly disheartening.

"The problem is that the political climate is so antiprisoner, and prisoners have been so demonized, that they are not even getting out [on compassionate release]," she told me. "The system's refusal to release dying prisoners is both inhumane and unconscionable."

Advocates might sometimes be given to hyperbole, but where the issue of compassionate release for dying prisoners is concerned, the words do not ever seem strong enough. Of all of the aspects of female incarceration that I have researched, the lack of compassion and humanity extended to people dying painfully, often at a young age, is unfathomable. No excuse or justification for it has ever made sense to me. The delay or denial of compassionate release to dying women for their sake, and for the sake of their families, friends, and young children, is a profound example of what "cruel and unusual" punishment looks and feels like, particularly when the very illnesses that prisoners are dying from have been ignored or treated poorly by prison medical staff.

One of the many disturbing stories that I came across several years ago was that of Tina Balagno, an HIV-positive prisoner with a history of drug addiction. Balagno started complaining of severe leg pain when she was admitted to Central California Women's Facility in June 1998. She had been distracted by the leg pain just long enough to not notice the initial emergence of lumps in one of her breasts. Balagno reported both conditions and finally got an appointment to see a doctor, who took no interest in her leg pains but found a malignancy in her breast. Her family urged immediate treatment. In November, Balagno was admitted into surgery for what she thought would be a lumpectomy. When she came to, she looked down and realized that her entire breast had been removed—without her knowledge or permission.

Worse still, Balagno's unexpected mastectomy was accompanied by neither chemotherapy nor radiation treatment. (Perhaps the idea had been that the more radical surgery meant that the state could save money on the costs of follow-up treatment). Like most other women suffering from chronic and terminal illnesses, Balagno received only an over-the-counter pain reliever for her pain.

Balagno was sent back to prison. The pain in her legs grew worse, but the medical department never examined her. Two months after her surgery, Balagno fell into a coma after suffering two seizures. Balagno was finally diagnosed with metastasized bone cancer—the cause of her persistent leg pain. Balagno's family pleaded for compassionate release so that they could be in her presence until the moment of her death.

Perhaps because they realized that Balagno could not make a run for it, California prison officials released Balagno to her family, just one week before her death. She died on February 10, 1999, at age forty.

After Balagno's death, her sister, Deborah Teczon, had this to say: "She was treated [by the prison] as if her life meant nothing. I'm here today to say her life meant *everything* to me and my family. No one in this world should have to go through the pain that Tina endured.

"Tina never wanted to get sick in jail, because she knew the system would do nothing for her," she added. "Tina's fears were confirmed. They waited so long that the cancer destroyed her. I cannot understand how the medical staff can live with themselves. They took an oath to save lives. This uncivilized way of acting and thinking is completely unacceptable. Prisoners are not just a number; they are living, breathing people."

Chapter 5: Trying to Stay Sane

"My heart aches when I hear a mentally ill woman crying out for help. They get lonely, and no one tends to them, and staff are not equipped to handle them. I try my best to reach out to the ones I'm able to through the ventilation system to calm them down, or to help take their minds away from here. I ask them why they go off, and they say they are bored here, and have nothing to do and no one to talk to."

—Christina Francis, serving her second Security Housing Unit term in Valley State Prison for Women

"They're trying to confine the mind. And that's what got us in there in the first place, that we were feeling secluded or isolated. . . . If you can survive [punitive segregation], you can survive anything. But when you get out, it feels like you've lost something."

—A female prisoner serving her fifth month in segregation, name withheld at her request, New Mexico Women's Correctional Facility

My original inspiration for this book came from the first time I walked through a women's supermaximum facility known as a Security Housing Unit, on the grounds of Valley State Prison for Women (VSPW), in October 2000.

I had traveled to VSPW, in Chowchilla, California, to sit in on an all-day legislative hearing within the prison. The hearing centered around female prisoners' complaints about rampant medical negligence and sexual abuse by staff. Sadly, several of the brave women who testified have died in the years since then, including Charisse Shumate, the lead plaintiff in a major class-action suit against what was then known as the California Department of Corrections. Filed in 1995, the suit was settled in 1997 when the state, without admitting wrongdoing, agreed to institute prisonwide changes to improve overall healthcare services.[1]

In the years before I visited the world's largest women's prison complex, of which VSPW constitutes one-half, I had tried to understand as much as possible about the wide variety of complaints and class-action lawsuits pertaining to the health and civil rights violations that were occuring with increasing frequency in juvenile detention facilities, jails, and prisons nationwide. I had also made an effort to learn more about prison culture itself, including the frustration of prison employees who felt the sting of pejorative stereotypes about their profession, as well as internal frustrations about trying to effect progressive change within the framework of massive, overburdened prison bureaucracies.

Yet absolutely nothing in my background could have prepared me for the day after the hearing, when I returned to VSPW for a prison tour that concluded at the facility's Administrative Segregation Unit (Ad Seg) and Security Housing Unit (SHU).

From the outside, the building looked almost like any other at VSPW. But that's where any of the similarities ended—and where my awareness of the severity of mental illness among women in prison deepened immeasurably.

My guide for the day, Public Information Officer Pat Callahan, had asked me whether I really wanted to go into the building, because, he explained, the behavior of the women there could sometimes a hard thing for an outsider to understand. I thanked him for the opportunity to back out but explained that this portion of the tour was just as important as any other. Years later, I would come to appreciate the experience for a multitude of reasons, not the least of which was the refusal of other women's prisons to let me see their equivalent of punitive segregation.

When we reached the door to the Ad Seg/SHU building, Lieutenant Callahan directed me to hand my ID and visitor's pass over to him. A fishing-type line with a clip on the end was lowered from a small window toward the top of the building. I looked up at what I later understood to be the control room area, as the officer peered down to try to compare my face to the one on my identification card.

A sharp click signalled the opening of the door, and we were in the building. The first thing to hit my senses was the chaotic sound of muffled screams. I noticed that the naturally bright sky of our outdoor environment had completely disappeared; here, there was nothing but artificial light shining inside the building day and night. The next things to reach my senses were the disagreeable scent and feel of stale air, even as the main physical space outside the cells was so spotless as to approximate the sterility of a medical environment.

One side of this building is dedicated to Ad Seg. At the time of my visit, just over forty women were being held while staff investigated or waited for rulings on the nature of their infractions against prison rules. By policy, the women confined here are allowed no possessions, no personal decorations, and limited contact with family members. They looked uniformly miserable.

Locked behind steel doors, the women are only to stare only into the unit itself; the outside windows are painted so that prisoners cannot see in or out. Once the women noticed me, a civilian carrying a notepad and jotting notes, many of them rushed to their small vertical windows. Some began to shout out for me to come talk to them, while others stared with something akin to curiosity, or else what I took to be hardened hostility.

The latter was also the attitude mirrored most closely by the guards concentrated on the ground floor, who sat with their sack lunches, reviewing paperwork, jotting down notes, and discussing prisoner conduct. Their occasional glares in my direction heightened my sense that outsiders were an unwelcome and bothersome presence here.[2]

I turned around to get a 360-degree view of this side of the building, and I spotted a woman sitting in a small cage with bars on the ground floor of the unit. I had actually walked past her already and had apparently been so overwhelmed initially that I had overlooked her very presence. But there she sat, in a zoo-style cage, using a combination of hand signals and loud shouts to try to communicate with some of the other women in the Ad Seg unit. My look of disbelief did not go unnoticed. For a brief moment, our eyes met. She turned her head and tried to pull off a dignified look, despite her disheveled hair and clothing. Despite this attempt to cover her emotions, the humiliation of being seen locked in a cage in this chaotic environment was transparent, and painful to witness.

Some women's stints in Ad Seg amount to a maximum of ten days "in the hole" for a minor infraction. A small number of women actually end up here because they have requested protective custody, either because they are worried about being hurt or, in some cases, because they are suffering emotional distress and consider the isolation preferable to stimuli from the general population. Women with more serious infractions, or whose cases are still being investigated, can sit in their cells for much longer, subject to thirty-day reviews. These women remain in Ad Seg either until they are cleared of the infraction and deemed safe enough to return to the general population, or until the prison's Institutional Classification Committee rules that the prisoner should do time in the SHU. As cold and harsh as the Ad Seg environment seemed, at least, I reasoned to myself, this was a temporary situation for the prisoners.

I crossed over to the SHU to see what fate awaited the women there. (Technically, this is the only SHU for women in the state prison system. The other women's prison in the complex, Central California Women's Facility (CCWF), also has a combined Ad Seg and death row with most of the hallmarks—but not the name—of a SHU for women.)

No partition separated the nearly identical-appearing wings. But here, the prisoners' sense of desperation and mental illness were even more palpable. Many of these women appeared to already be in various states of full-blown psychiatric crisis. These women were disturbed, but they came across as a danger more to themselves than to the people around them, and they were certainly far from representing the "worst of the worst," a phrase often used to describe female and male supermax prisoners.

In this twenty-two- to twenty-three-hour-a-day lockdown facility, I took in as much of the emotionally and visually jarring environment as I could. I will admit that the sights and sounds from this experience echoed in my own nightmares for weeks on end. Even now, several years after my visit, I am haunted by what I witnessed there.

While I stood in the unit and tried to make myself as inconspicuous as possible, most of the forty-four women imprisoned in the SHU yelled and screamed nonstop—either through their call boxes, used to communicate with prison guards or mental health workers, or through the ventilation system. Some women appeared to just be yelling and screaming to themselves disjointedly or hysterically, while other women were trying to communicate with one another. Some of the women had their sallow faces pressed up against the cell windows. They stared but said nothing. These women's expressions were hollow, their pupils wide and dark as bottomless pools of despair. Their eyelids were heavy and, in the case of a couple of women, brimming with tears.

Many of these women looked like they were no longer even functioning at anything higher than a basic survival level, manifested through either total resignation or full-blown rage. Several women in the SHU cells were drooling, a clear side effect of many of the psychotropic medicines that they were on. The only steady movement past these women's cells appeared to be the regular rounds made by the SHU's pill-dispensing medical technicians.

Cassie Pierson, a staff attorney at Legal Services for Prisoners with Children, spent several years interviewing women in the SHU at VSPW, in preparation for a report that she submitted to the California State Legislature. I talked to her shortly after my visit there about the prevalence of psychiatric medications administered to so many of the women there.

"The use of psychotropic drugs as a solution to the problems of women who present compromised mental health, or even those who don't, is a huge problem," Pierson told me. "A vast number of the women in the SHU are on some type of psychiatric medication, many of them on multiple drugs at high doses. I have talked with women who can hardly speak, or whose eyes roll back into their heads because of the high levels of drugs they are on."

In both Ad Seg and the SHU, policy dictates that all meals and psychiatric drugs are given to the prisoners through a small slot that only a prison employee can open. Women are either single celled or double celled—with no privacy allowed—in small, bare cells with a combination toilet-and-sink metal unit. A built-in concrete slab serves as a bed frame, atop which a thin, single mattress, two sheets, and one thin blanket are allowed.

The SHU windows looking into the facility cannot be covered by the prisoner for any reason, even if a woman is using the toilet, for instance, or changing a sanitary pad. "Papering," or covering any window, is strictly prohibited and subject to disciplinary action, and can even result in a forcible cell extraction. One of the primary tools used in those extractions—a large Plexiglas shield—was placed within the prisoners' line of sight, as if to remind the women that acting out was likely to have serious consequences. (By prison policy, the cell extractions must be announced and deemed necessary for the safety of the prisoner and/or the officers, although the necessity of chemical sprays, batons, and multiple officers converging to tackle a single woman in a small cell is a questionable practice, at best.)

"A significant proportion of women in the SHU suffer from mental health problems which may make it particularly difficult for them to cope with the conditions imposed," reported Amnesty International USA of their experiences at the VSPW SHU. "Some have histories of sexual and physical abuse, depression, and attempted suicide."

Unfortunately, some of those attempts are successful. When I walked through the Ad Seg unit at CCWF in 2006, one woman began to yell that she had not received her meds in many days and was suffering as a result. Another woman banged on her window to get my attention and hollered about a recent hanging suicide of a woman in the unit.

According to CCWF staff, the prison has had four suicides in the past two years, all of which happened in either Ad Seg or the adjacent Enhanced Outpatient Program, where severely mentally ill women are housed in identical cells but are given limited counseling and some freedom of movement within the pod during the day.

California broke a new state record when forty-four female and male prisoners killed themselves in 2005. An investigator appointed by U.S. District Judge

Lawrence Karlton to look into mental healthcare in the state prison system—and the reasons behind the increase in suicides—found that prisoners in "overcrowded and understaffed Administrative Segregation units are killing themselves in unprecedented numbers. . . . Confining a suicidal inmate to their cell for twenty-four hours a day only enhances isolation and is antitherapeutic."[3]

New York's state prison has also been exposed for shoddy mental healthcare practices. There, the control units are also known as SHUs, although they are colloquially known as "the box." One of the most powerful exposés of the agony of many of the men and women confined to these SHUs was written by Mary Beth Pfeiffer, who focused on the tragic story of Jessica Lee Roger for *The New York Times*.

Roger survived an abusive childhood at the hands of her mentally ill mother, who left the family when Roger was just eleven. She was stuck with a heavy-drinking father and soon ended up in juvenile mental institutions and psychiatric emergency rooms. She first attempted suicide at age thirteen and was eventually arrested and charged at age sixteen for a fight with her sister. Because New York criminal law dictates that felonies can be considered adult crimes starting when the perpetrator is sixteen, Roger was sentenced to a 1,200-day prison term.

Roger lashed out and kicked a jail guard while she was in custody and was charged with second-degree assault on an officer. She received a three-and-a-half-year to seven-year sentence, to be served out at Bedford Hills Correctional Facility. Predictably, her mental illness intensified and manifested itself in the prison through furious outbursts, which in turn were punished as infractions. Roger spent a total of 250 days confined to her cell and another 160 days in the SHU, where she was locked up twenty-three hours a day. Pfeiffer was able to locate some of the letters that Roger sent to her mother during that time:

"Mommy these people are stressing me out again. They took my sheets, my blankets, and my mattress out of my cell because I keep hiding under the bed and covering myself so they can't see me. . . . Mommy the feeling of hurting myself is getting stronger."

On August 17, 2002, Roger gave in once and for all. After several suicide attempts, she strangled herself with a bedsheet. She was twenty-one years old.[4]

Across the country, women like Roger, who end up in prisons—or, worse yet, in control units—have very little access to any kind of real psychiatric care. In the SHU at VSPW, they are at least accorded a few small privileges, especially when compared with women in Ad Seg, including the opportunity to have a limited number of possessions, books, and letter-writing materials; and to purchase prison-issue television sets or radios. SHU prisoners are not allowed to have clocks or watches and are allowed out of their cells for only a few possible reasons. Those reasons include eligibility to attend up to ten hours of group therapy per week, which is administered in a large closet–sized room within the SHU. The room is easily the most antithetical setting to therapy imaginable: a few adjacent cages contain nothing but round metal stools. The cages face a video monitor. According to a social worker on the day I visited VSPW, twelve-step programming and other "educational" videos were occupying most of the "therapy" time.

Women are also allowed to leave their cells for a few rushed, fifteen-minute showers per week (even there, the women are tethered to the shower stalls with very small "modesty" screens that still reveal much of their bodies), as well as for one hour of daily recreation time in a small, bare, razor wire–surrounded concrete yard. Women are either given "walk alone" status or are allowed to mingle with a few other SHU inmates during this hour.

The women with SHU status are also allowed out of the facility for occasional noncontact visits with immediate family members or legal counsel, or to be seen for a serious medical or full-blown psychiatric emergency, as determined by staff. Every movement in or out of a cell dictates that the woman must strip down and agree to a squat-and-cough inspection. Through the whole process, the woman is handcuffed, shackled at her arms and feet, and always escorted by at least two guards. Phone access, any kind of prison labor, vocational training, or access to educational classes are not allowed.

Small wonder that so many of these women appear as disturbed as they do. Beyond these few limited ventures outside their tiny cells, the women can quickly lose their perspective about what time it is, what date it is, and even how long they've been locked up. Some women begin to hallucinate, some withdraw into themselves, and others simply grow more and more hostile, wanting to seek an outlet for their mounting anger, and even to seek revenge in any way possible.

When I spoke several years ago with attorney Ellen Barry, the founder of Legal Services for Prisoners in San Francisco, she had numerous concerns about the placement of women in control units. One of her clients had entered the VSPW SHU without a mental illness diagnosis, but Barry explained that the woman had subsequently "been driven crazy" by the experience.

"Women do their time differently from men," Barry explained. "I don't want to ever imply that conditions for men are better, or that conditions for women are worse, because those are meaningless dichotomies. For men, the isolation is horrendous and people literally go nuts being so isolated. For women, I would argue that it takes on an even more significant dimension because of the way that gender differences play out in society. Women turn to each other for support and basic survival in ways that men don't do as often. So the isolation issue takes on an even deeper [meaning] for women."[5]

Scientific and psychiatric research has helped to explain why people tend to do so poorly in isolative, punitive conditions. We know that after a few days in lockup, a person's brain-wave patterns begin to shift to those typical of stupor and delirium. Even as far back as 1952, research showed that when researchers eliminate sight, sound, and tactile stimulation, people can begin to hallucinate within two days.[6]

Stuart Grassian was the first psychiatrist to identify a specific set of symptoms developed by prisoners in segregated, solitary confinement units, something that he named the "SHU Syndrome." Dr. Terry Kupers, a noted expert on psychiatric care in prisons, has continued in this vein, having interviewed and testified to the psychological state of hundreds of SHU prisoners. He agrees with Grassian's research that even SHU prisoners who do not become psychotic can manifest psychotic features, including "massive free-floating anxiety, hyper-responsiveness to external stimuli, perceptual distortions and hallucinations, a feeling of unreality, difficulty with concentration and memory, acute confusional states, the emergence of primitive aggressive fantasies, persecutory ideation, motor excitement, violent destructive or self-mutilatory outbursts, and rapid subsidence of symptoms upon termination of isolation."[7]

Although women in the SHU still have their sight and the sound of screaming women, they are most certainly limited in what they can see and hear and touch—and all of it is cold and concrete. For most women who already come from dysfunctional and/or abusive backgrounds, it is a traumatizing or retraumatizing experience.

"We're agitated, we're angry," one SHU inmate at VSPW explains in the cable television documentary *Lockdown: Women Behind Bars*. "The place is crazy. It's very evil, very mean, very painful. . . . We fight a lot because we're so angry."[8]

Spitting at guards is one of the most common ways in which the women seek revenge; known spitters have signs posted outside their cells and are made to wear "spit masks" to cover their nose and mouth every time they are allowed out of their cell. Officers who work in the SHU can also wear thin plastic spit guards in addition to their stab-proof vests, although stabbings are actually a rare occurrence among female prisoners in the SHU, according to Lieutenant Callahan.

"Gassing" is the other way in which SHU inmates are known to try to retaliate for real or perceived wrongs at the hands of staff. The prisoner will wait until her food slot is opened and then throw some kind of fluid—a drink or urine, usually—at the staff member on the other side. Other prisoners smear their cells and windows with their own feces to try to get attention or to try to keep officers away from them.

Former VSPW SHU prisoner Christina Francis explained to me that she joined in many unit-wide protests (banging on doors, screaming, and throwing food trays through food slots are usually the extent of those strategies) to try to help the "5150s," as the mentally ill are referred to in police code. These reasons for these protests included situations where women who had defecated all over their cells were being forcefully extracted from their cells. Francis's testimony closely matched that of every other prisoner who has contacted me about the experience of watching or going through a cell extraction. (I have also had the opportunity to view a few videotapes of cell extractions at other prisons, and their only variance is in the degree of brutality and/or the amount of warning time given to a prisoner before the doors are flung open and the person is tackled to the floor.)

"They gear up in riot gear and get out the video camera," Francis explained. "They shoot some type of smoke bomb that makes it almost impossible to breathe. They have a huge shield, batons, OC pepper spray, and other devices that are used to restrain [the woman], and one that is used to hog-tie."

Francis also complained about the fact that officers wield far too much retaliatory power over the fate of the prisoners, seemingly without proper checks and balances, including the ultimate length of their stay in the SHU. In California and many other states, even acts of self-harm are punishable offenses, subject to more infractions on a prisoner's record or additional SHU time, or forwarded to prosecutors for new felony charges.

Washington state's prison system was once a focal point of criticism regarding the punishment of women who self-mutilated or attempted suicide. The Washington Department of Corrections reached a settlement agreement in *Hallett v. Payne* in 1995 to improve their medical/dental/mental healthcare services, but complaints continued. According to court transcripts, for instance, one bipolar twenty-nine-year-old prisoner suffering from post-traumatic stress disorder cut herself with a razor blade in December 1998. For that act, she was punished with a loss of ten days of her accrued "good conduct" time. In another case, a thirty-nine-year-old woman housed in the prison's mental health ward for severe psychiatric problems actually cut the brachial artery in her upper arm to try to kill herself. When she recovered from lifesaving surgery, she was fined $50 for medical expenses and given extra work duty.[9]

While it is true that these prison employees have the authority to send a severely disturbed prisoner to a hospital, it is more likely that she would be sent to a prison suicide-watch cell—usually a bleak, cold, empty room with either a simple toilet or a drain in the middle—into which the inmate is thrust naked (as I witnessed the first time I visited VSPW) or wearing a suicide-resistant garment or blanket.[10] She is checked on every fifteen minutes to make sure she doesn't kill herself, but other than this surveillance, the conditions of confinement in these cells have always struck me as an unusually cruel response to a woman's suicidal feelings.

In 1997, when Californian Sheryl Jefferson was twenty-nine, she was sent to prison for the first time, at the California Institution for Women. She was placed under ninety-day psychiatric "observation" because she was exhibiting some symptoms of mental distress.

"It was one of the most horrifying experiences I've ever had," Jefferson told me. "I had to strip in front of male and female guards. For the first fourteen days [under suicide watch], I lay naked in a cell by myself, in a room with a broken window. There were roaches crawling all over the walls." The psych unit was full of women who talked to themselves all night, or who imagined people who weren't there, scenarios that Jefferson found heartbreaking and incredibly difficult to witness. Jefferson wasn't even suicidal, much less psychotic; she was eventually diagnosed with depression and a lesser form of bipolar disorder. The experience, as she put it, was actually more emotionally traumatic than growing up in a dysfunctional, alcoholic home.

The other alternative is for the SHU prisoner to be moved to CCWF's Enhanced Outpatient Program (EOP), which unfortunately sounds far more pleasant than it is. The EOP, Ad Seg, and fifteen women on death row (behind their own enclosures) are contained within the same building. The so-called condemned women and prisoners placed in the EOP must live with the sound of the screams and rage of the Ad Seg women. (In fact, when I visited, Ad Seg had overflowed into the EOP side, so there was not even any physical separation in place.)

The women sent to the EOP are essentially just allowed a bit more movement in the television "day room," although they do have more access to speaking with medication-dispensing employees. They do not truly receive any kind of intensive therapy; medications management is the primary purpose here. Additionally, the women's cells are nearly identical to those in the SHU, and the prisoners are still watched over by mostly male prison guards in what amounts to a very chaotic, discipline-focused environment.

The very serious issue of how emotionally distressed and suicidal women are dealt with in prison is not limited to California. In Virginia, Jennifer Blake, a prisoner at the Fluvanna Correctional Center for Women, has been sent to the

SHU twice—the first time for complaining about a male officer who watched her while she took a shower. Blake tells me the story of another prisoner who was a known self-mutilator. In July 2006, according to Blake, that woman asked a sergeant to place her in a suicide-watch cell, saying that she had an overwhelming urge to cut herself. Blake says she watched as the sergeant ignored the woman's repeated requests and sent her back to her cell. The last time she was sent back to her cell, the woman cut her own throat and wrist open in a genuine suicide attempt. She barely survived.

In an ongoing battle over the poor quality of medical and mental healthcare in Wisconsin's largest women's prison, (Taycheedah Correctional Institution or TCI), the American Civil Liberties Union has focused attention on conditions in the TCI SHU.[11] The Department of Justice (DOJ) also launched a yearlong investigation into conditions at TCI, finding in July 2005 that forty-four of fifty-nine women in the SHU had "serious mental illness and were observed to be in significant distress." One woman had gone into a psychotic state and was witnessed drinking her urine and eating her own feces. The cause of her incarceration in the SHU was based on disciplinary infractions and "disrespect." Investigators also found a severely mentally ill fifteen-year-old girl there who had been serving a long SHU term.

"Placing an unmedicated, mentally ill teenager in segregation, with little or no stimulation and no education services, causes psychological damage that may be irreversible," the DOJ investigators cautioned.[12]

Mentally ill juveniles also suffer tremendously when they are incarcerated. According to the Center on Juvenile and Criminal Justice, institutionalized youth in detention centers and adult prisons are eight times more likely than adults to attempt suicide.[13] In 2005, a study of mental health services for juveniles in detention facilities, commissioned by Representative Henry Waxman (D–Los Angeles), reported that many children and teens (some as young as eight years of age) spend up to two months in confinement simply waiting to receive community mental healthcare. In many cases, the children have committed no crime, but parents—alarmed by their children's emotional problems—call the police to lock up their kids until that mental healthcare can be accessed.[14]

"Youngsters in prison face daunting odds," writes Sasha Abramsky in his book *American Furies*. Abramsky references the case of a sixteen-year-old girl in a Florida women's prison who hung herself with her bedsheets in November 2000. He also references reports that emerged in August 2004 of suicidal girl inmates who were "stripped naked and locked in a dark room, while other girl prisoners were forced to eat their own vomit."[15]

Acts like these seem incomprehensible to most of us. Under any circumstance, they are absolutely inexcusable. But in condemning such brutality, it is important to try to remember that we, as a society, are allowing (although unknowingly so, where most Americans are concerned) the mentally ill to be incarcerated in facilities where personnel have little or no training in mental healthcare. Flared tensions on both sides of any kind of a restrictive control unit or strip cell actually make sense in a twisted way, if we view the escalation in the context of such a hostile and dehumanizing environment for prisoners and officers alike.

During my visit to the VSPW SHU, I watched as one guard tore apart an inmate's room, in all likelihood because of some suspicion that the prisoner possessed contraband. The prisoner was not present—she had been removed from her cell. The guard set about tearing through her few belongings (guards are not obligated to leave prisoner cells as they found them) and then tossed her thin mattress from the second floor of the SHU down to the first floor, with something akin to a joyful brusqueness. He seemed to take particular delight in the loud sound that the mattress made when it hit the floor, just a few feet from where I was standing.

Sadistic responses to suffering prisoners may not make a lot of sense to out-siders, but the stresses of dealing with the mentally ill in this kind of environment are very real and not at all specific to California. Psychiatric staff are generally overworked or barely present in supermax facilities. Those who do work on-site, including one social worker whom I interviewed in the VSPW, readily admit to being exhausted and overwhelmed by the environment and the myriad pressing needs of the mentally ill prisoners in particular.

Although I consider VSPW's SHU one of the most extreme examples of the unnecessary severity of a women's control unit, my experiences with divergent prison and jail cultures throughout the United States have convinced me that a high level of ignorance or outright hostility toward the mentally ill prevails. Con-sequently, prison guards faced with the most disruptive, emotionally disturbed prisoners can sometimes lash out in ways that do little more than ensure pro-longed agitation and suffering.

In his book *Prison Madness,* Terry Kupers, an expert in psychiatric issues in prison, is emphatic about the need to begin to separate mental health and disci-plinary issues.

"When behaviors on the part of mentally disordered prisoners—including suicide attempts, self-mutilation, rule-breaking, and even some minor violent incidents—are secondary to their mental disorder, they should not be handled entirely as disciplinary infractions requiring punishment," writes Kupers. "Too often, disruptive acts are merely punished and the possibility that they reflect an imminent psychotic episode or a need for immediate psychiatric attention is never even considered."[16]

Without this recognition, a vicious cycle of SHU incarceration and rein-carceration can quickly develop, as a prisoner's frustration, anger, and/or men-tal anguish intensify and turn into rule-breaking or self-destructive behavior.

In this kind of punitive, highly restrictive environment, deescalation seems to lose its significance, as many guards assume a defensive, even vengeful, attitude toward the behavior of prisoners who do not seem to respond well to orders or commands.

"There is a huge problem managing and treating felons who are considered both 'mad' and 'bad,'" according to Kupers, who believes that long-term control units should actually be abolished, although short-term segregation can be effective if used in concert with some kind of intensive mental health intervention or deescalation-focused therapeutic process.[17"]

Most prison systems lack treatment settings and programs for these prisoners. For instance, most state prisons, refused admittance to a psychiatric inpatient unit if inmates have a record of repeated violent episodes," writes Kupers in *Prison Madness*. "They tend to wind up in supermaximum [confinement], where the harsh conditions and forced idleness worsen their mental disorders, followed by more disruptive behaviors on their part and even longer terms in lockup."[18]

On average mentally ill men and women are locked up for fifteen months longer than their nondiagnosed counterparts.[19] This disparity is likely to be related to the fact that the mentally ill are put into a stressful environment that can exacerbate preexisting conditions, especially because of the difficulty many have in following strict rules, dealing with loud noises and constant chaos, and being cut off from human contact.

In a 2002 report on the mentally ill in prison, Human Rights Watch noted that prisoners with mental illness are very likely to be physically and/or sexually abused and poked fun at by some prisoners, who call them "bugs."[20] (Other terms I've heard include "kooks" and "dings," while medications are called "ding biscuits.") Jail and prison guards can be just as culpable as prisoners when it comes to using this kind of terminology.

In February 2007, I visited the women's division of the Los Angeles County Jail, located near Watts. Los Angeles County now has the nation's biggest jail system, spread throughout numerous facilities. Women in jail custody are now concentrated in the Lynwood facility, and they numbered between 2,500 and 2,800 on the day that I visited (the facility was unable to provide an exact number for me). The L.A. County Jails also function, de facto, as the largest psychiatric system in the nation, with 3,400 mentally ill inmates.[21]

On the day that I walked through the jail, there were roughly one hundred women in their mental observation units. Notably, this was the only area I was not walked into during my tour. But I got a taste of how mentally ill women were considered when Deputy Claudia Rodriguera, the tough, but amiable woman giving me the tour pointed in the direction of those units and casually referred to them as "cuckoo town."

The inmates in "cuckoo town," Rodriguera chuckled, "are the loonies." These women, she explained, are "hell" to work around, and frustrate her and other deputies the most because "they don't follow orders, throw urine and feces, and scream constantly." As a result, the women are only allowed to access restricted programming and exercise, and are fed in their cells.

All of this sounded very familiar to me, although I was not able to see the actual conditions of confinement for myself. I was actually taken to the women's "hole," a small, intense pod with a central command station (staffed by two female deputies)—the kind of twenty-three-hour-per-day lockdown that exemplifies control units across the country. Here, as in most such units, the women are allowed no phone calls or belongings, and are fed in their cells.

I asked Rodriguera what kinds of infractions would get a woman sent to the "hole." "All kinds of things," she responded. "Spitting, fighting, destruction of property, profanities, or resisting orders."

"Also," she added, as she squared her shoulders and lifted her head proudly, "if you call me a bitch, you're out of here."

The comment made me think about what I had heard from other female officers about how women prisoners can actually be more difficult to work with, because they are more likely to try to push the buttons of a woman guarding them. I also thought back to one of the things that prisoners and advocates alike had been telling me for years—that women are often locked down for behaviors that are almost expected of men in prison, at least to a certain degree. These actions include mouthing off to an officer, spitting on the ground or near an officer, passively resisting an order, or displaying anger in some other fashion (but not necessarily acting on it). This is not to say that men never get locked down for these things, but it usually takes something more severe—an assault or direct resistance to an order, for instance, to actually be thrown into solitary confinement.[22] With that said, I've noted an overall trend toward harsh, reactive punishment in female and male prisons for even the smallest and least serious infractions.

Nearly one-quarter of prisoners in control units are estimated to be mentally ill, and nearly 45 percent of those women and men try to commit suicide at some point during their incarceration.[23] Whether mental illnesses are preexisting or manifest themselves after lockdown in control units is hard to ascertain, but there is no question that the environment makes an inmate's mental health worse, not better. Supermaxes look and feel like oppressive and unnecessarily cruel forms of punishment, and the people contained within them react accordingly.

What percentage of control-unit prisoners were already manifesting symptoms of mental illness versus how many began to manifest symptoms of mental illness only after they were locked down has not yet been the subject of a comprehensive study. But the end result is that the control units look and feel like unfeeling, punitive, and repressive environments that do damage to the heart, body, and mind.

"In seg, you are isolated, it's freezing cold, you shower three times a week, and you might get a book to read if you're lucky," Blake says of her time in the Fluvanna SHU in Virginia. "The classic retaliation [by guards] is putting someone in seg under 'investigation status.' They can say you're being investigated and leave you in seg for an indefinite amount of time."

Rahema Carter spent five years between VSPW and CCWF, including nearly two years locked up in CCWF's SHU, and was finally released from the prison in 2005. Carter's memories of the experience—and of the treatment of the mentally ill—are scarring, painful reminders of the cruelty inflicted and witnessed there.

"The Security Housing Unit is where the inmates are treated the most inhumane," she tells me. "The mentally ill are placed there, left to soil themselves, kick, scream, bang their heads against the concrete."

Cindy Boskofsky, an Alaskan Aleut transgendered woman and former prison guard in Washington state, killed her lover, another female prison guard. Boskofsky alleges she committed the murder only after enduring repeated physical abuse. Because of her knowledge of prison operations in Washington, and the fact that she had killed a prison guard, she was deemed too dangerous to stay in the state. She was transferred into the federal system, where she has spent nearly the entire time in SHUs in various states, including California, Connecticut, and Florida.

"The conditions here . . . are in violation of our Eighth Amendment rights of the Constitution," she wrote to me about the FCI Danbury SHU in Connecticut. "There are three people to a cell that is about six feet by eight feet. The person on the floor (me) has a mattress that is up under the toilet. We get stepped on, [our] toothpaste is hard and chunky, [we have] no shampoo or deodorant [or] proper clothing."

The accounts from all of the women who have written or talked to me about their experiences in control units are startling in their similarity, although there is some variance in the ways the women explain the abuse and deprivation.

One might rightly ask how things even got to this point. To understand that, it is important to have a bit of context and history where the "evolution" of control units has been concerned.

In California, the first SHUs were built in the 1980s and were originally supposed to have been designed for the "worst of the worst": the sexual predators and uncontrollably violent inmates who posed a safety risk to other prisoners and correctional officers alike. There are now five official SHUs in California today, including the women's SHU at VSPW.

"The SHU was built on the premise that harmony inside California prisons depended on walling off . . . the most volatile offenders," the *Los Angeles Times* reported in a lengthy exposé on the brutality and corruption within the Corcoran SHU during the '80s and '90s. "Its purpose was not unlike that of a toxic landfill, taking the most dangerous chemicals from around the state and mixing the brew into one confined chamber, hoping it wouldn't explode."[24]

The intensive use of control units is actually a fairly recent trend in modern American prison practices. Roughly around the mid-'80s, prisoners rarely spent more than thirty days in the "hole."[25] Looking back further in history, SHUs are part of a legacy of solitary confinement that harkens back to practices started in the United States in the early part of the nineteenth century, particularly with the opening of the Eastern State Penitentiary in Philadelphia and the Auburn prison in New York.

In both prisons, the practice of solitary confinement was considered revolutionary in getting prisoners to reflect on their crimes, and to force a person's transformation into a repentant citizen. At Eastern State, prisoners were allowed no contact with one another, and were allowed only the sole possession of a bible. They could not write to or visit with loved ones, were referenced only by their prison numbers, and were led through hallways with hoods on to block out any visual stimuli or sense of their environment. At Auburn, the primary difference was that prisoners were actually made to work long hours around each other in the daytime, but they were forbidden conversation, gestures, or any contact whatsoever with each other. Both prison systems were soon replicated in many jails and prisons in the United States.[26]

The practice did not work as it had been planned, and criticism mounted from reformers who had toured these institutions, including the English novelist Charles Dickens, who likened a prisoner in solitary confinement at Eastern to a "man buried alive."[27] Then, as today, prisoners were suffering mental breakdowns from which they could never return to a state of normalcy. Many men began to mutilate themselves, swallow sharp objects, or commit suicide. By the late nineteenth century, most of these prisons or solitary confinement units were shut down, although horrific practices in some prisons continued, including iron jackets, gags, reduced rations, and torturous forms of psychological experimentation.[28]

Several decades passed before solitary confinement made a strong comeback in American prisons. After the 1963 closure of the notorious island prison U.S. Penitentiary Alcatraz, federal prison administrators created an intensive, high-security prison from which more volatile male criminals could not escape. In 1972, the nation's first supermaximum facility for high-risk male prisoners throughout the U.S. federal prison system—generally, those inmates deemed too violent to control in the general population—was established in the form of a high-security unit within USP Marion in Illinois. In 1983, after the murder of two officers in the prison, the entire prison was placed on twenty-four-hour lockdown. Shortly thereafter, the director of the Federal Bureau of Prisons, Norman Carlson, pushed for a newer, even more sophisticated maximum-security prison. He got his wish when, in 1994, ADX Florence opened for business as a male federal prison utilizing high-tech, omnipresent surveillance and security systems in solitary confinement as operating principles.[29]

ADX Florence is known as the first real supermax in the United States. Other terms for this kind of supermax—whether in reference to an entire prison or one of the units within a larger prison—include the catchall descriptor "control unit," including Security Housing Units; Intensive, Special, Closed, or Restrictive Management Units; or the more insidious-sounding Behavioral Modification Units. Currently, there is no female-only supermaximum prison, although one for political prisoners did exist in the United States until 1989 in Lexington, Kentucky.[30]

Whichever way the supermax is dressed up, the restrictive, harshly punitive, and deprivation-oriented conditions of confinement are still similar across the board. University of Washington anthropologist Lorna Rhodes, a national expert on supermaximum facilities, puts the number of people locked within such units at 40,000 to 45,000 men, women, and juveniles serving time in adult prisons.[31] The Commission on Safety and Abuse in America's Prisons released a figure of nearly 81,000 men and women in some form of segregation, whether in protective custody, Ad Seg, or a disciplinary control unit. (These numbers are based on data from 2000 and are very likely to have grown since then.)[32]

Conditions for prisoners in segregation have not gone without notice and criticism, as major editorials in leading newspapers and magazines have called into question both the treatment of the mentally ill and the use of control units themselves.[33]

Civil liberties and mental health advocates have put increased pressure on prisons make their their supermaxes more humane, and some administrations have responded with promises to do so. But those promises have rarely yielded dramatic change without court-issued mandates. To date, class-action lawsuits regarding supermax conditions, particularly regarding the treatment of the mentally ill within those units, have been filed in at least 80 percent of states, with limited success.[34]

In June 2006, after a year of research and open hearings held across the country, the nonpartisan Commission on Safety and Abuse in America's Prisons released a series of commonsensical recommendations pertaining to the increased use of solitary confinement and control units. The commission emphasized that segregation should be used only as a last resort, and, if necessary, it should be ensured that segregated prisoners have "regular and meaningful human contact and are free from extreme physical conditions that cause lasting harm."[35] Noting that the use of disciplinary segregation increased by 68 percent from 1995 to 2000 (dramatically outpacing the 28 percent overall prison population growth), the commission questioned the notion that placing prisoners in isolation was actually helping to reduce overall prison violence against inmates or correctional officers, citing individual prison reports on the issue, as well as anecdotal testimony from control-unit guards themselves. The commission expressed particular concern about the fact that prisoners are sometimes released directly into society, straight out of segregation. Prisoners released directly from such units have a 64 percent recidivism rate, compared with 41 percent of offenders released from a prison's general population.[36]

To put it in the words of criminologist Hans Toch, "Supermax prisons may turn out to be crucibles and breeding grounds of violent recidivism. . . . [Prisoners] may become 'the worst of the worst' because they have been dealt with as such."[37]

Regardless, the perceived need for supermaxes persists. Rhetoric about the necessity of these units tends to revolve around mention of the high-profile male terrorists, assassins, serial killers, major drug traffickers, and racist gang members incarcerated in supermaxes. (The most infamous among them include Ted Kaczynski, Charles Manson, Eric Robert Rudolph, and Terry Nichols.)

The public imagination is clearly still held captive by these images and these larger-than-life criminal personae. But the reality of female control-unit confinement is something that is just beginning to seep into the American consciousness. As is the case with generalizations about men in supermax facilities, perceptions of women on lockdown represent a very one-sided version of a much more complicated issue. Take, for instance, the aforementioned documentary *Lockdown: Women Behind Bars*, which seems to have set out to demonstrate that women in prison represent an equal—if not greater—threat than their male counterparts to the safety and security of prisons.

The film opens with ominous narration about the women whom we, the viewers, are about to see filmed in VSPW's SHU: "This is where California keeps its dangerous inmates. If you think women in prison are soft, think again."

From that moment forward, the documentary is clearly slanted in an apparent attempt to provide compelling visual evidence that the SHU is necessary for females who had proven themselves unmanageable in the general population. Filmmakers go to great lengths to focus on close-ups of screaming, angry women in the SHU, and quote a male SHU guard as saying, "This is a violent world." At six feet, weighing 250 pounds, the officer is shown suiting up with a stab-proof vest, his expandable baton, and a canister of OC pepper spray.[38]

From his perspective as a man untrained in mental illness, immersed in an environment full of women in various states of distress and rage, the SHU is likely to feel exactly that way. But it is my contention that most of the violence in women's control units appears to be of the psychic kind, wounding the humanity of both the female prisoners and the people charged with keeping them in line.

Whether the people employed to control these SHUs realize this is, of course, a different matter altogether.

As we know, the majority of female prisoners in the United States (as well as in the United Kingdom) suffer from mental illness, and they do so at far higher rates than those of their male counterparts. In state prisons nationwide, female rates of mental illness manifest at 73.1 percent of inmates, compared to 55 percent for men. A total of 61.2 percent of women exhibit mental health problems in federal prisons, versus 43.6 percent for men. The highest figures are found in local jails, the first entry point in the criminal justice system for people who run afoul of the law. There, fully 75.4 percent of women exhibit mental health problems. Men with some form of mental illness are also the most prevalent in jails, at 62.8 percent of the population.[39]

Prisoners suffering from mental disorders are very likely to have been abused as children and to have been homeless the year before their arrest. Three out of four are dependent on drugs when they are arrested. Once in prison, mentally ill prisoners are twice as likely as fellow inmates to get injured in a fight.[40]

Mentally ill women tend to cycle through the system for years or even decades, as is the case of Monica Lopez (a pseudonym), who explained to me that she began to manifest psychiatric disorders in her preteen years. Without any kind of treatment, Lopez had her first encounter with lockup at age twelve. Now thirty-eight, Lopez says that the continuing escalation in several of her diagnosed mental illnesses has destabilized her life to the extent that she has bounced in and out of jails in New York, New Orleans, Miami, and Puerto Rico, her native state. Lopez is now in a state prison in California, where she refuses to take the medications being given to her in lieu of counseling.

Some of the most important research findings to emerge in the past few years about the prevalence of the mentally ill in jails and prisons have been those of

Bernard E. Harcourt, a professor of law and criminology at the University of Chicago. Harcourt makes the compelling argument that our current prison culture of control is "by no means new." More specifically, Harcourt points to the fact that Americans were actually institutionalized at even higher rates than the current rates of incarceration throughout the 1940s and '50s, and most of them were women.[41] Back then, emotionally disturbed or socially "deviant" women were institutionalized en masse in mental hospitals, asylums, and "reformatories." In his research, Harcourt asks several provocative questions, including why it is that we diagnosed "deviance" in such radically different ways over the course of the twentieth century. He also asks us to consider whether prisons and mental hospitals have always included large numbers of unnecessarily incarcerated individuals.

"Whatever the answers," Harcourt writes, "the pendulum has swung too far—possibly off its hinges."[42]

From the 1960s through the 1980s, the deinstitutionalization and closure of asylums and mental hospitals were supposed to have been replaced by a comprehensive network of community mental health services, aided by advances in psychiatric medicines. But the community-based mental healthcare that President John F. Kennedy envisioned when he set this plan in motion never materialized. Matters were exacerbated by the Reagan administration's general disregard for mental healthcare or social welfare of any kind. The nail in the coffin for truly affordable mental healthcare finally came in the 1990s, when Congress closed the one remaining loophole in the Medicaid system that provided reimbursement for inpatient psychiatric care.[43]

Some of the people who cannot access mental healthcare work through the illnesses on their own, developing a semblance of a functional life. Some are taken care of by spouses, friends, or families who do what they can to help their loved ones. But many who suffer from more acute mental illnesses end up turning to drugs for self-medication and commit petty or serious criminal acts to support those habits. They often slip into periods of homelessness, marked by the likelihood of victimization and the worsening of their psychological states. Involvement in the criminal justice system is the next step, the logical consequence of this life of physical and emotional instability, in a country with little or no existing safety net. It doesn't have to end up with incarceration for the mentally ill offender, but far too commonly it does.

This is why our society should begin to seriously explore alternatives to incarcerating mentally ill persons, especially those who commit nonviolent crimes. To put the sole blame for the poor treatment of mentally ill prisoners on jail and prison personnel is to look at only one end of this dysfunctional continuum. Most corrections employees are not trained to any real extent in psychology or social work, and most are generally uneducated about the common symptoms of various psychiatric disorders and states of emotional distress. Effectively, we are asking men and women who have taken jobs as prison guards to handle a population that has the real or perceived capacity to terrify them or threaten their safety. That's not to say that prisons and their employees should be off the hook for how people are being treated in their institutions, regardless of their mental health. Civility, constitutional treatment of individuals, and innate recognition of someone's humanity are not too much to ask of anyone.

With regard to the issues of incarcerated mentally ill people, basic education could certainly be provided to correctional staff, with minimal cost and the potential for great efficacy. Just as training related to the Prison Rape Elimination Act has already had a positive impact on some jails and prisons in terms of reducing incidence and increasing reporting of improper sexual conduct, even minimal education in mental health issues for staff and prisoners alike would be very likely to result in overall reductions in staff/prisoner tensions, workplace stress, and prisoner-on-prisoner violence, as well as the need to put so many people on lockdown.

Furthermore, guards could easily be taught to calm and talk people down from fits of paranoia, anxiety, or distress, as do police officers who specialize in diffusing domestic violence situations, and situations involving disruptive or dangerous mentally ill persons. Resorting to an escalation in verbal and physical aggression rarely works in the long term, as a distraught individual is more likely to exhibit confusion, panic, and hostility. (I will not disagree, however, that prison guards need to be trained to break up fights, and, occasionally, to "take down" a truly violent or self-destructive prisoner who is acting out in a way that is clearly dangerous to others or to him/herself.)

Only on rare occasions have I met a prison guard with a deep level of understanding about the behaviors of mentally ill prisoners—and I am certainly grateful to have spoken with them. Higher-up prison administrators, psychologists, and social workers have also expressed true compassion and a depth of knowledge about mental illness in their prison populations. Both are in evidence, for instance, among many corrections personnel who work with the general population of female prisoners at Washington Corrections Center for Women (WCCW), despite the aforementioned issues that have surfaced in the past several years regarding the punishment of self-harming women.

Jim Walton, a psychiatric social worker, is one of several at WCCW who has gone out of his way to ensure that female prisoners receive as much preventative mental healthcare as possible for the duration of their incarceration—as well as in preparation for the stressors associated with release back into the community. This assistance is particularly important, he told me, for women who have not been in the "free world" for some time and who feel as though prisons are actually the safest places they have ever known. Walton told me that the prisoners who have been incarcerated for long periods of time are unaccustomed to everything from cell phones to debit cards, and are terrified of trying to get caught up on everything.

Walton also supervises training in suicide prevention, schizophrenia, post-traumatic stress disorder, and other mental illnesses. "The staff has been very receptive to this training," he said. "The biggest part is breaking down those old stereotypes and misconceptions about women and mental illness."

As Walton knows, insights and deeper levels of understanding about mental illness do not simply filter down to the rank and file unless an actual effort toward that end is undertaken.

Aside from WCCW, I found one of the most prominent exceptions to the generally poor approach toward mentally ill inmates in the San Francisco County women's jail. Here, Sheriff Michael Hennessey has held his position for the last twenty years, having come to enforcement from a most unlikely position, as an attorney and founder of the San Francisco Jail Project in 1975. His goal then was to assist in the legal defense of indigent prisoners—as well as to improve conditions for women in jail.

When I visited the main women's jail in downtown San Francisco in October 2006, I was able to spend the better part of two days in the women's portion of that jail, as well as in the psych ward. The latter was the most revealing. To begin with, my unannounced visit to the psych ward was not greeted with alarm by any of the guards or the mental healthcare workers, at least half of whom were women.

I was, frankly, surprised that the ward housed both genders, although male and female prisoners in acute states of agitation were never allowed to interact with one another, and certainly never to room with one another. But I still expressed my reservations about the wisdom of maintaining both male and female prisoners with mental illness in the same unit, until I peered into one larger room and saw an art therapy and group counseling session in progress. Men and women sat across the table from one another, focused on their projects and on the therapeutic process, all being led by a social worker. That group happened to let out while I was still in the unit, and I watched as the prisoners returned to their cells without handcuffs or strip searches. Some of them waved curiously in my direction, before heading off to their rooms.

From what I later understood, several of these prisoners had entered the jail as highly disruptive people in various states of distress. Careful monitoring and medication management, and an emphasis on giving inmates the opportunity to gain appropriate measures of trust within days or weeks—rather than months or years—had gotten many of the women and men to a more functional state. The way the jail staff appeared to treat and respect the essential humanity of the prisoners, while maintaining healthy boundaries, was downright refreshing compared to the level of callous disregard that I had witnessed elsewhere.

To be sure, many things could also be bettered about this jail system, including the space limitations of the building, which is overcrowded. Even the sheriff and his staff pointed to things that could be improved. This kind of willingness shows a more dynamic, open approach to bettering workplace conditions, counseling and education services, and the overall quality of life for prisoners.

"We deal with a lot of minor offenders that really shouldn't be in jail," Sheriff Hennessey told me. "The real underlying problem is often mental illness. If we don't want them back, our city resources should be oriented in such a way to provide them with the services they need to [stabilize] in our community.

"I'm also not Pollyannaish about excusing the behavior of people with mental illness," he added. "Should we just say that they don't need to suffer consequences for serious crimes? No. But a lot of minor offenders still come back time and time again [and] clutter up our jails instead of being in the treatment that they need."

A few dozen of the jailed women who were not acutely psychotic or self-harming in the general population did indeed talk to me of suffering from serious depression and anxiety, and of having extremely abusive and violent pasts that they wanted more help with than the staff could provide.

Many of these women would, of course, be better served by intensive treatment programs and community-based transitional care. But for a jail, I was struck by the overall calm that pervaded the environment. Ultimately, it served as the best contrast of my research travels, reminding me that what I had witnessed in female control units—and heard so many women describe—was an extreme and problematic response to a subpopulation of prisoners who were almost guaranteed to fare poorly in highly confining, punitive environments.

The overuse of jails and prisons to "treat" mental illness in our society is obviously problematic in itself. Worse still is the notion that sanity and "proper" conduct can somehow be forced upon prisoners through punishing them for erratic, self-harming, and self-destructive behaviors, including employing the barbaric practice of placing these individuals in smaller and smaller cages behind prison walls. One can only hope that reason will eventually prevail over the common practice of subjecting human beings to this kind of self-perpetuating madness.

Chapter 6: Criminalizing Motherhood

"I ended up with the first person that I believed loved me, and we had a daughter. I still struggled with depression and attempted suicide. I am guilty of many things: not getting help for my depression, using drugs, drinking, and being a poor excuse for a mother."

—Rhonda Leland, incarcerated at Valley State Prison for Women in central California

"No other group of mothers lays claim to the unspeakable in quite the same way that pregnant drug users do. Even when women made substantial strides during pregnancy to reduce the risk of drug use to their babies . . . throughout, the image of the ideal mythical mother loomed over these women's shoulders and over the shoulders of people with the power to determine their futures."

—Sheigla Murphy and Marsha Rosenbaum, in *Pregnant Women on Drugs*

Regina McKnight is doing twelve years in a South Carolina prison for murder. She didn't kill an abusive man, shoot an unarmed cashier in a robbery, or run over someone with her car. Her crime? Eight and a half months into her pregnancy, she gave birth to a five-pound, stillborn baby.

As McKnight grieved and held the lifeless body of her third daughter, Mercedes, she could never have imagined that she was about to become the first woman in America convicted for murder by using cocaine while pregnant.[1] McKnight's obvious devastation about the stillbirth didn't matter, nor did the fact that she carried the baby to term and had no intent to harm her. More important, the prosecutors could not cite any conclusive scientific research linking cocaine use to her stillbirth.

What did matter was that South Carolina prosecutors were hell-bent on using McKnight as an example of what happens to any pregnant woman who uses drugs at some point during her pregnancy. Although studies have demonstrated an actual detrimental effect on the fetus as a result of legal substances—namely, tobacco and heavy alcohol—the lack of any provable research regarding the impact of illicit drug use on fetuses didn't bother the prosecutors. Apparently, it was not punishment enough that McKnight grieved over the fact that her child wasn't born alive. What mattered was that McKnight, an African American woman, was a bad mother in the eyes of South Carolina male prosecutors.

Also of no small significance was that South Carolina was using the McKnight case to head up a political crusade inspired by the state's former conservative and pro-life attorney general, Charlie Condon, in what would eventually become a national trend of prosecuting pregnant women who didn't live exemplary lives prior to the birth of their children—even going to the extreme of filing charges after healthy babies were born. Condon rose to power when he was state attorney general with statements such as, "You don't have the right to have a drug-impaired child. . . . The child comes from God. We think we're in line with how most people feel in this country. We recognize the fetus as a fellow South Carolinian. And the right to privacy does not overcome the right to life."[2] A framed photograph of Pat Buchanan on Condon's office wall read, "To Charlie Condon, who is saving lives while others prattle on about the rights of drug addicts."[3]

But drug use and addiction among women are hardly as simple as Condon would like to believe, in terms of why women turn to any kind of substance for relief of emotional or physical pain, and consequently why many of them can't just stop all such use when they become pregnant.

"Women who are addicted to drugs cannot simply stop their use, because addiction is a chronic, relapsing disease whose recovery takes time," claims the New York–based National Advocates for Pregnant Women (NAPW). "Nevertheless, addiction is frequently regarded as a moral failing, and pregnant addicted women are presumed to be selfish and uncaring. Many of these women, however, were sexually abused as children or beaten as adults, and turned to drugs to numb the pain of the abuse and trauma they were experiencing."[4]

It would be one thing if drug treatment and counseling were widely available in the United States. However, unless a woman has access to considerable financial resources and strong familial support, she is quite likely to fall through the cracks and end up having to face her struggles on her own. Of the estimated 675,000 pregnant women annually who need some kind of drug or alcohol treatment, less than 11 percent are expected to get the treatment they desire.[5]

Charleston, South Carolina, was the first and only city to test pregnant women for drug use and report the findings to police without the woman's consent or the necessity of securing a warrant. Although that practice was stopped in March 2001 when the U.S. Supreme Court ruled that the process was violation of the Fourth Amendment, a fair amount of damage was done, as several women did end up being charged with crimes or losing their children.[6] Before the ruling came down, most of the women targeted were African American and from lower-income backgrounds, reaching a total of 80 percent of all women arrested.

Dorothy Roberts, a professor at Northwestern University and author of *Killing the Black Body*, said that the sight of these women being led to jail in handcuffs and shackles "conjured up the image of pregnant slave women."[7]

The U.S. Supreme Court declined in October 2003 to review the McKnight case, despite the pleas of twenty-six highly respected professional medical and health advocacy groups, including the American Public Health Association, the American Psychiatric Association, and the National Stillbirth Society.

"The prosecution, conviction, and sentencing of Ms. McKnight for her stillbirth not only distorts the law, but contradicts the clear weight of available medical evidence, violates fundamental notions of public health, and undermines the physician–patient relationship," the organizations stated in their amicus curaie brief to the court. "Tens of thousands of women suffer from stillbirths each year. In a substantial number of these cases, medical professionals are unable to provide parents with an explanation . . . of how or why the stillbirth occurred. As in the case of Regina McKnight, parents typically experience stillbirths as unexpected and undesired personal tragedies."[8]

In a 2002 interview before the South Carolina Supreme Court hearing, assistant state attorney Greg Hembree said that McKnight (who received a twenty-year sentence for homicide with an eight-year suspension) willfully killed her baby "because of her selfishness or her own personal desires."[9] Hembree also admitted openly to *The New York Times* that future cases could involve women whose pregnancies ended after they drank too much alcohol, or consumed other legal substances with the knowledge that they could be harmful.[10]

"This should be shocking to the American public, and should offend any true valuing of motherhood," NAPW Executive Director Lynn Paltrow told me just after the South Carolina Supreme Court upheld McKnight's conviction in 1993, in a sharply divided three-to-two vote. "In a country where a pregnant woman has no legal right to safe housing, healthcare, treatment for addiction, or mental healthcare . . . [when] she who has no rights carries a fetus, that fetus apparently has all those rights, which must be provided by a woman who must ensure that the fetus is healthy, as deemed by her community and by her government."

Pregnant women who use drugs have never earned public sympathy. In the 1970s, the demonization of drug-using mothers was reserved largely for women who used heroin; in the 1980s, the hysteria moved on to the ultimately false expectation of thousands of "crack babies" born to black women.

"The image of poor inner-city African Americans whose mothering instincts had been destroyed by crack was highly publicized and widely accepted. Numerous media stories reported that the coming generation would comprise untold numbers of permanently impaired crack babies," write Sheigla Murphy and Marsha Rosenbaum in *Pregnant Women on Drugs: Combating Stereotypes and Stigma.* "Journalists predicted that these impaired infants would topple the healthcare delivery and educational systems due to their expensive and lifelong problems."[11]

But this medical crisis never happened to the extent that the public was warned it would. In fact, most of the children, despite being born with cocaine in their systems, were able (with proper parenting and attention to their needs) to catch up to their peers quickly in educational achievement and social skills.[12] This is not to discount the scourge of crack cocaine in low-income communities, or to belittle the struggles that many of the children and their parents or foster parents would face when children were exposed to alcohol and drugs (whether in utero or as young children in an unhealthy, addiction-soaked environment). I am just pointing out that the "crack epidemic" of babies simply did not manifest itself as expected. Since then, the past two decades have seen this phenomenon of government-and media-driven hysteria expanded to methamphetamine and polysubstance use. No woman has yet been prosecuted for smoking tobacco, which has some of the strongest actual links to fetal damage, along with our very legal and most abused substance, alcohol.

And what of the prevalence of domestic verbal, emotional, or physical abuse in women's lives, and how these stressors impact the likelihood of a miscarriage or a stillbirth? What of poverty, which would seem to be the greatest indicator of pregnancy complications and infant mortality because of limited access to appropriate nutrition, medical care, health insurance, and safe, secure housing? National studies have, in fact, pointed to poverty as a greater indicator of a child's well-being than cocaine exposure in the womb.[13]

The reason is not very difficult to deduce. The prevalence of adult and child poverty points to serious social welfare deficiencies in the United States.[14] For all the conservative talk about saving fetuses from drug-using mothers, the United States might have more serious issues to contemplate, including the fact that this country is now tied with the poorly developed and economically devastated nations of Malta and Slovakia for the second-worst infant mortality rate among developed nations—about six per one thousand live births.[15]

Pointing to these issues is typically the furthest thing from serving the need for convenient, sensational fodder for pro-life political tirades and election campaigns. In this pull-yourself-up-by-your-own-bootstraps, class-stratified country that forces its inhabitants to make do with a bare-bones safety net, it has always been far easier to target the individual, regardless of their past and present hardships. Blaming pregnant women is simply more convenient, all the way around—exclusive of the prevalence of abuse in their childhoods and their adult lives; their poverty and/or homelessness; evidence of post-traumatic stress disorder, depression, or other mental illnesses; and any ongoing battles with drug, tobacco, and/or alcohol addiction.

As Murphy and Rosenbaum rightly point out, "no woman inhabits the all-giving-mother role entirely, but drug-using mothers may miss by the most. Mother as fetal poisoner, or user of illegal drugs, is the antithesis of the prevailing myth of mother as unflagging, unselfish caregiver."[16]

Preventative and intervention-focused strategies that should be the emphasis in dealing with high-risk pregnant women do not fare well in the face of sloganeering and regressive legislation.

"Medical knowledge about addiction and dependency treatment demonstrates that patients do not, and cannot, simply stop their drug use as a result of threats of arrest or other negative consequences," explain NAPW's Julie B. Ehrlich and Paltrow. "This is one reason why threat-based approaches do not work to stop drug use or protect children. Such approaches have, in fact, been shown to deter pregnant women not from using drugs, but rather from seeking prenatal care and what little drug and alcohol treatment may be available to them."[17]

In retrospect, South Carolina's early insistence on persecuting pregnant women can be viewed as a profoundly disturbing indicator of things to come. Indeed, prosecutorial "success" in McKnight's case emboldened South Carolina to go after other women, sometimes even retroactively, despite the fact that they had attempted to carry their babies to term. This was the case for Angelia Shannette Kennedy, who allegedly smoked cocaine during her pregnancy. She suffered a stillbirth in 1998 but was charged with homicide five years after the fact. Rather than face courtroom and media persecution of her character, Kennedy pled guilty to three counts of criminal child endangerment and received a five-year prison sentence.

To date, South Carolina has pursued at least eighty cases against women, mostly poor women and women of color, on similar charges, emboldened by a 1997 South Carolina Supreme Court decision in *Cornelia Witner v. State of South Carolina* that anything that a pregnant woman does to cause "potential harm" to her fetus can constitute child abuse.[18] Among the most outrageous are the "homicide by child abuse" charges against Jennifer Lee Arrowood, who suffered a placental abruption and had a stillbirth. The state charged that Arrowood had used drugs, and she received a ten-year prison term in January 2006. In July 2006, Hannah Lauren Jolly, who gave birth to a newborn and legally gave her child up for adoption, was subsequently tracked down, arrested, and charged for "unlawful child neglect" because the child had tested positive for drugs. Amy Sue Earls, who used cocaine during her pregnancy, delivered a healthy child (who did test positive for cocaine) but was still sentenced to twenty months in prison, plus three years' probation. During that time, the court has forbidden her to get pregnant.[19]

Ironically, South Carolina ranks lowest in the nation for spending on drug and alcohol treatment programs.[20] Although South Carolina leads the pack in the prosecution of pregnant women, the blatant hypocrisy of local and state governments when it comes to their alleged concern for the well-being of substance-using mothers and their children has spread across the nation. At minimum, the list of states criminalizing certain behaviors during pregnancy includes Alabama, Arkansas, Idaho, Hawaii, Maryland, Massachusetts, New Jersey, New York, Oklahoma, South Dakota, Virginia, and Wyoming. Several of these states have actually passed (or have pending legislation) criminalizing mothers-to-be who use substances while pregnant, including Alabama's Chemical Endangerment of a Child law, which encourages citizens, law enforcement, and social workers to turn in pregnant women suspected of drug use. This law has already resulted in several arrests of young women, with bonds set as high as $200,000, an amount usually reserved for the most serious criminal acts.

"We urge drug users, especially pregnant mothers, to seek help for their drug addiction," Covington County Sheriff's Office Investigator Greg Jackson said after one such arrest. "[B]ut when you're caught, you will be prosecuted."[21]

Garrett's Law in Arkansas also gives permission to medical personnel to report the mothers of newborn infants for parental neglect. According to a study commissioned by the Arkansas Department of Health and Human Services, of the 412 referrals made between fall 2005 and fall 2006, the most common was for marijuana, cited in more than half of the cases. Once again, these laws result in both rhetoric and repressive practices—but no tangible evidence of improved care for the mother or the child. As this study revealed, only 5 percent of children removed from their parents received any medical treatment related to the mother's drug use.[22] The University of Arkansas for Medical Sciences has tried to address this issue with its Antenatal and Neonatal Guidelines, Education and Learning System (ANGELS) program, which works with doctors throughout the state to help pregnant women engaging in high-risk behaviors (including use of drugs, alcohol, and cigarettes) to address the underlying emotional issues and traumas that help to explain why women lack the necessary coping skills to stay healthy. Despite the overwhelming need for such a program, funding has been lacking; the program was forced to downsize in 2005.[23]

Regardless of such failures in the provision of services to needy mothers and their children, prosecutorial zeal for going after pregnant women has spread with insidious stealth. Prosecutors in Talbot County in Baltimore, Maryland, went after Kelly Lynn Cruz in January 2005 for "reckless endangerment" because traces of cocaine were found in her and her child. Cruz is now serving a two-and-a-half-year term, although the ACLU is appealing her case to a higher court.

"Nobody thinks it's a great idea to take cocaine while pregnant," ACLU attorney David Rocah told the *Baltimore Sun*. "But the unanimous view of medical and public health professionals and drug treatment is that if you want to stop people from doing that, the way to do that is to provide them with meaningful access to drug treatment, and not criminally prosecute them."[24]

Shortly after the McKnight prosecution in 2003, Honolulu city prosecutors went after a thirty-one-year-old native Hawaiian, Tayshea Aiwohi, for the death of her two-day-old son, who was born four weeks premature. The prosecutor's office charged Aiwohi with manslaughter for using crystal methamphetamine during her pregnancy. It was the first time in Hawaii's history that such criminal charges had been brought against a woman. Aiwohi's defense attorney said that the prosecution was "perverse" and suggested under the same rationale that pregnant women could be prosecuted if they "don't eat right."[25]

Such conjecture may not be as far fetched as it sounds. Already, in some cases, even legal drug use can be grounds for criminal prosecution, whether a pregnancy, stillbirth, miscarriage, or abortion is concerned. Consider the case of eighteen-year-old Amber Abreu, who aborted her twenty-four-week-old fetus by taking an overdose of misoprostol, an antiulcer medication that is one of the key ingredients of the RU-486 "abortion pill." Born in the Dominican Republic, the teen mom-to-be, unaware of the confidential resources available to her, was not only terrified of the reaction of her immigrant mother, but had already been spurned by the baby's father. When the medications did not work as she had hoped, Abreu gave premature birth to a one-pound baby in Lawrence, Massachusetts, in January 2007. Amber was charged with manslaughter and "procuring a miscarriage," because her baby, Ashley, survived for only four days after she was born.[26]

Then there is the case of Julie Starks, who found herself in the middle of a methamphetamine trailer drug bust in Rogers County, Oklahoma. Seven months pregnant, Starks was thrown into an unsanitary county jail for thirty-six days, where she acquired a bladder and urinary tract infection, lost weight, and eventually went into premature contractions. "It was nasty, just nasty," she said of the experience. "There were ten people in a cell for six. The bathroom and the sink were out in the open. I didn't get any milk; no prenatal vitamins for two weeks."[27]

Although Starks had been present in the trailer when the police drug raid took place, she had not been using the drug. Still, she was charged because she could have been exposed to the chemicals used to make methamphetamine. Although her baby boy was born healthy, with no drugs or toxic chemicals in his system, Starks was found guilty by the court because she had "deprived" her fetus by being around drugs. Unemployed and facing the likelihood of a prison term, Starks was saved by a criminal defense attorney, Barbara Teichner, who took the case pro bono all the way to the Oklahoma Supreme Court. The court ruled in Starks's favor in 2001.[28]

Any government that attempts to define or approve what constitutes acceptable motherhood extends a dangerous and inconsistent reach into women's lives. Such policies represent a crucial intersection between the war on drugs; civil liberties and the right to privacy; and the battle over the reproductive rights of women. Women like McKnight, among many others, are the victims of major players in the criminal justice system and legislature who believe in judging and punishing women for what happens to their bodies. The criminalization of motherhood is a definitive step toward a government that would have the power to tell us what constitutes acceptable pregnancy and motherhood. Regrettably, the distinguishing line between "good" versus "bad" pregnancy and mothering, established by people with the power to prosecute and incarcerate our citizens, is altogether precarious.

Only one aspect of the criminalization of reproductive choices, healthy or unhealthy as they may be, seems to remain the same: Women are always the targets of the unpredictable gusts of political and religious machinations that seek punishment and retribution—not genuine concern for parents' and children's well-being—as their primary aims.

*"I am no longer a victim but a survivor, and I really know that all that
I have experienced and endured has been for a purpose."*
—Sara Kruzan, serving life without the possibility of parole at the Central
California Women's Facility for killing her pimp at the age of sixteen

*"It wasn't our anniversary or any other special day / Last night he threw me
into a wall and choked me / It seemed like a nightmare / I couldn't believe
it was real / I woke up this morning, sore and bruised / I know that he
must be sorry / Because he gave me flowers today."*
— Sandra Widner from Georgia's Pulaski State Prison, sentenced to
fifteen years for shooting her boyfriend during a violent altercation

Maria Suarez was just sixteen years old in 1976, when she was smuggled from Mexico into the United States. Shortly after arriving, Suarez was sold for $200 to a sixty-eight-year-old man by the name of Anselmo Covarrubias.

In the Los Angeles suburb of Azusa, Covarrubias was known in his neighborhood as a witch doctor. Suarez was told that she would be cooking and cleaning for him. Three days after moving into his house, Suarez was raped, beginning a vicious cycle of constant sexual, physical, and emotional abuse for the next five years of her life. For all intents and purposes, Suarez had been sold into modern-day slavery.

On August 27, 1981, Covarrubias was found bludgeoned to death with a table leg. As was common practice across the country in this era for felony trials involving violence or murder, evidence of prior abuse was not seriously considered in trial. Nor was expert testimony about the effects of domestic violence allowed. Suarez's servitude to a man more than fifty years her senior did not have any bearing on her guilty verdict or her sentencing. In July 1982, at age twenty-one, Suarez was convicted of first-degree murder, sentenced to life, and sent to the California Institution for Women. She prayed that something would come to light that would set her free, but even the sworn testimony on the part of the couple who had admitted to killing Covarrubias—insisting that the extent of Suarez's involvement had been her washing off the table leg in a panic and hiding it under the house—did not alter her sentence.

Two decades passed. Suarez had spent her adult life in prison. Even into her forties, she continued to maintain that she was innocent of the crime for which she had received a life sentence.

Like Suarez, women accused of murdering men are frequently sentenced to multidecade or life sentences, even when the murder was their one and only violent criminal act. Although there are no comprehensive national statistics on the sentencing of battered women (states and prison systems are not required to record the circumstances surrounding a murder, only the kind of murder charge for which a person is sentenced), researchers and advocates of these women point to an inordinately zealous approach on the part of prosecutors who charge abused women with first-degree murder. By some estimates, only one-quarter of women who claim self-defense are acquitted of murder charges, even with evidence of severe, ongoing violence at the hands of an intimate partner.[1]

Like Suarez, it seems that most women who kill are viewed as having transgressed the boundaries of existing gender roles to an inexcusable extent and are punished accordingly. Often these women become the subjects of lurid fascination and sensational media coverage.

This is not to say that men who murder are socially condoned (that is, unless they are members of the armed forces or law enforcement), but to acknowledge that there is an aspect of male violence that is better understood and subject to far less judgment, particularly when an act of violence is seen in the context of an imminent or immediate threat. American culture is drenched in the imagery of male violence, whether in the form of shoot-'em-up video games or such television shows as Fox's explicitly brutal terrorism–focused series *24*, even the far more hokey *Walker, Texas Ranger*. Pop culture consumers seem to possess endless fascination with extreme violence and flock to thrillers and horror movies that often depict men who stalk, rape, torture, mutilate, dismember, and kill women in disturbingly graphic scenes. (This ever-escalating gruesome imagery in mainstream films is tantamount to something I have started to think of as "hardcore horror pornography.") Most of these movies are fictional, but several blockbusters, including *Summer of Sam* and *Zodiac*, have revolved around real-life serial killers.

Programs and movies about men who murder are also sensational in nature, but they rarely set out to give viewers any kind of general insight into fundamental explanations of male criminal behavior. By comparison, programs like the E! channel's *Women Who Kill* (as a part of their *E! True Hollywood Story* series) seek to answer the overarching question of why women turn to murderous violence. As the show's promotional material reads, "How does a match made in heaven turn into hell on earth?"

Episodes of *Women Who Kill* usually feature women who are serving life sentences, including Margaret Rudin, who was convicted of killing a man she later described as an abusive alcoholic. Unfortunately for her claim of innocence, Rudin waited four months to file a missing persons report on her husband, which added to the suspicion that she had committed the murder, although no hard evidence was ever produced. Notably, although Rudin was not convicted of theft, embezzlement, or robbery, the show still described her as a "a gold digger with a dark side."

Oxygen's series *Snapped* goes a step further to posit the archaic concept that there is "something far more sinister to the fairer sex than 'sugar and spice and everything nice.'" The premise of each episode is to examine whether women accused of murder are cutthroat, cunning, cold-blooded, and conniving killers—all of these words are used at one point or another. Only toward the end of the show are the women proven innocent, given respite from the underlying assumption of having committed murder for "greed," a word that flashes prominently across the screen at the beginning of each episode, along with "deceit" and "murder."

"From millionaire brides with everything to lose, to small-town sweethearts who should simply know better, these shocking but true stories turn common assumptions about crime and criminals upside down," reads the promotional material for *Snapped.*

"Let's be honest," the show's website once read, "we've all had at least one moment in which we felt as though we could snap. Even if you're in the 'perfect relationship,' chances are, you've probably said (or even just fleetingly thought), 'I'm going to kill my husband!' So what separates those of us who do from those who don't?"

Nearly every episode of this program is replete with stereotypes and initial comments about a woman's "beautiful" or "gorgeous" appearance, which quickly devolve into suppositions about her drug use, her enjoyment of material possessions, or her sexual adventures (as demonstrated through blurred reenactments in which women are coupled with half-naked men). Above all, every episode hones in on the perceived heartlessness of women accused of murder. In one case, the narrator points to the scandalous behavior of a married woman who is having an affair with a man "ten years younger" than she, although the age difference is hardly even noteworthy in modern-day relationships—and certainly wouldn't even warrant mention if the genders were reversed. In another episode, a woman is torn apart for engaging in a "swinging" lifestyle, although it is soon revealed that both husband and wife openly engaged in sex with other couples. (The husband, of course, is not criticized for his sexual choices.)

Relying on family members, psychologists, and reporters for most of the "analysis" of women's motives, the producers of *Snapped* are particularly fond of bringing females to the show who rip the accused killers to shreds. One female forensic psychologist, Dr. Helen Smith, is brought on the show over and over again, and she appears to enjoy making sweeping statements about "women who kill." She also comments that "women through the centuries" have used poison to kill men, and contends that women who kill "don't even think they're killing. . . . [Instead, they] think they're getting rid of the problem."

In one segment of *Snapped,* Carolyn Warmus is introduced as a "young temptress" with "blond hair, a voluptuous figure, and sassy personality [who] got what Carolyn wanted, including men." As those "temptresses" are wont to do, Warmus began an affair with a married man, and then "the sexy nymphet . . . turned her charms on [a] private dick," whom she ostensibly cajoled into providing her with a silencer-enabled gun. Her adulterous relationship ended when her lover's wife was murdered. Although the evidence in her case does seem to point toward her guilt, the language used to describe her is, once again, focused on her appearance and suppositions about her sexuality. Warmus is described as arriving in the courtroom "dressed to kill . . . arriving every day in very short, very tight miniskirts and designer clothes." With her mainstream "girl next door" looks and fair skin, she is described as the embodiment of a "femme fatale," a "sexy, dangerous blond bombshell that seemed to step right out of the hard-boiled detective films and pulp novels of the '40s."

The phrasing of this sentence is very telling, because a modern-day woman is actually being compared to a pulp fiction female archetype popularized in the 1930s and '40s. Back then, it wasn't particularly shocking that such depictions of women existed, particularly as the genre was a widespread form of titillating entertainment before the advent of television. Some pulp fiction even served the societal function of pushing the existing boundaries of what constituted acceptable displays of women's sexuality, including lesbian relationships. What *is* shocking is that this kind of language is still employed to describe women in the twenty-first century. Modern-day "true crime" books and television shows may or may not use this kind of phrasing, but they continue to spin stories of women who kill, and do so with a heaping dose of hyperbole and conjecture not unlike that of the language of pulp fiction.

None of this is to say that women who have harmed or murdered others couldn't possibly be operating in the world with little or no conscience. Citing clinical research and her own work with trauma survivors, Harvard University psychologist Martha Stout estimates the ratio of sociopaths in American society to be an alarming one in twenty-five, which she believes is applicable to men and women alike.[2]

Are there cunning, narcissistic women in the world who act without conscience, to the point of manipulating, robbing, or killing for revenge, thrill, or

profit? Sure. Why not? The female gender doesn't ascribe essential, ethical character traits any more than being born as a man means that a person has an inherent
proclivity for violence or rape. Stout also points out that researchers know far
less about nonviolent, nonincarcerated sociopaths than they do about those who
have lashed out in some discernable fashion, because members of the former
group are much harder to detect in our society. We know even less about females
with this personality disorder, says Stout, because "women are less physical and
more verbal in the way they express things. For a sociopath who is a woman, one
would expect more social manipulation. Of course, women can be violent, but
it's less likely."[3]

Aileen Wuornos was one of those women who did turn violent. She captured
the nation's attention after she was tracked down for murdering seven middle-aged
men in Florida. Wuornos was painted as a sociopath no different from her male
counterparts, but the comparison loses some of its validity upon closer examination of her life story.

To begin with, her father was a child molester who killed himself in prison
in 1969. Wuornos's mother abandoned her children and left them in the care of
her parents, in whose house she was abused both sexually and physically. Wuornos
had nothing remotely akin to a normal childhood. She was pregnant by the age
of fourteen, possibly by her brother, who had sex with her. After she gave up her
child for adoption, Wuornos's family promptly disowned her. Without any kind
of a support structure to speak of, Wuornos had to take refuge in an abandoned
car and was forced to learn to live on her own, drifting into an existence filled with
depression, rage, alcoholism, auto theft, and prostitution. She endured repeated
sexual and physical violence at the hands of the men who picked her up at truck
stops, on the side of highways, and on the streets of whichever city or town she
wandered through.

Wuornos was arrested many times yet was never charged with murder until she was tracked down as the woman who had shot half a dozen johns in their cars. Once on trial, Wuornos did not deny that she had murdered the men but defended her actions as a reaction to men's attempts to brutalize her. Wuornos's claims of self-defense were ultimately dismissed, although it later turned out that the first man she killed actually had been a convicted rapist who had served ten years in another state for a brutal attack.

When she was found guilty and sentenced to death by lethal injection, Wuornos made it clear that she wanted to die, actively pursuing a quick execution to the point of firing her lawyers and halting every possibility of an appeal. But Wuornos still wanted to be treated with basic human decency until the moment of her execution. While on death row in a Florida state prison, she wrote a twenty-five-page complaint to the court, pleading for an end to the relentless physical and psychological abuse by male guards assigned to the unit. Wuornos complained of being served inedible food that had been urinated on and cooked in dirt, and of having to overhear guards who wanted to drive her to suicide and wanted to rape her before she met her fate.[4]

Wuornos's impending execution was not protested on any significant level, by either men or women. Before she was put to death, psychologist Robert Butterworth noted that people seemed to truly want Wuornos to be executed. No doubt, her primary affinity for lesbian relationships played some part in this lack of outrage. But Butterworth speculated that her rough exterior and fierce demeanor were even greater factors in public eagerness to have Wuornos executed. "If a woman sheds herself of her femininity," he observed, "all sympathy evaporates."[5]

Wuornos is an extreme example of how women are evaluated and judged based on the "purity" of their lives prior to committing a serious act of violence. Women who do not pass an unspoken test of an acceptable level of suffering and "good" female behavior beforehand seem to be viewed very negatively and, as many criminologists have suggested, sentenced more harshly.

"The binary opposition of angels and demons is replicated in the opposition of 'real' battered women and women engaged in 'mutual combat,' and other 'unfeminine' conduct," writes Kathleen J. Ferraro in her book *Neither Angels Nor Demons*. "'Real battered women' are portrayed as being overcome by their partner's violence and abuse. Sympathy is reserved for such women who must also adhere to feminine prescriptions for good mothering, sexual fidelity, and sobriety. . . . Women who are strong and resistant to male dominance and prescribed domesticity are not easily recognized as belonging to this category of pathetic victims."[6]

When Charlize Theron set out to produce and star in the 1993 blockbuster movie about Wuornos's adult life, she titled the film *Monster*. The movie was a huge success, hyping Theron's willingness to gain thirty pounds on her slim frame, to act sans glamorous makeup, and to wear prosthetic teeth. When she won Best Actress for her role as Wuornos, Theron's acceptance speech at the seventy-sixth Academy Awards ceremony was full of glowing words about her own life: "This has been such an incredible year. I can't believe this," she enthused, thanking her supporters and her boyfriend, to whom she referred as her "partner in crime." She also raved about her costar, Christina Ricci, whom she called "the unsung hero" of the film.[7] Oddly, there was not a single mention of the woman who had inspired the film, much less the fact that that same day would have been Wuornos's forty-eighth birthday.

A person like Wuornos, who decides to take on the role of judge, jury, and executioner, should certainly not escape punishment. When a person is found guilty of murder or another serious violent crime, sentencing should be influenced by the severity and surrounding circumstances of the offense, as well as by an assessment of the likelihood of a person's rehabilitation and reintegration into society.

No matter what the circumstances, the taking of someone's life should not be celebrated. Yet many men who are clearly beyond rehabilitation, those responsible for repeat sexual violence and murder, enjoy a peculiar kind of celebrity status after their convictions.

Writing about Ted Bundy, forensic psychologist Katherine Ramsland noted that the notorious serial killer offered his "services" to law enforcement, trying to track down the man who had come to be known as the Green River Killer. (Both men were responsible for serial rapes and murders in the Seattle area.)

"Bundy's keen interest had confirmed for investigators another disturbing notion," Ramsland writes in *The Human Predator*. "With the plethora of books on such cases now available, and the detailed coverage on television, they could learn from one another, especially from any mistakes made. . . . The media had clearly played a part in creating the cult of the serial killer persona."[8]

Histories of child or adult abuse are present in the lives of some men who become rapists and killers, but the rates of abuse in the lives of violent sociopaths are no higher than those in the general population. "About fifty percent of the variant seems to be accounted for by heredity," Stout said in an interview with *Salon*. "The other fifty percent would be shaped by something in the environment. The interesting thing is that we haven't been able to determine what that is."[9]

Men like Gary Ridgway, who was finally pinpointed as the Green River Killer, have escaped the death penalty in exchange for information, despite having committed multiple serial murders and having never suffered any kind of abuse or violence at the hands of the people they killed. By contrast, Wuornos, who was molested, beaten, and raped many times over, went to her death as a "monster."

The word "monster" as a descriptive term for women who kill has an interesting history. In 1848, renowned Italian criminologist Cesare Lombroso wrote that female criminals were living "monsters." He emphasized that women had intrinsic natures of "maternity, piety, and weakness" and concluded that when these qualities failed and resulted in a woman's criminal behavior, "her wickedness must have been enormous before it could triumph over so many obstacles."[10]

Although Lombroso's perspectives on women would no longer be entertained in the field of criminology, his ideas have certainly met their match in today's popular entertainment. Despite major progress toward civil, political, and personal rights for American women, our society still clearly struggles with a disturbing prevalence of emotional, verbal, sexual, and physical abuse toward girls and women. In light of statistics like these, it is clear that domestic violence in the United States is a problem of enormous magnitude:

- An average of three American women are murdered by their husbands or boyfriends each day.[11] One in three women reports having been sexually and/or physically abused by a male partner at some point in her life.[12]

- Many experts on public health and domestic violence believe that as many as three million American women are subject to some form of domestic abuse annually.[13] Half of them do not report their victimization.[14]

- More than nine times as many women are murdered by a man they know than by a male stranger. Six in ten female homicide victims are wives or girlfriends of the men who kill them.[15]

- In 2005, there were 2,004 women killed; 90 percent (1,793) were murdered by men. Of the 5,271 men killed in the same year, all but 10 percent (524) were killed by other men.[16]

- According to the U.S. Conference of Mayors, at least half of twenty-four major cities surveyed attributed the primary cause of women's homelessness to domestic violence.[17] Although some cities have a minimal or nonexistent "turn-away" rate for women seeking refuge in domestic violence shelters, Washington, D.C., and Seattle have the two highest turn-away rates for people seeking shelter from domestic abuse; the turn-away rate at Seattle's domestic violence shelters is 90 percent.[18]

- Women experiencing domestic violence do not leave their relationships for a number of reasons, including the fear of retaliation against them or their children; a strong sense of loyalty and a desire to "protect" their partners from arrest or public opinion; and/or the humiliation or disbelief they believe they would likely experience if they disclosed the abuse to friends or family members.[19]

- Seventy-five percent of murder–suicides occur in the home.[20]

Abusive men subject their partners to familiar cycles of domestic violence and predictable methods of control, but their female victims are quite different from one another. Some battered women who injure or kill their partners grew up in truly dysfunctional homes and were subjected to multiple forms of abuse. They learned early on that their lives were disposable, that their bodies were punching bags or sexual goods for men to use as they pleased. If these girls did leave home, they often ended up with much older men who actively seek this kind of vulnerability and a built-in expectation and acceptance of abuse.

Some battered women are on the low end of the economic spectrum, with minimal schooling or vocational training, and are thus more likely to become dependent on their mates for income.

But the idea that all battered women have little or no socioeconomic power in society was dispelled long ago. Many abused women are, in fact, professionals with advanced degrees, nice houses and cars, and an appearance of the model American family. In Seattle, Jewish Family Service's Project DVORA has worked to bring the largely invisible phenomenon of domestic violence in Jewish homes to public attention. Based on the limited research available, indications are that 15 to 25 percent of Jewish women have experienced intimate physical violence, and that one-third have suffered psychological abuse.[21] According to another study, seven in ten incidents of family violence in Jewish homes are never reported.[22]

An October 2006 article in *Essence* magazine revealed that Prince George's County in Maryland, the wealthiest majority African American county in the nation, had an incredibly high rate of intimate-partner homicide. According to the Maryland Network Against Domestic Violence, forty-eight people, mostly women, were murdered there between 2001 and 2006 as a result of domestic violence. The rate was second only to Baltimore County, which had seventy-two deaths.[23]

Battered women are often the wives or girlfriends of men in the military or law enforcement. They have particular cause for concern that their reports of abuse would be likely to be dismissed, downplayed, or covered up. According to one recent study, as many as 40 percent of women involved with a man in law enforcement are abused at home.[24] One of the most well-known and tragic cases was that of Crystal Brame, the wife of Tacoma Police Department Chief David Brame.

David's abuse of his wife, as well as his history of sexual harassment of other women, were altogether ignored, although many of his superiors and peers had known about such behavior on his part for a long time. Not surprisingly, Crystal felt that she had no real way out, because no one would step up to protect her or keep her husband away from her and her children. When she finally got up the nerve to leave David and filed for divorce, her worst nightmare came true: On April 26, 2003, David shot Crystal in a public parking lot in front of their children and then committed suicide on the spot.[25]

These are among the things that we know about women who are the victims of domestic violence, or who do not survive the abuse that they had to endure. To offer but one day's worth of an example, I scanned the April 4, 2007, issue of the *Seattle Post-Intelligencer* and noticed reports of two separate incidents of women who were murdered after they tried to leave abusive relationships:

"A domestic dispute disrupted in gunfire at CNN's headquarters complex Tuesday, killing a woman and critically wounding the exboyfriend who pulled a gun on her," read one of the stories.

The other story had to do with a Seattle woman, Rebecca Griego, who had obtained a restraining order against an abusive exboyfriend and feared for her life. Her fear, as it turned out, was far from unwarranted. "Before Monday's shooting, Griego had for months feared [Jonathan] Rowan, who had harassed her, her family, her dog, and even threatened her life," it was reported. "She had taken out a restraining order against him March 6 and sent colleagues his picture, warning them he might appear on campus. On Monday morning, he showed up at her [University of Washington] office and fired six shots, killing them both."[26]

Both of the stories made national news and then quickly fell off the media radar. This didn't come as a surprise to me, as most one-on-one murder–suicides by male perpetrators tend to fade away one or two days after they occur, just as the sentences meted out to men convicted of serious crimes against women do not even enter the realm of public debate or outrage for more than a few days. Often, there is no discussion whatsoever.

To illustrate just how lenient some male criminals' sentences are, consider what took place in April 2007. In that month, a man who pleaded guilty to running a prostitution ring was sentenced to serve just six years and eight months in federal prison. That man, Juan Baldera-Orosco, was found guilty of bringing in hundreds of women from Latin America and forcing them to have sex in thirteen states with as many as *forty men a day*, something that would constitute outright torture by any international standard.[27] There was barely any media coverage of this case, much less any public outrage.

On the surface, it might seem for some that a near-seven-year prison sentence is fitting for the crime of running a prostitution ring of forcibly indentured women smuggled in from other countries. But when we stop to consider that a nonviolent woman with no criminal record whatsoever can be sentenced to multidecade and life terms for crimes ranging from conspiracy drug charges to an act of violence or murder committed against an abusive male partner, it is worth asking how equitable our justice system truly is. [28]

There is no question that abusive relationships resulting in the murders of women by current or former male partners are alarmingly common in the United States. Most abused girls and women suffer in silence and are lucky if they are able to finally break free without severe retaliation, stalking, or threats of violence. But then there are the women who do finally retaliate and fire back—sometimes quite literally. These kinds of murders are certainly not random and very rarely happen without some kind of preexisting relationship. According to one study, 75 percent of incidents involving women who commit homicide occur in the context of male-initiated violence.[29]

Ferraro writes that when abused women lash out to injure or kill their abusive partners, they usually believe that "there was nothing else that would protect them."[30]

In my interviews with women who killed their abusers, not one woman ever expressed a preexisting plan to kill a male partner, although several admitted that they wouldn't take their decision back after the fact, as they believed it was more than likely that they would have died if they had not acted in self-defense.

Many of these women also describe an excruciating amount of psychological abuse in their relationships, something that they consider far worse and more damaging in the long term than any amount of physical violence. "I would rather be hit than have to be verbally assaulted for hours on end," one woman told me, requesting anonymity because of her fear that someone in the future would realize her vulnerability.

This kind of abuse can range from "gaslighting" (convincing a woman of her insanity or skewed perceptions of reality) to repeating degrading statements in order to wear down a woman's self-esteem and personal boundaries.

Unfortunately, the interrogation of those women who eventually kill their abusive partners still tends to revolve around the same line of questioning, whether by law enforcement or prosecutors: Why didn't you just leave? Why didn't you contact the police? Why didn't you tell your family? Why did you stay with him for so long? How could you have loved him and then killed him for abusing you?

Researchers and advocates specializing in domestic violence and women's retaliatory violence say that these kinds of questions are both predictable and insulting, given what we now know about the complicated reasons why women stay in abusive relationships. Instead, they say, the prevalence of domestic violence experienced by girls and women begs a different kind of question: "Why do so few women resort to violence in the face of such horrendous victimization?" as criminologists Meda Chesney-Lind and Lisa Pasko ask in *The Female Offender: Girls, Women, and Crime.*[31]

In her essay "Stages of Gendered Disadvantage in the Lives of Convicted Battered Women," Elizabeth Dermody Leonard points out that "the question of 'why doesn't she leave?' reveals the widespread gender bias of our society. The question makes the woman, rather than the abusive man, responsible for stopping the violence. This bias suggests an implicit acceptance of the abuser's actions as falling within a normative range of male behavior."[32]

The most obvious reasons why women stay in abusive relationships include severe psychological and physical intimidation; anxiety about being alone or not knowing how to live independently; fear of sinking into poverty and homelessness; a sense of shame and even protection of a man's reputation in the community; the well-being of children; feelings of immense anxiety and worthlessness; and other variables. Again, the impact of the physical violence in these relationships often pales in comparison to the psychological damage, including the onset or intensification of post-traumatic stress disorder.[33] In essence, the psychology of abuse freezes the woman in a situation that feels inescapable, particularly if the abuse is part of a lineage of sexual, physical, and emotional abuse.

A girl or woman immersed in this kind of relationship often has the sense that she is under constant siege, has to walk on eggshells, and cannot figure out how to extricate herself from the relationship. With all of this in mind, it should be more understandable in the eyes of both the public and courts of law that when women finally do snap, they do not do so without cause. Unfortunately, those who have never walked in the shoes of an abused person may not understand as readily the anguish that accompanies a woman's life lived in abject terror and fear of a person who, at some point, seemed to care about her and love her.

"The history of violence in these relationships shaped women's construction of meaning of behavior that might appear innocuous," writes Ferraro in *Neither Angels nor Demons*. "[These] women developed nuanced knowledge of men's facial expressions, tone of voice, and body language. They knew when he was in a particularly bad mood. Many women referred to the strange look that came over their partners' faces or into their eyes that made them look 'evil' or 'like somebody else.'"[34]

My interviews with girls or adult women serving time for murdering their abusers point to the frequency with which the man's own gun or rifle is used to kill him. (This is often the same weapon that their boyfriends or husbands once pointed at them, raped them with, or threatened to kill them with.) Unlike the various ways in which men kill women—strangulation, drowning, beating, torture, and so forth—women tend to use guns or knives to kill, because men are generally larger and stronger than women. When women pull the trigger, it is not uncommon to hear them describe a state of bodily dissociation, or of "blacking out" in the moments leading up to and after the act of violence toward the men who had been abusing them.

One woman in prison whom I interviewed several times, Sandra Widner, exhibited nearly all of these issues, including her ability to read even the slightest changes in her live-in boyfriend's body language and verbalization. Life with Truett Turner was a constant cycle of abuse, remorse, and apology; a short period of calm; and yet another episode of rage that was always blamed on her.

Widner stayed with Turner for two and a half years, although she moved out on two occasions, vowing to never return. (The third time she moved back in with Turner, he told her that it would be the last time that she did so.) The couple lived in Calhoun County, Georgia, and some aspects of their relationship satisfied Widner's desire to be loved and protected. But the red flags began to fly very early on. Turner would insist on having sex with her on his schedule, never on hers. He began to control their finances by deciding how the couple's money would be allocated. This was followed by verbal bullying and irrational jealousy about any amount of time that Widner spent away from him, to the point that Turner would sulk or lash out when he decided that Widner had been gone for too long with family or friends.

Turner would explode into violent rages at three- to six-month intervals. Afterward, he would always apologize profusely, bringing her flowers and gifts and promising never to hurt her again. (Domestic violence experts have identified this part of the abuse cycle as the "honeymoon phase.") Predictably, the cycle of abuse went on and on.

On January 12, 2002, Widner returned home from a friend's funeral, a woman who had committed suicide two days before. She parked close to the door, as she usually did, having had to flee many times from Turner's violent outbursts. Right away, Widner could sense something was wrong. Turner was in the living room, waiting for her in stone-cold silence. He had been drinking, and several empty beer bottles were scattered around. Widner saw and sensed that something was very wrong but tried to stay calm. She changed clothes, grabbed a beer, and then asked him what was going on.

Without warning, Turner jumped out of his chair and struck her with such force that she fell back on her couch, spilling her beer. Turner exploded in rage over the fact that she had spilled the beer, and picked up the can to hurl it against the wall, breaking a ceramic plate on impact. Widner used the opportunity to try to get out of his way, while Turner began to yell at her for staying so late with her friends, although he had been asked to attend the funeral and had declined. "You care about them more than you do me!" she remembers him shouting.

The fight escalated quickly. Turner hit her again, knocking her over a chair. He lifted his arm, fist clenched, to hit her again. But this time, she reacted by kicking him. Turner recovered and started to head for the bedroom, an act that struck immediate fear in Widner's heart—his shotgun was stowed at the head of their bed. Widner made a fast break for the door and rushed to her car's front seat, scrambling to find her purse and keys. To her horror, she realized that they were not in the front seat. The screen door slammed, and Widner looked up to see Turner running across the porch and down the steps toward her.

What she remembers next comes to her in bits and pieces, like a halting, freeze-frame recollection. Guns in that part of the country are more common than not. Widner kept, but had never fired, a Taurus .38 in her glove compartment.

"I hurriedly opened the holster," she remembers, "and dropped it to the floor [of the car]. I stepped out of the car with the pistol raised over my head and fired a shot in the air. Turner stopped on the second step only a few feet away from me. I began yelling, 'Let me get my things and I'll leave!'"

Turner backed away. Widner took steps forward until she was on the porch, watching him reach toward the door. It was a bluff. He turned quickly to raise his hand to hit her.

That, says Widner, was when she "blacked out." From what we now know, Widner shot him once at close range. She insists that she didn't even realize that she had fired the gun until she saw Turner "gasping for breath." At first, Widner couldn't seem to grasp what was happening. Widner's recollection is that she got on her knees to flip him over, saw him bleeding from his stomach, put her gun down, and immediately called 911. The county 911 radio log filed earlier that day, with mundane reports of broken gas pumps and a complaint at a high school gym, shows a call from Widner at 7:36 PM, pleading for an ambulance. "Truett Turner's residence," the log reads. "[Widner] said . . . he was shot. Try to give directions, but was unable to do bery hystacal [sic]!" The last four words are thickly underlined twice.

The startling sequence of events transpired so quickly that, just slightly more than fifteen minutes after Widner had walked into their home, Turner was dead, and Widner's life had changed forever.

Widner was arrested on the spot, pleading guilty a few months later to voluntary manslaughter. She was sentenced to fifteen years in the state penitentiary;

her attorney immediately filed an appeal, while Widner began to serve out her sentence in Pulaski State Prison. Just one year into her sentence, the Georgia Sentencing Review Panel, given the task of ascertaining whether lengthy prison terms in the state had been fairly meted out, ruled that Widner had clearly killed Turner in self-defense. Her sentence was reduced to eight years, but Widner's sense of relief was soon tempered by word that the man who had prosecuted her, Georgia Circuit Court District Attorney J. Brown Moseley, had decided to sue the Sentencing Panel to get the decision reversed. Although his suit was dismissed shortly, Moseley owed to take his campaign against this "murderess" all the way up to the Georgia Supreme Court.[35]

Widner is likely to serve eight years in prison, which is still a long time for a woman who killed in self-defense, especially compared to the sentences handed to so many men convicted of premeditated, large-scale crimes for profit—including that of the aforementioned man who ran a prostitution ring of immigrant women sold into sexual servitude, only to serve less than seven years in prison.

Sentences such as his pale in comparison to those slapped on women like Flozelle Woodmore and Sara Kruzan, who still sit in prison on life sentences, despite the fact that they were both teenagers when they killed the men who had used and abused them relentlessly.

Woodmore was just thirteen years old when she began a relationship with a man five years her senior, Clifton "Sweet Thing" Morrow, in South Central Los Angeles. Woodmore had sought out love and companionship, but just one year into the relationship, she was already being beaten and raped. "I used to believe it was his right to hit me, force me to have sex, etc.," she told me. "I didn't feel pretty unless he hit me or forced me to have sex."

Pregnant with his child by the age of fifteen, she was already completely immersed in a relationship from which she felt she could not escape. (Woodmore

could not even have gotten a restraining order if she had wanted to; nonemanci-
pated minors cannot obtain them without involvement from a guardian or parent.) To dull the pain of the abuse, of being beaten, forced to have an abortion,
stabbed, and pushed down a flight of stairs, Woodmore turned to alcohol.

At the age of eighteen, she finally got up the courage to leave, looking for
protection in the arms of another man. As is common for men who batter and
intimidate their partners, Morrow wasn't willing to let her go. The physical
altercation that ensued, according to Woodmore, escalated quickly after Morrow
assaulted their two-year-old son, Clifton, Jr. She retaliated by firing a single shot
from a .357 magnum in her possession, killing Morrow on the spot.

Arrested half an hour later at her mother's house, Woodmore admitted to
the murder immediately, expressing both shock and deep remorse. Although she
told me that she couldn't even begin to process what had happened, Woodmore
felt that she needed to be punished in some way. In 1987, her attorney negotiated
a second-degree murder plea that carried a fifteen-to-life prison sentence. Robert
W. Armstrong, the Superior Court judge overseeing the proceedings, believed that
she would serve "much less" than fifteen years.[36]

Twenty years later, Woodmore is still incarcerated at the Central California Women's Facility (CCWF) in Chowchilla. She has stayed clear of infractions,
earned her GED, and taken on the role of counseling other women coming into
the system with histories of abuse. Woodmore has made a point of attending
domestic violence support groups, and is president of the CCWF Alcoholics
Anonymous group, supporting other lifers and long-timers in their mutual effort
to retain a positive attitude despite their circumstances—and the possibility that
they might die in prison.

After a few years of correspondence, I finally met Woodmore in person in July
2006. She was in truly low spirits, having been denied parole for the fifth time by

the governor's office, despite an exhaustive investigation by the California Board of Prison Terms into the severity of the abuse that she suffered at the hands of the man whom she murdered. That investigation concluded with an unequivocal recommendation for her immediate parole, but democratic Governor Gray Davis overturned the recommendation. (His decision was not completely surprising, considering the extent of his financial and political connections to the influential California Correctional Peace Officers Association, a conservative union that does not typically support the early release of prisoners, particularly those sentenced for murder or "three strikes.") Shortly after Davis took office, he proclaimed his disdain for letting any person convicted of any kind of homicide go free: "If you take someone else's life, forget it."[37] Republican Governor Arnold Schwarzenegger has followed suit by denying Woodmore's appeal two times.

Woodmore told me that she was doing everything she could to not sink into despair, keeping her composure throughout my group interview with her and other long-timers or lifers at CCWF. Only toward the end did Woodmore's eyes well up with tears, when another woman, who had entered the system as a teenager and was serving a life sentence, asked why society was not willing to "give us a second chance."

I met Sara Kruzan on the same day of my visit to CCWF, entirely by accident. In the heat of the midday sun, I had already toured several prison workplaces, ranging from television repair shops to the prison's unique fire department, which trains women to a level on par with any fire department in the "free world" to fight fires throughout the greater Chowchilla/Modesto area. (The women are entrusted to staff the dispatch command, drive the fire engines off prison grounds, and do what needs to be done to quell fires in one of the driest and most fire-prone parts of the state. It's worth noting that not one of these prisoners has attempted to escape.)

The particular shop where I met Kruzan housed a large-scale sewing operation where prisoners were hired to sew flags and fulfill other special orders from state agencies, at a pay rate ranging from forty to seventy-five cents per hour. The air in the shop was excruciatingly hot and humid; a large fan in the room was doing nothing but blowing heat throughout the warehouse. Thankfully, the prisoners had at least been dismissed a few hours early because the conditions were so unbearable.

The civilian manager of the sewing operation had a small, air-conditioned office, where I gladly took refuge to try to cool down. I sat down to try to prevent my body from collapsing from heat exhaustion. After a few minutes, I was able to focus on my surroundings and noticed two quiet prisoners at opposite ends of the office. They were among the select few in the prison who are entrusted with taking care of financial records, inventory, and other administrative tasks.

One of them, a gregarious woman in her thirties, noted that I didn't look like I was a prison employee and forthrightly asked who I was. When I told her I was working on a book about women in prison, she immediately pointed toward the other woman in the office, who had clearly been listening to our conversation but was not uttering a word.

"You need to talk to Sara," she insisted. "You need to hear her story."

Sara Kruzan looked up at me with a shy but intense expression. As I found out in the months after our chance meeting, she hadn't planned on working late that day. "I wanted to leave really bad, but it just seemed as if it wasn't meant," she said.

Kruzan later told me that when she saw me walk into the office, she thought to herself that I was her "voice to the outside."

Here, I need to digress for a moment. Listening to the stories of people who live and work in prisons has become such a part of my life that I sometimes lose sight of what it means for a "free world" person to walk into a prisoner's environment. Six years prior to this visit to CCWF, I remember walking through the adjacent Valley State Prison for Women and having several women sitting against a wall make eye contact and ask humbly that I talk to them. I was wearing a headscarf and heeled boots, attire that is typical for me but does not necessarily reflect any kind of fashion trend. One of the women said that she hadn't seen how women on the "outside" dress themselves in well over fifteen years. "Is that what women are wearing now?" she asked with shy curiosity.

It struck me then that what I thought I understood about the alienation that prisoners feel from the world around them was far deeper than I had realized. Prisoners' concept of life on the outside is frozen in time, and for the females who enter the system as teenagers and spend the next several decades in prison, the sense of disconnection is even more profound. The people who guard them are always in uniform. There are no opportunities for the vast majority of incarcerated persons to see the outside world, outside of what's broadcast on television—something that rarely reflects how people actually dress and act in the real world. The everyday use of cell phones, ATMs, PDAs, cordless headsets, laptops, and many other norms in modern-day American society is altogether foreign to women who started doing lengthy sentences in the 1970s, '80s, and early '90s. Small wonder then that so many former prisoners are reincarcerated shortly after being released. Among other hurdles, most women and men coming out of prison have no practical preparation whatsoever for the significant societal changes that have occurred since they were locked up.

Back at CCWF, I asked Kruzan to sit and talk to me in a more private section of the office, and her life experience prior to incarceration began to come out in bits and pieces.

At first she spoke haltingly, looking down at the floor as she conveyed her story to me. But what emerged was one of the most disturbing stories I had ever heard in my years of interviewing prisoners.

Kruzan started prostituting by the time she was eleven years old. A thirty-seven-year-old pimp, George Howard, assumed the role of introducing Kruzan to a harsh, fast-paced street life of drugs, fast money, and guns. He controlled her movements and "dates," and abused her when he felt she deserved it. Like Woodmore, Kruzan could not even fathom leaving her situation. Although her relationship with her pimp was utterly abusive and unhealthy, she had no real sense of how damaging it was to her psyche, to the point that she became a teenager, as she put it in her own words, who "lacked any moral scruples." Her compatriots in the "life"—a street term for people surviving in the underground economy—were female prostitutes and men engaged in violent criminal conduct.

As a prostitute and street hustler, Kruzan's life became predictable, despite the damaging nature of just about everything that she was going through. But on March 10, 1994, everything changed. Three of her male associates talked Kruzan, then sixteen years of age, into a convoluted scenario to rob Howard. They handed her a gun before she joined Howard in the honeymoon suite of a hotel in Riverside, California—his plan was to spend the night with this girl who "belonged" to him. Once there, Kruzan says she got on the phone with another one of the three men, James Earl Hampton. He told her that he was just a few blocks from Kruzan's mother's house, and instructed her to rob Howard of the typically large amount of money in his wallet, and to "leave no witnesses, or he would handle it 'his' way." Kruzan said she didn't think she had an alternative, because either she or her mother would face severe retribution of one kind or another if she did not do what she was told. In a matter of minutes after the phone call, Kruzan shot and killed Howard, raced out of the hotel with his wallet, jumped into a waiting car, and delivered it to Hampton.

Hampton took the money, the car, and the gun. He returned after a few days, kidnapped her, and warned her to never talk about what had happened. But Kruzan got in touch with her mother about what had happened, trying to figure out what to do. Unfortunately, Hampton got word that Kruzan was talking and had his sister make a phone call to the police, directing them to Kruzan. She was arrested four days after the shooting. Kruzan went to jury trial, but the three men never testified in her case, nor were they brought to trial on related charges. Evidence of Kruzan's history of abuse at the hands of the man she murdered was not introduced into evidence. Although she was only sixteen and had a clean record—despite her dangerous lifestyle up until that point—Kruzan was sentenced to life in prison without the possibility of parole, plus another four years tacked on for "lying in wait." Now twenty-eight, Kruzan has already served more than thirteen years of her sentence at CCWF. She has known nothing but life in a prison for her entire adult life.

Unlike Woodmore, who has formed close relationships with other lifers, Kruzan says that she has survived the experience by staying a loner. The strongest commonality between the two women is that both have refused to participate in the mix of drugs and violence in prison life, and have pursued their education, employment, and self-edification. Like so many other lifers, both are known as prisoners who pose no problems whatsoever to correctional employees.

Kruzan told me that it took serious effort for her to begin to develop healthy social skills, and that she struggled to begin to comprehend her life experiences as those of brutality and control by the men around her, particularly the man whom she killed. Today she defines herself as a survivor, with an exceptional degree of self-acceptance and the sense that her suffering has somehow been for the greater good of bringing attention to the myriad abuses suffered by other girls and women.

A few months after I met her, Kruzan wrote me with cautious optimism about a decision by the California Habeas Project to take on her case pro bono, to try to win her freedom from prison. This attempt at getting a court of law to recognize the needlessly harsh sentence handed down in her case is still in its very early stages; it is difficult to say what might happen, particularly in light of the constant denials of recommendations of parole for women like Woodmore.

One thing is for sure: Kruzan and Woodmore are more representative of the women serving out long sentences for killing their male partners than those portrayed as backstabbing, cold-blooded killers in popular media. They also represent the fact that prosecutors tend to go after women who kill even under abusive circumstances; with particular vehemence in persuing first-degree-murder charges and lengthy sentences.

I met some of these freed women in 2004, when I attended "Our Voices Within: Our Journey," an event held at The Women's Building in San Francisco's Mission district. One of the women who had been freed just a few months before the event, Mary Ramp, was a fifty-six-year-old disabled grandmother who had served more than fifteen years in prison for killing an extremely abusive husband. Ramp told me that she carried no bitterness in her heart about her lengthy period of incarceration and was only "overjoyed" to be able to rejoin her loving family in Stockton, California.

California stands at an interesting crossroads where the sentencing and parole of battered women are concerned. On the one hand, the state has passed bills and enacted several changes to the penal code that have allowed women to introduce evidence of abuse and domestic violence in their lives, even allowing such evidence to be introduced retroactively. (In this sense, California is far ahead of any other state in the nation.) One of the most significant recent developments was the change in California state law that allowed women to seek relief for all manner of felonious crimes committed under the duress of an abusive relationship—not just for the murder of a male partner. Also, the term "battering and its effects" in the California penal code has now replaced the far more problematic term "battered women's syndrome," which seemed to imply that the condition of being abused was a form of mental illness.

On the other hand, nearly a decade of concerted efforts to free women with serious histories of abuse has resulted in the parole of only twenty-seven women as of 2007. Although Andrea Bible, Habeas Project Coordinator of Legal Services for Prisoners with Children, says it is impossible to prove intentional discrimination, she notes that the vast majority of the women approved for release by the governor's office have been Euro-American, and that African American women like Woodmore are inexplicably denied, time after time.

Even pleas for the "compassionate release" of terminally ill women like Charisse "Happy" Shumate, a forty-six-year-old African American woman who killed her abusive male partner, have been ignored. Despite receiving approval from the then-named California Department of Corrections (CDC) for her release, as well as the support of several members of the California state legislature, Governor Davis let her compassionate-release paperwork languish on his desk. Whether because of his inability to relate to the plight of a black woman dying of cancer, or perhaps because of her role as the lead plaintiff in *Shumate v. Wilson,* a class-action lawsuit related to improving the standard of medical care for female prisoners, former Governor Davis ignored her plea for compassionate-release.

Shumate died behind bars on August 4, 2001, without ever hearing back from Davis.

The hurdles that incarcerated battered women are up against are tremendous. For most women, the likelihood of getting out early—or getting out of prison at all—is very small. In light of this, I am consistently amazed by how resilient so many of them are, wanting to assure me that they are working hard to keep their spirits up and not succumbing to despair about their lives. Although many of these women will never be given a second chance to prove themselves as worthwhile members of society, they are still grateful for having an opportunity to live without the terror of being beaten by their partners. Like Kruzan and Woodmore, many women feel as though they have gotten a chance to just live and know who they are as individuals.

As for Suarez? She was finally paroled from state prison but was promptly taken into custody by immigration officials who wanted to ship her off to Mexico, a country she had not seen since she was a child. Another legal battle ensued, and Suarez began to lose all hope. Fortunately for her, her advocates were unwilling to give up. Eventually, they were able to able to secure a temporary "I" visa for her, a new kind of visa that is strictly limited to people sold into slavery in the United States. At the time of this writing, Suarez was still waiting to hear whether the governor will grant her a full pardon.

For her part, Suarez has refused to let her abuse and her lengthy incarceration stop her in her tracks. These days, she has committed herself to counseling and rehabilitating male, mostly Latino, sex offenders in Los Angeles, at a nonprofit organization called About Face.[38]

Kruzan is still waiting to see if legal efforts on her behalf might result in some kind of "miracle," although she is cautious about expressing any kind of optimism, a sentiment that is more than understandable, given that she has lived with nothing but disappointment, brutality, and punishment.

In March 2007, Woodmore was denied parole for the sixth time, despite the urging of her sentencing judge and Morrow's own family that she should be freed. In a subsequent letter to me, she could not even find the words to express the depth of her sadness. Her advocates on the outside are still unwilling to give up, and with good reason. Woodmore deserves to have this once-perpetual cycle of repression and punishment broken for good and to have an opportunity to experience life free of alcoholism, free of fear and desperation.

There is simply no justice in keeping women like Woodmore from ever being able to breathe the air beyond prison walls, nor is there any justice in forcing women to die behind bars for defending their right to live.

Chapter 8: Women Loving Women

"Trying to have a relationship in prison, it can be done. But there are consequences to pay if you are caught in any sexual relationship."
—Beverly Henry, Central California Women's Facility

"I have always known that I'm attracted to women; coming to prison has let me open up and admit my feelings for women. And I'm one of the lucky ones. I have found my soul mate."
—Kathy O'Donnell, writing in the "Women Loving Women in Prison" issue of *Sinister Wisdom*

For just $14.98, Amazon.com shoppers can pick up a scintillating duo of movies promising lots of adult action having to do with *Nymphos Behind Bars*.

The two-pack of films includes *Lust for Freedom* and *Escape from Hell*. In the former, a prisoner named Crystal Breeze fights for her survival amidst "heart-stopping, brutal action and lesbian affairs." In the latter film, "two courageous and curvaceous" lesbians make a daring escape from a jungle penal colony.

The peculiar subgenre of campy, over-the-top, lesbians-in-prison films (and pulp fiction novels) was all the rage from the 1950s through the 1980s, with such films as *Caged* (1950), *Ilsa the Wicked Warden* (1978), *Caged Heat* (1974), and *Reform School Girls* (1986).

The popularity of lesbians-in-prison films seemed to wane in the 1990s but has made a curious comeback. The *Nymphos Behind Bars* movies appeared in 2006, although they did not reach the big screen. The award-winning *Chicago* (2002), on the other hand, enjoyed huge box office success and critical acclaim.

"Instead of nubile young actresses running around naked, *Chicago* is characterized by much more tease and innuendo," writes Kris Scott Marti on AfterEllen.com. "The suggestively lesbian warden, Matron "Mama" Morton, played by Queen Latifah, exercises her lecherousness through persuasion instead of force. As she lays down the law to the fresh meat, she sings, 'When you're good to Mama, Mama's good to you.'"[1]

Television has also gotten into the mix, introducing one of the most popular BBC shows of all time, *Bad Girls,* in which predatory lesbians are a constant presence and a threat to newbie inmates. Even the popular and pro-lesbian cable series *The L Word* features an episode in which Bette (Jennifer Beals) and her extramarital fling, Candace (Ion Overman), are locked up together after a political demonstration. Bad food, verbally abusive guards, and humiliating strip searches aren't the focal point, though. What matters is that the two, apparently so excited by being locked up, get it on in the cellblock.

All of this seems to make for great fodder for the male imagination, and perhaps even for the female imagination, given the recent release of *Bad Girls Behind Bars* by a lesbian filmmaker, Sharon Zurek. "Imagine taking four women in prison movies and editing them together so it seems as though it's one big happy prison of bad girls," reads the promotional material. At least the intent with the film was to highlight the absurdity of these kinds of films, but the question still needs to be asked: Do any of these movies or television shows represent any aspect of the lives of real female prisoners in same-sex relationships?

Hardly.

If anything, same-sex relationships are inherently risky in prison, because nearly every facility has strict rules expressly prohibiting sexual contact between prisoners. Some facilities go so far as to prohibit hand-holding or anything but a brief hug. Violations are subject to major write-ups and even periods of extensive isolation.

"Homophobia is used to control and stigmatize women in all areas of the criminal [justice] system," reads a 2001 newsletter editorial from the California Coalition for Women Prisoners. "Any positive expression of sexuality can lead to retaliation by prison staff. Always looking for ways to tighten control in the prisons, guards may separate lovers from each other and move them to different units, often arbitrarily and with the knowledge that this will only bring disappointment and anger to the couple. According to one prisoner, 'homosecting' is the number-one reason that women are sent to the SHU (Security Housing Unit) to endure . . . solitary confinement."

"In most cases, couples never live together, and once separated, we are ridiculed and talked about [by the prison guards], written up and [subject to] character assassination," says a lesbian prisoner, Marie Bandrup, who is incarcerated at the Central California Women's Facility (CCWF).

"It's not good to get too comfortable in here," agrees Beverly Henry, fifty-seven, who is also doing time at CCWF. "Chopper," as fellow prisoners know her, was slapped with a fifteen-year "second strike" prison sentence for possessing roughly $5 worth of heroin.

Life circumstances made her a tough, rebellious woman, and prison has definitely made her even less willing to bow down to any form of authority. Fortunately, that toughness hasn't come at the cost of compassion. In fact, as someone living with both HIV and hepatitis C, Chopper has become an outspoken advocate and leading figure in the ongoing fight for the needs of chronically and terminally ill prisoners.

For the first time in her life, Chopper also found real, unconditional love in the arms of another female prisoner. She never thought prison would be the place to find this kind of love, but that's exactly what happened. Like any woman in prison, Beverly has her own story, her own share of struggle and pain, and her own time to serve. But what she truly has in common with many female inmates in prisons across the country is that she's been able to deal with her prison time with the love of a woman at her side.

Barbed prison walls and armed guards are everyday reminders of the fact that women can't kiss their girlfriends or walk together holding hands. There are always exceptions, on certain yards, depending on how the correctional officer in charge views the phenomenon of same-sex love.

From the early 1900s onward, researchers and criminologists have largely disregarded women's sexual relationships in prison as temporary and transitional. One male psychologist wrote in 1913 about the "Perversion Not Commonly Noted" between women in prison in the *Journal of Abnormal Psychology*. The author made particular mention of the "unnatural" relationships he had witnessed between white and black female prisoners. Writing in 1962, sociologists Halleck and Herski put forth the theory that same-sex relationships in women's prisons were the abnormal result of early developmental problems and consequent immature sexuality.[2]

Other researchers have focused their energies on prison families, including the formation of nonsexualized mother–daughter roles—or entirely female family structures, complete with a "married" father, mother, aunts, uncles, and children. Even more recent and progressive analysis, including Joycelyn M. Pollock's "Women, Prison & Crime," frames same-sex relationships as a "subcultural adaptation," noting that "women are 'in the life' only during their prison stay and revert back to a primarily heterosexual lifestyle upon release."[3]

Yet the reality of life for women who love women in prison is much more rich, dynamic, supportive, and complex than academics have been able to grasp. Some love relationships do, in fact, continue well after one partner's release from prison, although the denial of visitation for parolees makes such relationships very difficult to maintain.

"These relationships are far deeper and longer-lasting than what's been called 'situational homosexual sex,'" says Judy Greenspan, a prisoner advocate in California. "As anywhere, there's jealousy and possessiveness in prison. But it's also true that a lot of these relationships are far more fulfilling and supportive than the relationships that these women had on the streets with men."

During my July 2006 visit to CCWF, a walk through one of the outdoor prison yards revealed the sight of a woman seated on a grassy patch, her girlfriend lying sideways and resting her head on her lover's legs. I watched as the two women talked to each other in soft, soothing tones, and the seated woman stroked her lover's hair.

No one did anything to intervene, and the male and female prison guards near them seemed to not be bothered by the sight in the least; in fact, no one was paying them any attention at all. As I later found out, this was one of the rare areas of the prison where the correctional officers in charge of their unit actually recognized that allowing a limited amount of romantic physical contact between women helped to keep the environment calm and nurturing.

Our neighbors to the north have had similar approaches to those practiced in U.S. prisons (sexual contact or kissing is expressly prohibited in the provincial prisons, although hand-holding is sometimes allowed). A new precedent was set in February 2007 when a federal prison in Canada allowed a lesbian couple to exchange wedding vows.[4] Although the women's names were not disclosed, the marriage ceremony took place in the Edmonton Institution for Women, in Alberta. The event appears to be the first time in North American history that two women have been able to officially marry one another behind bars. But the marriage didn't change anything else where lesbian rights in prison were concerned: After the ceremony, the women were returned to their respective separate cells, with no honeymoon to be enjoyed.

These kinds of progressive leaps in the treatment of same-sex relationships in prison are the exception to the rule. Chopper's own relationship with her girlfriend, for instance, was a testament to perseverance. The two always felt like they were walking on eggshells for fear of being completely split apart. Chopper had to work particularly hard to prearrange secret locations for her and her girlfriend to meet outside, between work shifts, counts, and other movement restrictions, just to be able to sneak in a few precious moments in outdoor locations. For three years, the couple kept their relationship going through freezing winter lows and boiling summer days in central California.

On the outside, Chopper identified as a bisexual African American woman. On the inside, she proudly calls herself a lesbian and an "aggressive femme." Yet most female prisoners in romantic, emotional, and/or sexual relationships with other inmates would be hard pressed to define themselves as lesbian or even bisexual.

"Women in prison don't have to declare themselves," explains Greenspan. "These are women who love women. We have to realize that declaring yourself a lesbian can result in harassment from the guards. I've seen it used as a way to break up relationships or to put someone in [isolation or segregation]."

Greenspan's longstanding concern for prisoner rights—and for the lives of lesbians in prison—resulted in an unique "Women Loving Women in Prison" issue of the lesbian journal *Sinister Wisdom*.[5] Contributions came in from approximately sixty former and current prisoners across the United States, including an essay from a prisoner named Lorrie Flakes.

Before incarceration, Flakes had been a heterosexual woman in a long-term marriage. During incarceration, she found herself alone and utterly depressed by her new surroundings. Flakes surprised herself when she fell in love with a fellow prisoner: "This woman has changed my life forever," writes Flakes. "She found and moved into a place within my heart that I never knew existed. . . . Loving a woman is so very much different than loving a man. I've found something I now feel I've been looking for all of my life. We understand one another, we respect each other, and most of all we are both gentle, loving creatures that want no more out of life than a life of joy."

Anecdotally speaking, same-sex relationships in women's prisons rarely seem to be a matter of coercion or sexual violence, although intimidation and physical violence certainly do exist. However, one study published in the *Journal of Sex Research* indicated that 20 percent of female prisoners in a large prison had been coerced into some kind of a sexual relationship, and that other inmates had instigated one-half of those incidents. But even the researchers for this study admitted that "the female situation is not as violent and serious as what happens typically in a male prison."[6]

Female prisons tend to be environments in which women build relationships of various kinds in order to survive the emotional and physical stressors of incarceration. In many cases, these relationships last far longer than the period of incarceration—or for life, as is the case for many women who will never be released from prison.

Current and former prisoners interviewed for this article consistently put the number of lesbians in prison at 10 to 15 percent of the general population. Prisoners like Gricel Paz even say that they experienced more harassment for being gay on the outside than in prison.

"It's the normal day-to-day relationship to have in here," says Paz, forty-two, who has already served ten years for crimes related to her heroin addiction. "I'm very comfortable with who I am . . . I've always been very open as being a lesbian." Her openness about her sexual preference has caused Paz a fair amount of difficulty with guards, in the form of multiple infractions on her prison record.

According to the California Department of Corrections and Rehabilitation, prisoners may not engage in "illegal sexual acts," and must avoid placing themselves in situations that would encourage illegal sexual acts. Such acts include oral sex and mutual masturbation, but can also include "overt acts" like hip thrusts, sexually suggestive letters, or drawings that depict sexual acts. Women can be charged with misdemeanors for such acts, and subsequent violations can be prosecuted as felonies.[7] Several other prison systems, including the Kansas Department of Corrections, have made "lewd" contact by a prisoner eligible conduct for prosecution as a predator and sex offender.[8] Other state prison agencies, such as the Washington Department of Corrections (WDOC), have a confusing and even contradictory approach. A spokesperson for the WDOC explained it this way: "We do not have policies that specifically deal with inmates having sex with other inmates. . . . [But] an inmate would be infracted for having sex with another inmate and would go through a disciplinary hearing and receive a sanction."[9]

In this sense, things are only marginally better than when "Bo" Brown was incarcerated in 1978. Brown served eight years under high-security lockdown in the federal prison system, owing to her armed robberies in connection with the radical antiracist group the George Jackson Brigade.

As a self-proclaimed "butch dyke," Brown recalls that when she entered the federal prison system, officials stamped her prison clothing with an "H," for homosexual. Brown dealt with the situation as best she could, despite long stints in isolation and being moved from state to state according to the whims of prison administrators.

"I had a girlfriend in almost every joint I was in," Brown explains. "It was against the rules, but that didn't stop me or the other women."

In one prison, Brown recalls that the lesbian population ended up having an entire prison wing of their own. In another institution, Brown was able to live with her girlfriend in the same cell for six months of "domestic bliss." Bribing staff, challenging infractions, maintaining a level of respect with sympathetic guards, and working out secret signals are all parts of lesbian life in prison. But it takes only a homophobic snitch, an abusive guard, or an unexpected prison transfer for a loving relationship to be torn apart. Released in 1986, Brown has remained a prisoner advocate, particularly focused on the struggles of lesbian-identified prisoners.

The issues facing lesbians and bisexuals in the criminal justice system aren't just limited to what goes on behind bars. One study conducted by Victor Streib, a professor of law at Cleveland State University, points to the possibility that lesbians—or simply women who do not appear traditionally feminine—may be more likely to be meted harsher sentences, including the death penalty. Writing about female defendants facing capital murder charges, Streib finds that "prosecutors first must defeminize the defendant, trying to show that her crime is more 'manly.'"

"It would seem that to a typical Southern Baptist jury in a small Southern town, an effective means of defeminizing a female capital defendant is to show the jury that she is a lesbian," he adds. "The more 'manly' her sexuality, her dress, and her demeanor, the more easily the jury may forget that she is a woman. In essence, she is defeminized by her sexual orientation and then dehumanized by her crime. The jury is left with a gender-neutral monster deserving of little or no human compassion."[10]

Following that logic, lesbian and/or nonfeminine-appearing women who have entered prison as perceived gender deviants and ruthless criminals may very well have less of a shot at early release or parole.

On the one hand, the legal system may very well mete out more severe sentences to lesbians and/or women who do not fit an acceptable feminine profile. On the other hand, the higher courts do not seem to concern themselves with same-sex relationships between women. According to a 2002 Fourth Circuit Court of Appeals ruling, there is no fundamental right for prisoners to engage in homosexual acts. The court ruled specifically that prison administrators have the right to place openly gay male prisoners in single cells because of the potential threat of violence or sexual abuse from either party. But female prisoners, the court determined, are generally less violent and homophobic than their male counterparts, and therefore do not need to be covered by the ruling.[11]

No matter what the prevailing legal sentiment about lesbians and same-sex relationships is, there is rarely anything akin to privacy or "quiet time" for women in relationships with other women in prison. As such, intimate moments between prisoners are a precious experience, carefully negotiated and arranged between cellmates and lookouts.

"We learned to listen for keys and footsteps," concurs Vickie Nevis, forty-five, who did three years in prison for committing a solo bank robbery. "We had it down so good that if we heard something, I could be off my girlfriend's bunk, hop down, and be on the toilet in two seconds."

Why the toilet?

Because in the Dublin, California, federal prison where Nevis did her time, regulations stated that the only reason why a cell door could be closed was that a prisoner was using the toilet. Knowing this, Nevis and her longtime girlfriend would make love with their clothes on, listening for the slightest indication that a guard might be approaching. Nevis was able to keep sexual activity from being noticed by the staff for the entire duration of her prison term, but she counts herself among the few fortunate women who did not have to suffer repercussions for same-sex relationships.

"Sometimes people get busted just because they have fallen asleep together," explains Linda Evans, a former prisoner who was granted executive clemency in 2001 by President Clinton.

In the 1960s, Evans began her activism in antiracist and antiwar organizations, including Students for a Democratic Society (SDS), and later became active in women's liberation and lesbian movements in the 1970s and '80s. She was arrested in 1985 on charges of making false statements to acquire weapons. While in prison, she received an additional sentence for her participation in the "Resistance Conspiracy" case, involving a plot to carry out political bombings in Washington, D.C., and New York.

Evans was out as a lesbian during her entire sixteen years in prison. "The main thing that the [prison administration] does is that they try to break down any kind of supportive relationship," she recalls. "It doesn't matter whether it's sisterly or sexual in nature."

Evans had two intimate relationships with women on the inside. In 1996, she met and fell in love with her current partner, political activist and documentarian Eve Goldberg. The couple stayed together through the remaining years of Evans's incarceration, despite physical barriers and emotional struggles. Guards would crack down on even the slightest displays of affection between Evans and Goldberg when the two were allowed to visit. (Those rules are not enforced for heterosexual female prisoners, who can usually embrace and hold hands with their male partners.)

"Lesbian kisses weren't exactly popular with the guards," Evans says. "We were told repeatedly that we couldn't hold hands when we were walking around [in the visitation area]."

Since her release, Evans has been grateful for even the smallest of freedoms: the freedom to hold her lover's hand, the freedom to choose the food she wants to eat, and the freedom to travel. But the postprison adjustment period hasn't been easy for either her or Goldberg, whom Evans credits with "endless patience."

"In many ways, I'm still adjusting to life [after prison]. I have flashbacks, and I'm still so connected to the individuals I knew in prison," Evans says softly. "The suffering there is so intense, and the injustice is so overwhelming, that if I were to turn my back on it all, I wouldn't feel right."

That feeling is echoed by another committed lesbian couple whose relationship has stood the test of time—the furthest thing from the "situational" lesbianism that academics have emphasized. Pat and Nikki, who asked that only their first names be used, have been partners for nearly ten years. Their relationship began at the California Institution for Women in Corona. Both of the women had been sentenced to indeterminate life sentences, charged with first-degree murder. In Nikki's case, it was her male partner who actually pulled out a gun and killed another man, but under the felony murder rule at that time, her participation in lesser crimes with the killer made her eligible for sentencing as though she herself had pulled the trigger.

As lifers, Pat and Nikki were left alone to a greater degree than most women in the general population, because prison administrators and guards know that lifers are typically the least troublesome, violent, or demanding inmates. They were able to live together for a time, sharing their experiences and coming to life-changing realizations about how their self-conceptions had been totally warped by severely dysfunctional homes, and about their own lifelong struggles with alcohol and drugs as forms of escape and self-medication.

Pat, now fifty-nine, says that physical abuse was a constant in her life. She was raped at the age of thirteen; she had her first baby at fourteen and her second child at sixteen. She drank heavily for twenty-three years to escape the pain of her circumstances and could not see a way out of the lifestyle that she had been born into. When Pat entered the prison system, she had the equivalent of a fifth-grade education. On her part, Nikki was raped by her father at age four and then molested by her brother until she turned twelve.

For the two women, prison represented a remarkable turning point. Although neither of the women believe that they should have served nearly thirty-year sentences, Pat and Nikki admit that being removed from their hellish personal lives on the outside gave them their first real opportunities to pursue schooling, vocational training, sobriety, and counseling.

When they were finally released in 2004 and 2005, respectively, Pat and Nikki set about building a life and a home together in central California. The two women left prison with a sense that they had to do what they could to help the women still inside, as well as people in the "free world" who were likely to end up in prison.

Pat and Nikki became the first lifers to ever be allowed to go back to the state women's prisons, where they conduct reentry workshops and provide inspiration for women who feel hopeless about their futures. "A warden told us that she had seen a light go on in the women's eyes when we started to talk to them," Pat explains emotionally. "They've got their hope back since we've been back in, and we want to make sure it stays that way."

The couple's strength is that they are willing to speak openly to the women and prison administrators about nearly every aspect of their lives, including their histories of sexual abuse, alcoholism, and self-destructive lifestyle patterns. Animated, articulate, and extremely well versed in legal matters, the two have gotten to the point where they finish each other's sentences. Privately, they share in the joy of having liberated themselves, through love, from a life of certain self-destruction.

Of note, though, is that only one thing remains unspoken when Pat and Nikki go back to the world behind clicking electric doors and razor wire: the very nature of their relationship.

"If they knew we are a couple . . . "

Nikki trails off without finishing her sentence.

After everything is said and done, it's still abundantly clear that gains made in the public sphere toward the recognition of same-sex relationships haven't actually done much for breaking longtime prison taboos. From their standpoint, Pat and Nikki have made the decision that they don't want to risk the importance of their work with prisoners for the sake of being able to declare, once and for all, that they are truly in love.

Chapter 9: Living in the God Pod

"Don't forget that Jesus himself was a prisoner."

—New Mexico Department of Corrections Secretary Joe Williams, at the
American Correctional Conference in Phoenix, Arizona, January 2005

*"Disobeying the promptings of the Holy Spirit will cause Him to be
grieved and will quench His power in your life."*

—From a workbook given to state prisoners in Grants, New Mexico

Betty Ramirez is a career correctional officer who actually loves her job.
She believes in the power of rehabilitation and redemption for the
women she is responsible for guarding and protecting. More than anything,
Ramirez believes they deserve a second chance—or a third, a fourth, or a fifth,
as the case may be. New Mexico's recidivism rate is the nation's third highest,
and, by the prison's own estimates, up to 85 percent of women who are incarcerated and released within this state will end up back in prison.

Nonetheless, Ramirez believes in the potential for rehabilitation of even the most hardened inmates. "Most of these women are sorry for what they have done," she says, "but have run into bad luck and bad situations."

A petite woman with a powerful presence, Ramirez is one of the few Corrections Corporation of America (CCA) employees who have been at the New Mexico Women's Correctional Facility (NMWCF) in Grants, New Mexico, from the very beginning, when the facility became the first privately run women's prison in the United States in 1989. The move signaled what later became a full-blown trend toward the privatization of incarceration in the United States. In the ensuing sixteen years, Ramirez watched the population at NMWCF increase dramatically, as growing numbers of nonviolent and addicted offenders were given longer sentences under more punitive drug-war laws. From 149 New Mexican female prisoners in early 1989 to 600 today, these women have had one or more children by the time they are incarcerated, on par with female prisoners in the rest of the country. Most come from backgrounds filled with abuse, neglect, poverty, drug and alcohol addiction, domestic violence, and limited educational and vocational opportunities.

Ramirez greets fellow correctional officers and inmates alike as she walks me through classes, workshops, and prison pods. One of our early stops includes a visit to two segregation pods where a few dozen women are locked down twenty-three hours a day in small, dark solitary confinement cells. Ramirez, who used to work in the segregation pods, acknowledges that this form of imprisonment can be very stressful for the inmates, who do not have contact with the outside world—let alone other inmates—for months or even years on end.

But there is one area of the prison that stands in particularly sharp contrast to the bleak desperation of the segregation pods: the God Pod, which is officially named Life Principles Community/Crossings Program. The God Pod is a program that prison officials consider a real success story within the confines of NMWCF.

As a housing pod, Crossings has been around since 2001, with the enthusiastic support of the prison administration and the prison's chaplain, Shirley Compton. More recently, CCA picked Crossings as one of eight sites nationwide to pioneer a new partnership with a fundamentalist Christian ministry named the Institute in Basic Life Principles (IBLP).

Although the Life Principles Community/Crossings Program is not the only example of religious activity at the prison, it is by far the most institutionalized and structured one. It also is the most problematic, from a First Amendment point of view. It is in this unit that the blurring of the line between church and state is most evident, signaling a growing trend toward Christian-based programming that has begun to truly influence (or, depending on one's perspective, to infiltrate) the nation's prisons. Publicly, federal prisons recognize a diversity of spiritual and religious practices. FCC Coleman in Central Florida, for instance, visibly posts the ackowledgement of several dozen religions, from Muslim to Jewish, from Wiccan to Rastafarian.

In hushed tones and letters, however, female inmates from a variety of backgrounds complained to me about the preferential treatment granted to women at FCC Coleman who sign up for religious programming in line with the Protestant faith of high-ranking prison officials, or of the warden himself. Numerous women at FCC Coleman spoke off the record for fear of retaliation regarding special privileges—ranging from the best prison jobs to the ability to leave the prison on furlough—granted in particular to those who joined the prison choir or converted to Protestantism.

In Madison, Wisconsin, former prisoner Carrie Wipplinger says that she was subjected to criticism and condescension by prison officials and inmates alike after she complained about prison mandated attendance at an overtly Christian "life skills" session put on by the Prison Fellowship. Once Wipplinger complained to the Freedom From Religion Foundation (FFRF) in the fall of 2006, flyers in the prison were changed to read ATTENDANCE IS STRONGLY RECOMMENDED. Widely advertised during the program was the availability of after-release services (including clothing, jobs, and housing) for women willing to join the program. According to the FFRF, no comparable secular programs have been made available by the prison.

"If I was somebody without money or connections," noted Wipplinger, thirty, a self-described atheist, "I would have been all over it."

"There's not much to do during the day in prison," she added, "so when Bible study is made available—with snacks that we don't otherwise get—people get excited about it, just because it's something to do."

Wipplinger was later shipped out from prison to a city office and was made to "volunteer" to stuff envelopes without pay. The enclosures advertised a faith-based, antidomestic-violence–themed "prayer breakfast." When she questioned the role of the city in promoting such an event, she was confronted with accusatory questions about whether she supported domestic violence. Wipplinger continued the work in silence, until she was finally relieved of her duties a few hours later.

Religious programming for prisoners has been around for as long as prisons have existed in this country, but the modern-day influx of fundamentalist and overtly patriarchal Christian sects working hand in hand with state or federally run prisons begs the obvious question of whether the constitutional imperative to separate church and state is being eroded behind prison walls.

A significant legal curveball was thrown toward this trend when the Justice Department had to cancel its proposal for a "single-faith residential reentry program" in October 2006. The plan had been for the Federal Bureau of Prisons to implement a variety of religious housing programs in as many as six federal prisons, but the plug was pulled after a lawsuit was brought by the FFRF.[1] However, one entirely "faith and character"–based prison for women already exists in Tampa, Florida, run by the Department of Corrections. "My expectation is you'll be better behaved, but more important, you'll be better prepared when you get out, " Governor Jeb Bush told Florida inmates about faith prisons in 2005.[2]

At NMWCF, volunteers from churches of various denominations come in to lead Catholic mass, baptisms, Bible studies, and other activities. The Kairos Prison Ministry, the mission of which is to "bring Christ's love and forgiveness to all incarcerated individuals," also has a presence. Even more prominently, an Albuquerque-based ministry named Wings has gained particular preference within the prison for conducting large-scale, Christian-based family reunification/pizza party events inside the Grants prison. At the 2005 American Correctional Association conference, Joe Williams, secretary of the New Mexico Department of Corrections, went so far as to fly out to the conference, using state monies, to support the work of Wings. One such workshop opened with prayer and revolved around singing Christian songs, as well as enacting aspects of the gospel as they related to the concept of inmate rehabilitation.

The federal government's increased emphasis on religion has impacted the scope of—and the amount of money available for—such programs. After it was created in 1998, President Bush's national Faith-Based Initiative funding rose to more than $2 billion by 2006, including funding for the Department of Justice's reentry initiative for prisoners.[3]

Most of the female state prisoners with whom I have corresponded have mentioned the presence of a Christian religious program behind bars. Most of these programs emphasize a particular denomination or evangelistic approach toward Christianity and provide special perks, including quieter housing, pizza parties, and ice cream which are rarities in prisons as a whole. Ostensibly, these programs are brought in by outside religious organizations, although the line between "state-funded" and "state-encouraged" is a fuzzy one.

The Faith-Based Initiative has not specifically provided money for the Crossings program, which is financed by New Mexico's general fund and funneled through the CCA. The program is also supported by seasonal, in-person sales of foodstuffs and hair products.

The administration's emphasis on the faith needs of people released from prison has channeled millions of dollars into ex-offender transition programs involving churches, while providing an overt justification for "volunteer," faith-based prison programs. Under President George W. Bush's tenure, the White House has gone to great lengths to say that these kinds of programs are voluntary and are therefore not intended to convert people to any particular religion or sect of Christianity.

But the "voluntary" nature of these programs has become a point of contention for many civil liberties organizations, including the FFRF and Americans United for Separation of Church and State. In 2005, FFRF, along with several New Mexico taxpayers, filed a lawsuit to stop money from going to the Crossings Program. FFRF attorneys representing the plaintiffs called the overt state sponsorship of a prison-based, single-faith residential religious program "unprecedented and . . . unconstitutional."[4]

"We are not trying to deny reasonable accommodations for prisoners' religious beliefs," FFRF President Annie Laurie Gaylor clarifies. "We have a problem with the state involved in adopting far-right, fundamentalist Christian doctrine and imposing it on prisoners as a form of rehabilitation."

The constitutional issues have yet to be sorted out by the courts, but there is no question that CCA's business interests seem to be driving this phenomenon. John Lanz, CCA's national director of industry and special programs, told me that the CCA has benefited greatly from its recent decision to partner with IBLP, because that relationship cements a "franchise-like approach . . . which helps maintain the integrity of the [Crossings] Program."

Both CCA's corporate headquarters and NMWCF's employees emphasized that everything that happens in the prison related to religious programming is voluntary; I was told that religious conversion was not a prerequisite for, or an end goal of, the program. One inmate in the program was absolutely convinced by this idea: "It's multifaith," she said of the Crossings Program. "Yes, we're Christian, but we would not turn anyone away."

But these statements are hard to believe upon closer examination of the materials the program uses.

"Have you received Jesus Christ as your personal savior?" reads one of the workbooks given to NMWCF prisoners. "The first function of faith is to believe in Christ for salvation," reads another section. "The Holy Spirit then takes up residence in your spirit and confirms that you are a Christian."

Despite what CCA officials say, the texts are intended to convert people to a fundamentalist interpretation of Christianity that revolves around a man named Bill Gothard.

Gothard, the unmarried real estate mogul at the head of the Illinois-based IBLP, has been in the business of American evangelism since 1964. Originally named the Institute in Basic Youth Conflicts, IBLP officially changed its name in 1990. All told, IBLP boasts that at least 2.5 million people have attended IBLP's seminars and ministries in the United States and many other countries, including Russia, Mongolia, Romania, and Taiwan.[5]

Gothard has gained success not only through his religious education programs and training centers, but also through an organization called the International Association of Character Cities (IACC) and its secular instruction program, Character First!, which is in wide use in many public institutions (including schools and city councils) across the United States. The IACC never publicizes its ties to the IBLP or Gothard, although this connection was made clear to me when I investigated a three-day IACC conference at the organization's Oklahoma City headquarters in 2005.[6]

The IBLP, on the other hand, makes no claims whatsoever of secularism, or even respect for other world religions or worldviews. Officially established "for the purpose of introducing people to the Lord Jesus Christ," IBLP declares that it does so by providing "training on how to find success by following God's principles found in Scripture."[7] That is to say Gothard's own interpretation of scripture, which represents an overtly patriarchal, hierarchical, and highly authoritarian interpretation of Jesus Christ's teachings.

To take but one example, Gothard's workbook materials distributed to the women in the NMWCF Crossings program includes a breakdown of "basic life principles," including "Moral Purity," "Yielding Rights," and "Proper Submission."

"Wives, submit yourselves unto your own husbands, as it is fit in the Lord," reads one of the biblical selections scattered throughout the IBLP workbooks. Emphasis is placed on "courting," rather than "dating," and on the need for Christians to respect, obey, and submit to church and government. These institutions and their rulers, as the workbooks explain, exist because of God's will. In one of the workbooks, women prisoners are told that "under extreme circumstances a wife may need to depart from her husband, but not to divorce him."

"Must we continue to respect an evil ruler as a minister of God?" reads one question in an IBLP workbook. ("*Yes*" is the answer.)

CCA has become so convinced of the power of the IBLP residential program that the company now plans to institute similar pods in every one of its owned prisons. As the nation's biggest private prison corporation, CCA now represents the fifth-largest prison system in the United States, with sixty-five thousand prisoner beds in sixty-four facilities—thirty-eight of which are company owned.

Legally, CCA is obligated to provide access to multifaith services where they are requested. But in selecting its religious "partners," CCA has opted exclusively for arrangements with Christian evangelical and fundamentalist groups. The vast majority of chaplains in CCA prisons are indeed Christian.

"It's difficult to find an imam or a rabbi for these positions," Lanz says, without a hint of irony.

The Life Principles Community/Crossings unit is clean, orderly, and decorated with handmade declarations of Christian love and obeisance. Scripture-based books and movies pack the shelves of a small library in the pod; prisoner cubicles are neat and colorful; and an invitingly intimate living-room area offers prisoners the comfort of couches, a microwave, and a decidedly peaceful ambience. As far as prison facilities go, this kind of environment is truly a rarity. Other pods in this prison are not as nicely furnished and are far more noisy and hectic. Some pods house nearly forty-five women, with one correctional officer on the floor trying to keep track of the women's movements. (Still, the relative comfort and privacy in the housing pods are far better than dismal women's prison conditions in neighboring states like Texas and Arizona, to say nothing of California's eight-women-to-a-cell "solution" to overcrowding.)

With thirty women in residence and another thirty-five on a waiting list, the Crossings pod is explicitly—and rigorously—religious. The program involves engaging in spiritual counseling and religious meetings, prayer walks, meditation, memorization of the New Testament, and 732 hours of activities ostensibly geared toward helping a woman succeed after her release from prison—with a mandate that the woman stays involved in a "faith community."

There is no regular television for the Crossings women, and no hip-hop or rock music to speak of. Even Christian rock music is explicitly frowned upon, in accordance with IBLP instructions. In one workbook, devotees are told that listening to rock music will lead to an addiction to it. "As in the case of a drug addict, a 'rock addict' will sacrifice God-given relationships with his parents and will neglect fellowship with Godly Christians in his compulsion to listen to his music. . . . Only God can free a 'rock addict' from the bondage of Satan's strongholds."

When the Crossings women join together to sing and dance to music, then, it is only to devotional music deemed appropriate. During my visit, several of the women performed expressive dances to such "approved" Christian songs as "I Can Only Imagine" and "Psalms Three," and the head of the choir got up to perform a vocal performance of "City Called Glory." The emotional intensity of these performances is clear; several women are, in fact, moved to tears. "It instills character in all of us," one inmate says. "It betters our lives through belief in God."

As for NMWCF's claim that the program is reducing recidivism, it is true that only a few women who graduated from that program have returned to prison. It is also true that those numbers are based on "graduates," not on the total number of women who have enrolled in the program and dropped out, or been removed for drug sales or using the program as a cover for other illicit activities.

Chaplain Compton says that she sees dramatic differences in the women who become a part of the Crossings program. The reason for the dramatic change, adds Compton, has everything to do with the transformative belief in a higher power.

"They realize that . . . they are helpless, and [that] God is in control if they allow him to be," says Compton.

Indeed, if the women do as they are told, they will be well on their way to turning themselves into obedient wives, daughters, and citizens who should never question authority.

"Telling these women to blindly submit to authority," responds FFRF's Gaylor, "is the worst kind of message to be sending to them."

Chapter 10: Shipping Women's Bodies

"It is an eighteen-hour round trip for us to [visit my sister]. I am nearly seventy, and my husband is seventy-two. There is no one else in the family close enough or physically able to make the trip to Florida. We live in South Carolina, and the rest of the family is in Virginia."
—Jane Young, sister of FCC Coleman (Florida) inmate Suzanne Thomas, who suffers from severe chronic pain, multiple injuries, neuropathy, and hepatitis B and C

"Our women have been moved around like chess pieces."
—Kat Brady, coordinator of the Community Alliance on Prisons in Honolulu, Hawaii

I t had already been an arduous, surreal journey for Hawaiian female prisoners sent to do their time on the mainland when they found themselves in a small, utterly foreign Southern town called Wheelright, Kentucky.

Among those women was Sarah Ah Mau, forty-three, one of the sixty-two Hawaiian female prisoners who first arrived in southern Texas in May 1997. From their island home, they had been transferred to the Crystal City Correctional

Center, roughly forty miles from the United States/Mexico border. According to prisoner and local news accounts, the facility was in dire shape, and the heat extremes were completely unfamiliar to the prisoners.

The prisoners, including Ah Mau, did what they could to fit in. Ah Mau gained the trust of the guards and facility officials, and was even allowed outside facility walls on work detail. The acclimation was short lived. In August 1998, all of the Hawaiian women were moved to the Central Oklahoma Correctional Facility (COCF), newly built by the Correctional Services Corporation, in the town of McLoud. The prisoners sent word back to Hawaii that the living conditions there were acceptable, even if they had yet to receive a visit from a single family member because of the cost and distance of travel.

But things went from tolerable to terrible in February 2003, when the Oklahoma Department of Corrections announced its intent to purchase the facility. By late summer of that year, the Hawaiian women reported to the Hawaii Department of Public Safety (DPS) that the overall operations and security at COCF were unbearable.[1] According to reports received by Kat Brady, coordinator of the Community Alliance on Prisons in Honolulu, the situation involved disgruntled unionized staff, lack of programs, sick-leave abuse, and "staff having sexual relationships with inmates."

The Hawaii DPS acted slowly eventually deciding against bringing the women home. Instead, the prisoners were moved yet again to another state. This time, they were sent to the Brush Correctional Facility (BCF) in Colorado, where the women found themselves with leaky rooftops, broken plumbing, a lack of drug treatment programs, and inadequate medical care.[2]

BCF prison employees were hired quickly and, as it turned out, without the requisite background checks. Allegations of sexual harassment and abuse were soon to follow. Initially dismissed by the GRW Corporation's internal investigators, many of the accusations turned out to be true. Not only had five convicted felons been hired as staff members, but four prison employees were soon charged with and convicted of criminal offenses ranging from running a cigarette smuggling ring to sexually abusing female prisoners. BCF's prison warden resigned and was later indicted as an accomplice in one of the sexual misconduct cases.[3]

It was clearly time to send the women somewhere else—that is, anywhere but back home, where Hawaii's sole female prison continued to pack three women into cells designed to accommodate one to two prisoners at most.[4]

Brady, who has stayed in continual contact with the female prisoners shipped out of Hawaii, says, "Most of these women would be better served in community programs to directly address their needs: drug addiction [and post-traumatic stress disorder] resulting from various forms of abuse and anger management."

The interstate transfers didn't stop there. The next stop for the Hawaiian women ended up in one of the most remote mainland locations imaginable. Located in the mountains of eastern Kentucky, Wheelwright (population 1,048) was once a successful coal-mining town with a Nashville Steel plant that employed three thousand people. That all changed in 1970, when the plant shut down; the town quickly dwindled in both population and resident income. Building a prison in 1993 on the site of a former coal camp seemed to be a great solution to this town's intractable problem of unemployment. Indeed, when the Corrections Corporation of America (CCA) bought the facility in 1999, the corporation quickly became the town's biggest employer.[5]

Private prisons know the advantages of moving into economically devastated rural communities—generous tax incentives, low construction costs, and a cheap labor market being key among them. Once the facilities are built, the private prison companies strive to keep them at maximum capacity.

That's exactly what CCA did with Otter Creek, initially bringing in male inmates from Indiana to fill the available cells. In July 2001, the Indiana prisoners staged a nine-hour riot, which was brought under control only after one hundred outside law enforcement officers had been brought in to subdue the prisoners. By 2005, Indiana had transferred the last of its state prisoners out of the facility, after which CCA converted Otter Creek into a 656-bed women's prison.[6]

Past riots weren't the concern of Hawaiian authorities—CCA was offering a great deal. According to the contract, each out-of-state inmate costs the State of Hawaii only $56 per day—compared to an on-island average of $108. (Entry-level guards make roughly $7.60 per hour.)[7] CCA also agreed that Hawaii could send out a new group of higher-security "close custody" inmates. Approximately forty such female prisoners were promptly shipped out to the CCA-run Otter Creek Correctional Center.

Today, female and male prisoners commonly find themselves commodities in the practice of interstate prison transfers. In 2006, the nation's most overcrowded state prison system, California's, finally gave in to the practice of shipping prisoners out of state resorting to mandatory transfers when they could not get enough "volunteers".[8] Many others, ranging from Washington state to Washington, D.C., have been doing so for many years.

If the fiscal bottom line is the primary consideration, it is particularly important for taxpayers to recognize the real potential for interstate transfers to have a damaging impact on the prisoners and their partners, children, and extended family members. Actual physical travel is usually cost prohibitive for the loved ones of prisoners—so much so that anecdotal evidence suggests that most prisoner families cannot visit out-of-state family members who are incarcerated. Letters are a good way of staying in touch, but where growing children are concerned, they are often insufficient to maintain and strengthen existing bonds. Telephone calls can help to strengthen such ties more directly, but they, unfortunately, are prohibitively expensive: Interstate phone calls can easily run from $20 to $40 for fifteen minutes.[9]

Another commonly overlooked dimension of interstate prison transfer is that the prisoners themselves are typically sent to culturally unfamiliar facilities, temperatures, and climates. Food can be so radically different from state to state (consider what a Hawaiian woman is accustomed to eating, compared with what a Tennessee state prison diet is likely to offer) that prisoners can stop eating altogether, or eat unhealthily by picking at their unfamiliar food. Prisoners sent interstate are supposed to be treated according to the laws and regulations granted by their home states. However, in my correspondence with both female and male inmates sent out of state, this appears to almost never be the case. Worse is that home-state law and prison regulation books are rarely available, making the prisoners' appeals or grievance requests even more difficult to file. Cultural unfamiliarity, distance, and detachment from family, isolation, and legal inequity—all of it adds up to an already bad formula for a prisoner's state of mind and overall well-being.

The results of a 1993 study on the recidivism rates of Hawaiian prisoners indicates how serious this issue is. The study found that *90 percent* of inmates sent to other states to do their time eventually returned to prison. (Those incarcerated in their home state had recidivism rates ranging from 47 to 57 percent.)[10]

Most of the prisoners transferred out of their home states (which include but are not limited to Alabama, Alaska, California, Colorado, North Dakota, Vermont, Washington, Washington, D.C., and Wyoming) end up in privately run facilities in rural communities. Typically, the guards hired for such prisons are undertrained and ill prepared for their stressful work environments. They are paid "fast-food restaurant wages," according to Ken Kopczynski, executive director of Private Corrections Institute (PCI), a prison watchdog group.

Incarcerated women in Alabama held at the notoriously decrepit and severely overcrowded Tutwiler Prison for Women—currently under federal court order to improve prison conditions—are now being shipped off to the Southwestern

Louisiana Correctional Facility in Basile, Louisiana. Run by LCS Corrections Services, the mixed-gender prison maintains that it keeps the men and women completely separate and charges the State of Alabama just $24 per day, per inmate. Starting pay for an LCS prison guard is $7 an hour, compared with $11 from the Alabama Department of Corrections.[11]

It would be one thing if the most violent or most difficult-to-manage inmates looking at long-term sentences were transferred out of the main prison because of the difficulty of maintaining them in the general inmate population. Instead, these women tend to be the "lowest-risk offenders," explains Gabriel Sayegh, director of the State Organizing and Policy Project for the New York–based Drug Policy Alliance. Typically, he says, the women are serving out nonviolent, drug-related sentences and are the most interested in accessing treatment and other programs available within a prison. The female prisoners who have been shipped to Louisiana feel as though they are being punished, rather than rewarded, for their good behavior in prison. The most common complaint has been that the women prisoners have very few family visits because of the distance required to travel from Alabama to Louisiana.

"My kids are the only thing that's helped me make it this two and a half years, the only thing that's kept me going," prisoner Kristie Godsey told *The Birmingham News*, referencing the fact that her parents have been unable to bring her daughters for a family visit. "How did we get chosen?" she pleaded. "We were the good inmates."[12]

Prisoners who end up in the federal system are very likely to experience interstate transfer during their incarceration, particularly if they are serving a longer sentence. Interstate placement decisions are made by the Federal Bureau of Prisons (BOP) without any apparent regard for the accessibility of prisoners' children, spouses, or extended family. Suzanne Thomas, fifty-six, is serving out a twenty-one-month sentence at FCC Coleman in central Florida. A first-time, nonviolent offender who lived in Virginia, Thomas was charged with money laundering for unwittingly accepting financial assistance from her younger son, who originally told Thomas that he had won the money gambling in Atlantic City. When it turned out that the money was from drug dealing, Thomas tried to stick with the story to protect her son. Her son was still indicted, and Thomas' house was brutally raided several times; in one such incident, the family dog was battered to the point of losing an eye.

Despite severe medical conditions caused by three near-fatal automobile accidents, the prosecutors went after Thomas. Her public defender took almost no interest in her case and convinced her to plead guilty, assuring her that she was likely to end up with home confinement. Instead, Thomas ended up with a twenty-one-month sentence and was shipped off to Florida.

"She has had numerous surgeries, and her spine is literally held together by metal rods, nuts, and bolts," explains her sister, Jane Young, who lives in South Carolina. "She contracted hepatitis B and C as a result of blood transfusions connected to the surgeries and now has peripheral neuropathy in addition to all the other problems."

To make matters worse, Thomas was prescribed improper blood pressure medications. Shortly thereafter, Thomas passed out, fell on a concrete prison floor, and cracked another vertebra and two ribs. She has suffered from a severe bladder infection that was allowed to progress, unchecked, for nearly four months, which has left Thomas unable to control her bladder. She now has osteoporosis and regular panic attacks, and she has lost a front tooth which the prison is unwilling to replace. But the worst thing, says Thomas, is being unable to see her low-income family except on rare occasion because of the sheer distance from South Carolina to Florida.

"It's so unreal," Thomas tells me. "They are simply not equipped for health problems here, and the BOP should not [transfer] prisoners here with those issues."

In many ways, Hawaii represents the most extreme example of these practices, because all of the transferred prisoners are sent far into the depths of the mainland. Today, Hawaii leads the nation in interstate prisoner transfers.[13] Nearly two thousand prisoners—roughly half of the state's adults convicted of felonies—are serving out their sentences in CCA-run prisons in Arizona, Kentucky, Mississippi, and Oklahoma. Notably, 41 percent of the "shipped" prisoners are indigenous Hawaiian natives, although they represent only 20 percent of the state's prison demographic.[14]

Such prisoners have no recourse for contesting their incarceration out of state. A 1983 U.S. Supreme Court ruling based on a Hawaiian prisoner's lawsuit held that prisoners have no right to be confined in a particular prison, region, or state. More recently, a Seventh Circuit Court of Appeals ruling reinforced that Supreme Court decision by deciding that parents in prison had no right to insist on staying in their home state for the sake of their children.[15] All subsequent legal challenges of out-of-state prison transfers have failed.

"These transfers are very problematic for a number of reasons," notes David Fathi of the ACLU's National Prison Project in Washington, D.C. "Visitation is all but impossible, and visitations are very important to prisoner mental health. [Visits] are usually correlated with positive prison adjustment behavior, as well as decreased recidivism rates."

These days, Otter Creek houses over 120 Hawaiian women alongside Kentucky state prisoners. Half of the Hawaiian women are serving crystal methamphetamine–related sentences, and most of them are incarcerated on nonviolent charges. Ninety-five percent of these women are mothers.[16] Not a single woman has gotten a visit from a child or other family member at the facility, and collect phone calls from the prison can run more than sixty cents per minute. Since arriving at Otter Creek, women at the facility have complained consistently about cold temperatures in cells, loss of property during their transfers, racial and sexual harassment, bizarre medical care and commissary hours (2:00–4:00 AM), and "drinking" water that has caused widespread diarrhea and vomiting.

Among other scandals that have begun to emerge from that facility, Eldon Tackett, a forty-three-year-old guard at Otter Creek, was accused of providing food and candy to a female prisoner in exchange for oral sex. In addition, the Kentucky-based *Floyd County Times* reported that Otter Creek's drug counselor, Tanya Crum, thirty-two, had been arrested for trafficking in methadone.[17]

Kat Brady, coordinator of the Hawaii-based Community Alliance for Prisoners, has been corresponding with both the inmates and their families. Brady was alarmed to find out that prisoners are regularly threatened with Administrative Segregation if they complain about medical conditions. In one situation, a Hawaiian inmate, who asked to remain nameless, wrote to Brady that she was constantly coughing up blood and had repeatedly asked for medical assistance. When the medical unit at the prison finally saw her, she was given a nasal moisturizer and told she simply had a sinus infection. The prisoner's condition worsened, and she was eventually rushed to the Hazard Regional Medical Center—in leg shackles and at gunpoint. The inmate had to have emergency surgery; one lung had completely filled with blood. Prison officials then ignored a follow-up appointment scheduled by the surgeon until Brady intervened on the woman's behalf. Another female inmate, who also requested anonymity, told prison staff about severe chest, arm, and leg pain for several months, only to be told that she would be placed in Administrative Segregation if she continued to complain. When she was eventually taken to the hospital in critical condition, triple bypass heart surgery had to be performed.[18]

It's possible that all of this would have escaped notice had it not been for Sarah Ah Mau. Ah Mau, serving a life sentence for second-degree murder, had been incarcerated since 1993. She had a shot at parole eligibility in August 2008. But in November 2005, Ah Mau started experiencing severe gastrointestinal distress. Family members, fellow prisoners, and Brady's contact with the prison itself suggest that Ah Mau's pleas for medical care were ridiculed, downplayed, or outright ignored by prison employees. As her stomach distended—and other body parts began to swell visibly—prisoners say that Ah Mau was fed castor oil and told to stop complaining unless she wanted to face disciplinary action. On New Year's Eve 2005, after two days in critical condition, her complaining stopped: Ah Mau was dead, of "unexplained" causes, at the age of forty-three.[19]

Ah Mau's death could likely have been prevented if her cries for help had been heeded when she began to show signs of severe physiological distress. Perhaps Ah Mau would have survived, or perhaps she would have died eventually from complications of whatever the underlying issues were. But the sluggish response and amateur medical "treatment" of her critical issues are inexcusable, even at the most surface level of analysis. (As of this writing, a plodding investigation into her death is still under way.)

Back in Hawaii, Ah Mau's death made the news but was not enough to warrant any kind of change in the state's policy on the interstate transfer of female prisoners. Apparently, this is the kind of price that many state correctional systems are willing to pay for the convenience of shipping women's bodies to the lowest bidder. All too often, cost-cutting measures for swelling prison budgets come before the dignity, safety, and well-being of the country's captives, whose very lives, as we see again and again, have been reduced simply to numbers of one kind or another.

Chapter 11: International Lockup

"If you're spending a lot of money on the corrections budget,
you've failed on the front end."
—Matt Lang, deputy warden, Alouette Correctional Centre for
Women, British Columbia, Canada

"God forbid that any of us are ever locked up in a jail or prison cell.
But if it ever happens, be very thankful that it's in the U.S.A."
—James A. Gondles, executive director of the American Correctional Association

C rime and punishment are not unique to America, but the American approaches to both *are* unique in this day and age.

Our nation's policies toward minor, nonviolent, and self-harming crimes
such as injection drug use and our severe and unforgiving punishment of even
our youngest, sickest, and oldest citizens, have put us at the very top of the world's
per capita imprisonment list, far surpassing China, Russia, Iran, and other countries that *we* have long derided for their governance and punishment practices. The

United States imprisons at least ten times more female prisoners than all Western European countries combined.[1]

For the purposes of comparison, however, it is most useful to look at those countries that espouse the ideals of some form of representative democracy. To be sure, no country in the Western world has found an ideal response to antisocial or otherwise dangerous criminal behavior. Mimicry of other systems should never be any nation or region's goal, as cultural differences and definitions of criminality are hardly monolithic—and attempts to make them so are bound to backfire. Some universal standards would, of course, be a boon to international human rights, although our world is still far from realizing such a goal.

In our own society, I personally would prefer to see the decriminalization or legalization of drug use (including a harm-reduction approach to people who are actively using drugs); the legalization of all forms of consensual sex (including sex work, except in cases where women or men are not selling their own sexual services, but are being "pimped out" by someone else); far more opportunities for truly therapeutic rehabilitation; prevention- and intervention-minded counseling; real vocational training (with real-world applicability); and regular and fair parole review. I would also prefer to see a deemphasis on petty infractions that worsen and lengthen a person's period of imprisonment; a deeper understanding of the role of abuse and domestic violence in nonviolent and violent crimes; and, yes, the arrest and incarceration of truly antisocial, predatory, violent people in society until they can be rehabilitated—or else watched over, according to the international rules governing humane captivity, for as long as is necessary.

In this sense, I am not an advocate of complete prison abolition, which I have heard some of my peers on the left posit as the logical solution to our sky-high imprisonment rates. At this chaotic point in American history, I think such a concept is absurdly unrealistic. Having witnessed the intergenerational impact of brutal, repeat crimes in society, and having spoken to and seen the cold remove of a few male killers and rapists in prison, I can say that prisons have a limited purpose in our society. At the same time, I strongly believe in the mass decarceration of male and female prisoners alike. We need only a small fraction of the nearly 5,000 jails and prisons that we have built across the nation, and our sentencing policies and approaches toward nonviolent, addiction-based, abuse-reactive, or self-destructive acts must be radically reconceptualized.

An exhaustive study of the criminal justice policies of Western nations does not fit into the scope of this work, but my visits to international women's prisons gave me great insight into what other methods of incarceration for women might actually be possible.

Looking into what other countries do with their jails and prisons—and how they do it—won't actually hurt or endanger us in any fashion. Yet it often seems as though we treat any external information as a threat to the premise that our methods of democracy and the way we "fight crime" are the only right ways to go about it. This is a curiously insular way of dealing with American mass incarceration, as it is one of the most serious and costly issues confronting our nation here and now.

Women's incarceration is no exception. In fact, looking at how other countries treat one of the most vulnerable groups in prison can give us particular insight into the underlying issues of mental illness, self-destructive impulses and actions, histories of abuse, and other common factors in the lives of females in the criminal justice system.

For these reasons, I decided to travel abroad to three women's prisons in three different countries—Canada, Finland, and the United Kingdom—to see how their approaches and priorities might differ from or mirror ours. I expected to see some of both, but what I witnessed surprised me to a greater extent than I had imagined.

Before getting into the specifics of these experiences, I should note that my visits to these women's prisons are not intended in any fashion to represent the entirety of those nations' respective prison systems, and certainly not those of the entire European Union. The United Kingdom, for instance, has numerous women's prisons, although Holloway is indeed its biggest (as well as the largest women's prison in all of the European Union). Unlike the other two countries I chose for comparison, Canada has two prison systems, provincial and federal, similar to the state and federal systems within the United States. (The prison that I visited was a provincial one.) One of the biggest differences between these three countries is that Finland has only one "closed" women's prison, which is to say a prison where women are locked up behind a strict perimeter. Finland also has "open" prisons that allow prisoners a far greater degree of movement and prison staff far less control over their activities, employment, possessions, and interactions with their families and the public.

A far more effective way of making a comparison is to look both at the per capita rates of incarceration and at what percentage of prisoners are women. Counting both genders, we know that the United States locks up 750 per 100,000 residents.[2] England and Wales imprison 148 per 100,000, while Canada's rate is 129 per 100,000. Finland comes in at 75 per 100,000. (Only Norway is lower, at 66 per 100,000.)[3] Notably, all of the countries I visited were experiencing faster growth rates of women's incarceration as compared to men's rates of incarceration, just as is the case in the United States.[4]

In the United States, women in both state and federal prisons represent 7.2 percent of the total prison population, and 13 percent of the total jail population.[5] The countries that I picked for comparison had lower percentages than ours, but not significantly so. Women constitute 5.5 percent of all prisoners in the United Kingdom, just over 6 percent of prisoners in Finland, and exactly

5 percent of prisoners in Canada.[6] Throughout the European Union, the percentage of women in the entire prison population has a wide range, from just above 2 percent (in northern Ireland) to nearly 9 percent (in the Netherlands). Only Portugal matches our rate exactly.[7]

Yet these kinds of statistics constitute just a small part of the total picture of female incarceration in Europe and Canada. My in-person visits helped to complete that picture through the experience of walking through prison yards, talking with and noting the behavior of prisoners and correctional employees (including guards, counselors, and medical staff). I also made a point of examining the condition of housing units and individual cells (including segregation units and cells) to observe whether women were allowed to express their individuality, culture, or religion though their clothing, hairstyles, makeup, and jewelry, and to examine the cleanliness of kitchens and the quality of prisoners' meals.

Before I share a few of my experiences from these international prison travels, I want to note that every one of these facilities not only accepted, but actually welcomed, my visit. This receptiveness contrasted sharply with the guarded concern, hesitation, and delays I encountered at many U.S. prisons and jails. (For instance, even though I had planned a visit to a Memphis women's prison, the staff failed to respond to my visitation request until after my trip was supposed to happen, while one of the biggest federal women's prisons, FCI Danbury, refused my visit altogether based on unexplained "security" reasons.)

None of the international prisons asked me to clear a background check, although I was certainly asked to present my passport at each location, and every prison asked my publisher to send a letter verifying that I was writing a book on the subject.

Officials in these countries allowed me, an outsider, into their prisons with no restrictions whatsoever in terms of what I was allowed to see, ranging from segregation units to lifer wards. Administrators did not even broach the idea that I would be limited in terms of whom I would be able to talk to—whether inmates, guards, or other prison employees—although some concern was expressed at Holloway about my talking with clearly mentally disturbed prisoners in states of agitation. If I requested a private, one-on-one interview with a prisoner or staff member, that request was granted without hesitation or a time limit.

I asked prisoners directly, independent of prison-employee supervision, whether any kind of cleanup had been ordered before my arrival. I found out that my visit had not been announced to anyone outside of the high-ranking prison officials with whom I had been corresponding and certain categories of prisoners with whom I had stated in advance that I wanted to spend some time, particularly recovering drug addicts in Finland. On the day of my visit, Holloway did announce the fact that I would be touring their prison, on a screen in the waiting room that stated my name, my city of origin, and the fact that I was authoring a book on women in prison. (This video screen was seen only by visitors and prison employees coming to work in the morning, not by inmates.)

Every facility was willing to share the materials and statistics that I requested, to respond quickly to my follow-up questions, and to discuss the aspects of their prisons that they found problematic or that they felt needed improvement. I also noticed some aspects of the prisons that I found either remarkably progressive or obviously regressive, although prison employees did not point them out. I was allowed to photograph the outside and inside of all three of the prisons, with the logical exceptions of control rooms handling security operations, close-up shots of locking mechanisms for cells and units, and prisoners without their express permission. By contrast, most prisons and jails in the United States did not allow any photography, with the exception of the women's prisons in Washington and New Mexico. Last, I found it interesting that all of the officials at the international prisons asked me if I would be willing to discuss what I thought about their prisons compared with detention facilities in the United States and abroad, something that I was rarely asked to do in the United States.

Here, then, are the highlights of my visits to the three women's prisons in the United Kingdom, Finland, and Canada.

HOLLOWAY PRISON (LONDON, ENGLAND)

Holloway used to be the United Kingdom's most notorious women's prison.

In truth, it still is. During my few days in England in the summer of 2006, locals at pubs, shops, or restaurants occasionally asked me if I was in their country for business or pleasure. When I responded that I was there to visit Holloway Prison, every single woman and man looked at me with an expression of shock and a fair amount of alarm. "Why would you want to go there?" was the most common response.

Some asked if I had a family member incarcerated at Holloway; others seemed to assume that I must be a bit daft, or at least confused about what I was actually getting myself into. A lengthier explanation of my research usually allayed some of their concerns, but the sense that Holloway has a scary reputation stuck nonetheless.

Holloway's notoriety, as I was to find out, was warranted not too long ago, but was completely divorced from the actual experience of the prison in the present day, a disconnect that was largely attributable to the leadership of the prison's new governor, Tony Hassall. (In the United Kingdom, a prison governor is the equivalent of a warden in the United States.)

A look back at British history a few hundred years ago reveals the genesis of Holloway's terrible reputation. In the late 1700s and very early 1800s, prison conditions in England were absolutely deplorable. Inmates lived in filth, sickness, and iron shackles; were fed horrible food; and were subject to all manner of abuses, including whippings, beatings, and death on the gallows. These conditions began to elicit concern as early as 1811, particularly as a result of Quaker emphasis on the potential of all human beings to seek and attain an "inner light," despite the nature of their crimes. The protofeminist Quaker Elizabeth Fry began to work directly with female prisoners, bringing them clothing and supportive sermons, as well as agitating publicly for reform in the prison system.[8]

The ensuing period of prison reform had numerous glitches along the way, as the British government continued to experiment with myriad systems of discipline and attempted reformation, many of which were truly oppressive in nature. These approaches included complete solitary confinement for the entire duration of a prisoner's sentence; exercise and movement through the prison with dark hoods on to prevent any awareness of one's surroundings; and mandated silence between prisoners at all times, even at work and in religious services. The practice, emulated widely throughout the Western world (including in the United States), finally began to lose favor when prisoners began to kill themselves in large numbers, or else go insane and never recover from the experience.[9] This moment in Western penological history appears to have temporarily affected the imposition of extended periods of solitary confinement. Regrettably, this practice made a complete rebound by the end of the twentieth century. (This time around, the use of modernized "control units" to punish people for any range of violations was expanded to imprisoned juveniles and women.)

In this historical context, British experiments with punishment and incarceration led to the 1851 opening of Holloway as a prison for both women and men (including such notable "deviants" as Oscar Wilde). Holloway did not become an all-women's prison until 1903. Among other kinds of female debtors and women deemed unfit for society, suffragettes were incarcerated at Holloway in great numbers. When I peered from a second-floor stairwell into the one remaining section of the original Victorian structure—a comfortable, well-kept yard with green shrubbery and the sight of women lounging, conversing, and smoking cigarettes—I was informed that this very same yard was the one where advocates for women's rights were once strung up, hosed with water, force-fed, and hung. The last woman was hung in the yard as recently as July 1955.[10]

The Holloway Prison of the 1990s and the very early part of the twenty-first century improved somewhat, but it's no wonder that the prison maintained its reputation. Cells and housing units were filthy and full of vermin, the food was below par, and guards were known for bullying prisoners and spouting racist comments. Northern Irish women who were part of the resistance against British occupation were also imprisoned here and were reportedly subjected to all kinds of abuse. In 1995, Her Majesty's Chief Inspector of Prisons (an entity completely separate from Her Majesty's Prison Service, with keys to all prisons and full rights to walk into any prison and report publicly any findings) walked out during an inspection in protest of and sheer disgust with the conditions at Holloway.[11]

Six years later, Chief Inspector David Ramsbotham was quoted as saying that the Holloway Prison was "virtually unmanageable" and that women did not need the same level of security as men. Their continued incarceration under strict prison conditions, he added, amounted to a "waste of public money."[12] Small wonder that this prison was the original inspiration for the award-winning BBC television series *Bad Girls,* which has aired since 1999. The show's three creators are all self-described feminists who have pronounced their opposition to the continued incarceration of nonviolent female offenders.[13] Although the television show does tread into overly sensational material and does exaggerate the notion that female prisons are truly dangerous places, the issues it raises fairly depict aspects of women's emotional and physical struggles before and during incarceration.

By 2004, both public and governmental pressure forced serious changes at Holloway, including the firing of numerous guards and other prison employees. The changes also included a complete overhaul of prison medical and mental healthcare and in-prison social services, as well as the hiring of more ex-offenders, women, and ethnic minorities on par with their representation in London. (Female prison guards now account for 67 percent of the correctional workforce at Holloway.) Internal audits became par for the course, in addition to regular civilian oversight visits and reviews. Another thing that I had never seen before was the ongoing presence of "family tours," which are intended to give prisoners' loved ones an idea of what the facility really looks like.

As such, my introduction to this British women's prison was far removed from its justifiably poor reputation of yore. Many of the most significant changes at Holloway have been the direct result of the new governor, Tony Hassall, and his emphasis on structural reform.

From Hassall's perspective, what happens to women when they're released should never be an afterthought, but a primary, guiding consideration that informs the programs available to them while they are still incarcerated. Furthermore, the idea that any woman should have to endure sexual violence, racism, xenophobia, or any form of cruelty in her punishment is clearly unacceptable under the new leadership at Holloway, something that is apparent all the way from the prison administrators to the prison guards.

Under Hassall's leadership, a library carrying newspapers and books in languages ranging from Amharic to Hindi was expanded, and classrooms and recreational facilities were upgraded, including the renovation of a generous-size gymnasium with a volleyball net and basketball court, as well as a large swimming pool. Prison grounds beautification had clearly become a priority, tended to by prisoners who are allowed to work without supervision.

In response to an ever-increasing population of non–English speaking detainees, multilingual computerized booths were installed. The prison offers regular, open access to all manner of religious services, ranging from the various Christian denominations to ceremonies for Rastafarians and Sikhs. Because many prisoners were suffering from poor nutrition and diet-related problems with their weight, Hassall and his administrative team helped to ensure that prison meals were improved substantially, to include fresh vegetables and fruits, as well as many dinner options and vegetarian options—most notably to the extent that correctional employees actually started eating some of the same food served to inmates. The prison canteen changed from carrying nothing but junk food to offering fresh food and products for ethnic minorities, ranging from halal food to cosmetics and hair products for women of color.

Perhaps most significant, prison employees have been given strict training about the unacceptability of racism (whether in the ranks or toward prisoners), as well as a far deeper understanding of women's emotional needs, including the mechanisms of self-harm and suicide prevention. A more finely tuned grievance process has also been instituted—including confidential reporting about any of kind of racist or sexual statement or physical attack.

"We encourage people to complain, because it's healthy," Governor Hassall told me. "We investigate every single complaint," he added. His assertion was backed by a comprehensive audit that I obtained of the prison's response to inmate grievances.

The last account of sexually inappropriate behavior had taken place approximately ten years prior to my visit, when a male guard was fired for indecent exposure. He was fired promptly. Governor Hassall and other staff explained that there had not been a single incident of a reported rape in anyone's recent memory, although it is problematic that the prison still considers some sexual contact between prisoners and staff to be "consensual" and not subject to punishment, if both parties agree on this. If the sexual contact is unwanted, it is immediately reported to the police. A woman who reports such a crime is never placed into solitary confinement pending an investigation, as is common practice in the United States, although a prisoner can be moved to another prison for her safety.

Governor Hassall also created a "first-night center," a quiet, peaceful unit in a separate area of the prison that allows incoming prisoners to be gently introduced to the experience of incarceration. Upon their arrival, women are given information about how the prison operates, what services are available to them, and how the grievance and appeal process works. Guards assigned to this unit are specially trained in suicide and self-harm prevention, as one-third of all suicides in U.K. prisons take place within the first week after a prisoner is locked up.[14]

Even outside the first-night center, prison guards and the equivalent of unit captains have been trained in suicide prevention and the concept of "trigger points" for women with histories of self-harm. A "listener" program was also instituted in the prison, so that female prisoners can place a crisis call that goes straight to the room of a trained prisoner, who will respond at any time of the day or night. Listeners are trained in providing nonjudgmental emotional support, suicide prevention, and active listening. Moreover, the listeners are strictly forbidden to report anything to staff that they hear from prisoners who request their help.

Unfortunately, this support network has not stemmed the frequency of cutting incidents, which happen at an alarming rate of seventy-one serious incidents per month, out of a total prison population of roughly five hundred women. While I was at Holloway, prison staff mentioned that a woman had cut herself so severely that blood was flowing out of her cell, although I was not witness to the sight. There had been numerous additional suicide attempts already by the summer of 2006, when I visited; By June 2007, six women had killed themselves in British prisons.[15]

I sat down to talk with one prison guard, Sue Chatten, who had taken it upon herself to focus particularly on self-harming women. Above and beyond her regular, paid work hours, Chatten often stayed after hours to talk to women in various states of distress, and women with whom she had made considerable progress in getting them to begin recognizing their value as human beings.

One imprisoned woman, Chatten recalled, indicated that she had been rejected for most of her life by the people around her. She was particularly prone to constant self-mutilation, something that is tended to medically but never punished by the prison. Chatten's intensive conversations with the woman, and her concern for the woman's well-being, seemed to pay off. One day, Chatten recalled with a smile, the woman wondered aloud why Chatten hadn't simply "given up" on her. "I told her that she was worth it," Chatten said, adding that she wouldn't give up on her, no matter how much she tried to push away the help.

To address this high level of self-destructive impulses at Holloway, support groups and individual counseling opportunities have been enhanced to include groups that promote understanding and alternatives to self-harm (cutting, burning, tearing out hair, scratching skin, banging one's head against the wall, and so on). Other groups are designed to help women heal from trauma and grief related to domestic and sexual violence. The prison also offers drug/alcohol relapse prevention groups; voluntary drug testing to help provide women with an incentive to stay clean without fearing punishment; and harm reduction–minded support groups, which operate on the premise that some women will continue to use drugs in prison. The prisoner's approach is that the damage women do to themselves can be minimized by educating them about cleaning needles and gradually reducing their substance dependency. While the goal is to get women to stop using drugs, these support groups do not insist on immediate abstinence as a precondition for participation. Drug "amnesty" drop boxes are also placed throughout the facility, so that women can deposit their illicit drugs without fear of repercussion if they decide to go clean.

Holloway has a dedicated detox unit, which serves roughly 250 women annually as they withdraw from opiates and other drugs. Regular medical supervision is a part of the process, and opiate substitutes are administered through a pharmacy window. As I expected, the feeling inside the detox unit was one of chaotic, emotional intensity. One woman sat moaning on the floor of a hallway while she rocked back and forth uncontrollably. The staff assigned to this unit did not take an aggressive attitude toward her. A male prison guard, for instance, was being harassed by a woman making irrational demands. He spoke to her firmly but calmly, and told her to settle down. After a few seconds of staring at him defiantly, the woman's tough veneer faded, and she started cracking jokes.

"Once you get past the bullshit," the guard said frankly, "they're brilliant. They've got untold talent, and we've just got to find it."

Other programs at the prison include art and drama therapy, prenatal care, yoga, baby massage, basic education and literacy, computer studies, life skills, mathematics, meditation, pottery, and creative writing. Prominent flyers are now posted throughout every hallway of the prison, explaining that racism or sexual abuse in any form is not tolerated (whether against prisoners or staff), and grievance forms are widely available.

Women prisoners wear their own clothes (with obvious restrictions surrounding overly revealing outfits), as do prison employees who are not guards. Both can wear their own style of makeup and jewelry, and can sport various hairstyles and colors. (A hair salon within the prison, Hairy Poppins, is a very popular spot.) Roughly 10 percent of the prison population—those preparing to transition into the "free world"—is allowed to leave the prison for outside work. Because they do not wear prison uniforms or any other identifiers of their status as prisoners, they are indistinguishable from civilians. In the last several years, not a single woman has absconded from the prison after being let out to work.

Unlike many U.S. prisons, Holloway is actually located on a very busy street, accessible by the underground subway and several bus lines. This struck me immediately as a completely different experience from my travels to American prisons, which are typically located in distant, remote towns, often with no form of public transit running anywhere near the facilities, making it difficult, if not impossible, for low-income families without cars (or with several jobs) to visit their loved ones.

At Holloway, there is no fence around the perimeter, no barbed wire, and no guards posted outside, although entrance into the prison involves a security check through two sets of locked doors. Visitors are not subject to walk through a metal detector, pat-downs, or examinations of their belongings or clothing, although a drug-detecting dog is occasionally walked through the visiting room. Touching is permitted between prisoners and their loved ones, although the line is drawn at any kind of sexual contact. A small tea shop is located in the visiting room, complete with scones and other edibles. Children coming to visit their mothers are received in a separate area, filled with stuffed animals, games, and toys, where guards wear civilian clothes so as not to traumatize them further than they might already be by having their mothers removed from their lives. Armed guards are unheard of (in fact, the staff expressed dismay that weapons of any kind even existed in American women's prisons), although protective gear, shields, and pepper spray are available if a cell extraction is ordered.

Segregation units at the prison, however, are as dismal as any I've seen. The ones at Holloway were particularly dingy and reeked of cigarette smoke. The major distinction is that women are not allowed to spend long periods of time in these cells—certainly not for the months and years forced on American prisoners—and are first adjudicated in an official hearing overseen by two officers. The prisoner is always allowed to bring written statements and witnesses to this hearing.

My tour of the prison's Mother and Baby Unit was particularly illuminating. While it had a rather narrow corridor and was certainly a bit too small for the thirteen women and their children, the unit was spotless and furnished with comfortable beds, changing rooms, play areas, couches, and a flower-filled outside yard. Holloway's Mother and Baby Unit allows women to keep their babies from birth to the age of nine months, while the country's other five women's prisons that have their own mother–baby units allow newborns to live with their moms until the age of eighteen months.

Not all women, of course, are allowed to keep their children, particularly if they test positive for drug use, if they have violent histories of abusing their children, if their babies are born very unhealthy, or if the women initiate fights with other women or staff in the unit. In fact, when I walked in, there was a fair amount of tension over the fact that some women did not want to attend a prisonwide meeting because they wanted to spend time with their children. Staff members were trying to negotiate a resolution, actually looking more upset than the mothers themselves at the temporary flare-up of emotion.

One of the most interesting aspects of this program for mothers and their babies is that it was designed around the realization that prison is not an ideal environment for babies to spend their first few months in. The obvious need for a mother–child bond was, of course, recognized as a good thing, completely contrary to the common practice in the United States of separating mothers from their babies at birth. The primary concern was actually that babies were not hearing and smelling the city into which they would eventually be transferred. The resolution of this concern was one that I hadn't considered before: Staff or volunteers take the babies outside in carriages. This way, the infants can hear traffic noises and the buzz of conversations, and can feel sunshine, fresh air, and drizzle on their faces.

All in all, I had never seen anything like this set of programs and services in any prison, male or female, and could barely contain my sense of curiosity about how a prison had made such a radical transformation in a short period of time. As we sat in his office to talk and drink the customary cup of English tea, Governor Hassall explained that the changes had not been made without rather heavy resistance from the Prison Service, as the plethora of new programs and services, and the obvious relaxation of a security-oriented prison, were seen as affronts to the very purpose of incarceration. "I knew what needed to be done," he told me, "and I was willing to face the consequences."

As it turned out, those consequences were minimal. Aside from a few vocal detractors in the public and the Prison Service, Governor Hassall got the green light for most of what he wanted to put in place. By his own admission, Holloway Prison is far from perfect, and many of its inherent problems stem from larger issues not unlike the inherent problems of America's criminal justice system.

For one thing, the United Kingdom's prison rates continue to grow year by year, and the women's incarceration growth rate has surpassed that of the men's, tripling from 1995 to 2005. (There are now over 4,300 women in the Prison Service's "Women's Estate.") Among incarcerated women, 80 to 90 percent are imprisoned for nonviolent crimes. Shoplifting is the primary reason why women are sent to prison, followed by drugs and prostitution. Recidivism rates are almost as high as those in our country: Over half of female ex-offenders are arrested again and convicted within two years of release.[16] Women sentenced to life (although there is no such thing as life without the possibility of parole in the United Kingdom) are almost always people who have killed their batterers, according to Hassall.

As is true in the United States, people of color (known as BMEs, for "black and minority ethnic groups") are disproportionately represented in England's jails and prisons. My visit to Holloway did reveal a large number of incarcerated black women—certainly higher than their demographic representation in England—but whites were still in the majority. Inclusive of both men and women, black people in England are six times more likely to be sent to prison than whites and are more likely to be imprisoned for a first offense than any other group.[17]

In terms of the actual living conditions at Holloway, there are aspects that are far healthier than any women's prison I have visited in the United States, including relative freedom of movement within the prison, comfortable grounds, humane and compassionate treatment across the board, the seriousness with which complaints are taken, and bona fide efforts toward resettling women after their release. Although some women are released without permanent housing, they never go without access to healthcare and some source of food, shelter, and social services.

On the negative end, the women at Holloway complained of not being able to shower regularly, and of the difficulty of obtaining enough sanitary pads and toiletries. Although the prison was not overcrowded, there was an expectation that that might soon be the case, as the British government was in the process of instituting the unfortunate strategy of moving noncriminal immigrants awaiting hearings or deportations into female and male criminal prisons. Overall, there did appear to be a shortage of staff, and adequate ramps and facilities for the disabled were noticeably lacking. In the lifer unit, inmates were allowed to decorate their units beautifully, to possess refrigerators, irons and ironing boards, carpets and curtains, and to live in relative comfort, peace, and solitude (if they so chose). But the remainder of the one-to-two-woman cells were rather dismal and dark, and horribly hot in the summertime (and, prisoners told me, far too cold in the winter). Cell drapes, beds, linens, and towels looked old and worn, and the long, dungeonlike hallways of the prison gave the indoor environment an eerie, mazelike feel.

In its strongest parallel with the United States, the United Kingdom has gravitated toward the regrettable practice in its criminal justice system of locking up far too many mentally ill persons, something that has sparked the greatest degree of public debate, especially in relation to the imprisonment of women and juveniles. According to reports, at least 70 percent of women in British prisons are mentally ill, and nearly 40 percent have tried to commit suicide. As is the case in the United States, at least half have been the victims of various forms of childhood abuse and/or domestic violence.[18]

A March 2007 editorial in the *Guardian* about the "Corston Report," regarding the plight of particularly vulnerable women in jails and prisons, summed up what seems to be an increasingly common sentiment in the United Kingdom: "Hell would freeze over before this government decided to close any prisons, but that should not detract from the message of this important review. Anybody with clear sight of the female penal estate knows that it incarcerates some of the most vulnerable and damaged members of society. A tour of any women's jail will produce sights and sounds that would cause a dry-stone wall to weep."[19]

HÄMEENLINNA PRISON (FINLAND)

Not so long ago, Finland's criminal justice system had a great deal in common with that of the United States. By the mid-1960s, this small Nordic country wedged between Sweden and Russia, with its own distinct (non-Scandinavian) language and fierce history of struggling for independence, had gone the route of heavy incarceration as a way of dealing with social ills. Chief among them were public drunkenness and all manner of nonviolent and violent crimes related to drinking.

The next thirty years saw Finland and the United States go in divergent directions. Violent crime had continued to go up in the two nations, but Finland decided to take a different approach from that of the American cousins that they (otherwise) admired so tremendously. Sentencing alternatives, victim restitution, intensive rehabilitation, treatment for the mentally ill, and reductions in the length of prison sentences cut Finnish incarceration by more than half and led to a decrease in crime, just as the United States was embarking on its multidecade strategy of prison-building and imprisoning people to fill those prisons.

Finland's prison population has begun to creep up in the last few years, but not dramatically so. In 2003, the total prison population (out of a nation of just slightly more than five million people) stood at 3,650. In 2006, that number had grown by a couple hundred, to 3,848, inclusive of both genders. There were 198 women locked up in 2003. In 2006, there were 245.

In a country of more than five million people, this number is notably low. Alternatives to sentencing are still a national priority. Central to the success of this idea is Finland's social welfare model, based on the premise that most people do become decent and productive citizens if given the necessary resources for healthy emotional and educational development, access to medical care and counseling, and the basic essentials of housing, food, and clothing. This is not to say that Finland is without its problems, but it is fair to say that overincarceration is not among those concerns.

With this in mind, I eagerly awaited my visit inside Finland's only "closed" women's prison. I was born in the country in 1970 and can still speak the language (albeit with occasional flaws in my diction and what seems like the vocabulary of a tenth grader). From Kouvola, a city close to the simple family cabin in Iitti where I go each summer, I hopped on a train to Hämeenlinna (the name of the city and the prison). From there, it was a fifteen-minute, scenic taxi ride to the facility that incarcerates separately both women and men.

Finland's prisons are run by the Prison Service of the Ministry of Justice, which also oversees probation, postrelease care and supervision, and alternative sentencing, such as community service and victim restitution. Altogether, there are seventeen "closed" prisons in Finland, as well as fifteen "open" prisons, which allow prisoners to leave daily for work and do not have security perimeters akin to those of the "closed" prisons. The nation's only mental hospital for prisoners is designed specifically for people who have committed crimes and are deemed too mentally ill to be placed in the general prison population, and there is one National Hospital Prison, adjacent to the Hämeenlinna prison.

The Hämeenlinna prison itself is located in a heavily wooded area, with only one security checkpoint. Here, as elsewhere, no cell phones or weapons are allowed inside, but there were otherwise no restrictions on my clothing or what I was allowed to carry on my person. The prison guards themselves wear comfortable uniforms and are not even equipped with pepper spray. Only women guards are allowed within the housing units where female prisoners live, with no exceptions.

My tour guide for the day, Anne Salmi, an educator and twenty-six-year veteran of the prison system, greeted me with the kind of formality and restrained demeanor to which I have long been accustomed in Finland. After all, this is a country where unnecessary smiles and conversation are shunned but civility and kindness are not. Our day started out promptly with the customary cup of Finnish coffee; the ritualistic nature of these kinds of caffeinated meetings throughout Europe and Canada has always struck me as an interesting way to defuse nervousness or conversational hesitation. Salmi is fluent in both English and Finnish, which made our conversation—or, more specifically, my kind of "Finnglish"—go smoothly.

"This is my life's work," Salmi explained to me right away. "I don't expect miracles from the women that I work with, because it is all about small steps."

Salmi's role at the prison is clearly more than that of a woman who oversees the educational programs for female prisoners. She serves a multipurpose function as counselor and confidant to prisoners and correctional employees alike, moving through the prison grounds with an air of easy confidence. This has been her "second home" for so long that it shows. Given the opportunity, Salmi made it clear early on that she had no interest in becoming a guard, a position that she saw as necessary but unfulfilling in terms of her desire to expand her knowledge and interact meaningfully with female prisoners.

The Hämeenlinna prison is not as small as one would expect for containing only a few hundred prisoners. The corridors are long, and the downstairs areas of the prison are filled with large-scale sewing and laundry operations, as well as extensive crafts workshops for men and women alike. Several classrooms, a cosmetology school, and a mother–baby unit are also part of the prison.

Women and men do not share housing units or cooking or working facilities, but they do wait in line for medical care in the same hallway and take educational classes together. "Doesn't that pose problems?" I asked. "Don't the men and women get distracted by each other's company?"

"Yes, of course, we have prisoners who fall in love," Salmi said, slightly bemused by the question itself.

And that seemed to be the extent of her concern—if that was even a concern to begin with. Sexual contact is forbidden in prison, but the prison staff just took flirtation and attraction to be parts of human nature.

Female prisoners have many needs, Salmi added, and the need for affection and comfort is just one of them. Mainly (and familiarly), those needs at Hämeenlinna manifest themselves in the women's desire to have someone to listen their stories, sometimes for the first time in their lives. Most are mothers, and they miss their children tremendously.

"You have to be firm, but not narrow minded," Salmi told me forthrightly. "You have to be willing to listen to prisoners' stories, to let them share their own stories."

There was one intensive drug rehabilitation unit for women in Hämeenlinna, in which personal storytelling and disclosure of past experiences, including childhood abuse, rape, and domestic violence, were a regular part of daily life. The unit was self-contained; women who agreed to live in the (more spacious) rooms had to agree to provide regular urine samples and to live without contact with the general population for a set period of time.

The women came from all over Finland, and their addictions ranged from heroin to prescription pills—and alcohol was always in the mix. All of the women admitted that while prison wasn't where they ever intended to end up, they were still glad for the opportunity to get sober and to live in relatively comfortable surroundings.

But then, in a lowered tone, one of the women admitted that it got very tiring being expected to "talk about addiction" every single day. Between the formerly drug-addicted "inspirational" speakers, the books about drug use, and the videos about drugs, one woman volunteered that they all actually ended up thinking more about doing drugs. The rest of the women in the group nodded their heads in agreement. As I've heard from other prisoners and users over the years, there really is such a thing as too much of an intensive recovery process that seems less about an individual's needs, and more about a set group curriculum intended to drive out a person's addiction, an approach that often backfires.

One of the key reasons why I wanted to visit a Finnish women's prison, aside from the fact that it is the only national women's prison, was that the country still has a relatively homogeneous ethnic population. Although refugee populations have begun to arrive over the last few decades from countries like Somalia, Finland has remained very white, very Nordic, and, depending on what area of Finland one might be traveling in, rather xenophobic.

The notable exception to the long-standing "whiteness" of Finland has been the presence of the Roma (gypsies) since the mid-1500s. Although the term is considered pejorative today, Finnish Roma have long been known as *mustalaisia*—roughly translated, "the black ones."

The Finnish Roma (population ten thousand) are not actually black, but they are typically a bit darker in skin tone—and certainly in hair color—than most Finns. Traditional Roma women wear formal, bejeweled tops and heavy, embroidered skirts with several layers of petticoats, so that when they walk down the street, they look almost as though they are floating. The Roma are just as much a part of the national fabric as any other Finn, but they have always been treated as second-class citizens, at least in part because of their nontraditional appearance, "ethnic" features, and insistence on keeping their own language and culture intact and largely unassimilated.

Discrimination toward the Roma has been around as long as they have; the most common assumption has always been that Roma men and women will rob and steal from a white person any chance they get. In truth, there are real parallels here with perceptions in the United States of low-income people in general, and low-income people of color specifically. Namely, the economic and cultural marginalization experienced by all of these groups has made it harder for them to find legitimate employment. Moreover, the idea of office work is anathema to the free-spirited Roma, who may not roam in caravans anymore but cannot fathom the idea of having to sit in a small cubicle for eight or nine hours a day. As a result, some Roma do turn to crime, but crime is not a way of life for most.

Much of this is intimately familiar to me because of my "darker" appearance in my Finnish childhood as a result of my mixed Finnish/Jewish ancestry, with some Roma heritage on both sides of my family. My features made me stand out in ways that made some white Finns wary of my presence, and resulted in Roma women encircling my younger sister and me, calling out, *"Sisko, sisko!"* (Sister, sister!) I knew what it was to have children and adults point at me, or even cross the street to get away from me—on one recent occasion as an adult, I was even refused service at a bar. I knew that discrimination against the Roma was still very much a Finnish reality, and so I wondered if Roma women would be disproportionately represented in this prison.

Indeed, they were. Although the prison did not actually keep statistics by ethnicity, varying accounts put the Roma prisoners (male and female) at about 20 to 25 percent of the total number of incarcerated persons—an extremely high percentage considering that Finnish Roma represent less than 0.2 percent of the national population.

One nontraditional Roma woman, in her early thirties, agreed to talk with me in her cell only after she changed into her new tracksuit and put on some powder and lipstick. Except for her features, she looked every bit the average Finnish woman. She lit up a cigarette and asked me where I was from. After the pleasantries, I asked her, point blank, what it was like for her to live in the prison, with a majority white population. "Oh, it's all right," she said. "They don't give me any problems. . . . The traditional [Roma] women are more critical of me because I wear pants."

I asked her what she was in prison for, and she chuckled. "Oh, I stabbed my husband a bunch of times!"

I was genuinely puzzled by her flippant description of such an unpleasant crime, until I remembered that dark humor is a part of both Finnish and Roma

culture as a way of dealing with life's adversities. As it turned out, there was cause
for it. A devoted mother of five, she had struggled to keep her family going, despite the fact that her husband had been beating her for many years. One day, she
decided to break with tradition and leave him. Her husband tried to stop her, and
she finally "snapped" and stabbed him multiple times. He lived but spent a bit of
time in the hospital. Her children are now in the care of other family members,
and she has no intention of ever allowing the man back into her life. Prison, she
told me, was the necessary break she needed to figure out what to do with her life
in the aftermath of the entire experience.

The cell where she lived was part of the women's wing of the prison, which
occupies a few floors. The very first thing to hit my senses when I walked into
the unit was the familiar smell of *pannukakku*, a traditional baked egg-and-flour
dessert that has no real American equivalent. (It is usually served with lingonberries
or another kind of jam.) I was confused about why there were prisoners cooking
their own food in their own small kitchen, something I've never seen before in a
prison housing unit, save for the sight of a woman making ramen in a microwave.

As it turned out, prisoners are actually given high-quality ingredients to
make any number of traditional Finnish foods two times a week, including rice
porridge and *mehukeitto* (a thick, potato starch–based berry soup), new potatoes
and fresh dill, and to access fresh milk and butter, and the dense, dark rye bread
favored by Finns. Prison kitchen prepared meals are provided every day; lack of
nutrition and hunger are certainly not issues at Hämeenlinna, nor has hunger
been a problem in the earlier part of these women's lives, which would at least
partly explain the lack of serious health concerns among the prisoners. (Cigarette
smoking, however, was omnipresent in all three of the countries that I visited,
unlike the United States, where tobacco has been banned in almost all women's
prisons, with limited success.)

Without exception, prisoners were always allowed to have the two dietary staples of Finnish existence: coffee and *pulla,* a cardamom-flavored coffee bread that is ubiquitous in all homes and coffee shops. With such an abundance of food, especially compared to most other prisons in the world, I couldn't help but chuckle when some of the women complain that their food is too traditional, and that they would like "exotic" foods like Mexican tacos, and more candy bars and potato chips.

A small library and dining area was at the front end of the long corridor, leading to cells arranged on either side of the hallway. There were one to two women per cell, usually based on their preference. Most of the women had decorated their cell doors with their first name and some kind of cheery image. (As at Holloway, no prisoner was addressed by prisoner number or last name.)

On average, the women locked up at Hämeenlinna were quite young, usually from eighteen to thirty-four years of age, and included several women (mostly Roma women) housed in the prison's spacious mother–baby unit. I was surprised to see that these prisoners, unlike normally reticent Finns, were actually enthusiastic about speaking with me. I was welcomed into several of their cells, packed neatly with stuffed animals, colorful linens and blankets (non–prison issue), clothes from home, hair accessories, makeup, books, fashion magazines, televisions, radios, and the like. Although the cells did have windows at the back, the living spaces were very small; there was scarcely enough room for me to move around. (A small slot is the only way that a prisoner can see out into the corridor once the cell doors are locked.)

Of immediate concern to me was the fact that I didn't notice any toilets in any of the cells; I could see only one small sink per room. This, as it turned out, was the chief complaint that all of the women had about the prison. In the daytime, the women were able to use the shared bathroom and shower area, but at night, they were locked into their cells for eight to nine hours with no access to the toilets.

"What do you do when you need to go to the bathroom?" I asked.

One of the prisoners in her midforties grimaced, and then pointed toward a small plastic potty in the closet. She told me that it was a humiliating experience to have to use the toilet in this fashion, especially in a shared cell, or if a woman was sick to her stomach or on her period. "I just try to hold it in all night," another woman told me. "I don't like the embarrassment of having to dump the [potty] out in the morning."

Salmi was clearly bothered by this too, and made it clear that some kind of an expansion was eventually planned for the women, so that they could have access to toilets at night. (From the sound of it, however, these plans were not happening in the near future.)

Educational opportunities were certainly plentiful at the prison for women at all levels of literacy, but I found it odd that nearly all of the women's vocational training—in a country where a woman is president and women have long held positions of power in government and business—centered largely on cosmetology, sewing, and laundry. Some women were involved in making stunningly beautiful crafts, linens, children's toys and clothes, kitchen accessories, and so forth, but they did not receive any of the profits from these sales.

I spoke with one thirty-four-year-old woman in the laundry area, who had been arrested for drug trafficking in England and was initially sent to Holloway to do her time. Upset by the conditions of confinement there, she asked to be repatriated back to Finland and was sent to the Hämeenlinna prison.

"Now I wish I could go back," she told me.

Her reasons for wanting to leave the prison had nothing to do with sexual or physical abuse, at the mere mention of which she marveled. "Nothing like that would ever happen here," she said, in all seriousness.

Her issue with the women's side of the prison was that the women felt as though they were being infantilized, subject to a kind of class discrimination and limitations on the real skill sets that they could acquire if only they were given the opportunity. Sewing and doing laundry, she emphasized, just guaranteed that the women wouldn't get far in their lives. I had to admit that for a country as focused on gender equality as Finland, I found this to be highly incongruous.

"This is like a children's playground," she said. "We are treated like children. It's like we exist in an air bubble."

There did seem to be a great deal of truth to what she told me, although the progressive nature of Finnish imprisonment was very apparent in other, significant ways. Namely, women who are mentally ill are usually sent to a mental hospital, not isolated in solitary confinement. As for those isolation cells *(rundi)* reserved for women who get into fights, no prisoner is allowed to spend more than five days in one; the average stay is three days. Finnish law dictates that no prisoner can be allowed to live in such a cell, as is common practice in the United States. Moreover, contagious diseases, serious health problems, and suicides were incredibly rare in the entire prison, as was any form of self-mutilation. The manner in which all guards and administrators addressed prisoners—and vice versa—was clearly based on a fundamental respect of each other's humanity, something that I had also witnessed at Holloway.

Some of the most progressive policies at Hämeenlinna were those that Salmi and the other staff didn't think were remarkable in the least. Namely, women were allowed monthly, unsupervised, overnight visits with their male partners in a small but comfortable room—regardless of whether they were married or not. When I asked if a same-sex couple would also be allowed to spend the night together, Salmi shrugged. "No one's asked yet, but if they do, of course we'd let them. If they're in a relationship, then that's that," she said.

The real shocker came just as I was about to leave. I watched a young woman come into the reception area of the prison. She didn't look like an employee, and my assumption was correct. As it turned out, she was a prisoner returning from a "vacation." I was utterly baffled. A vacation from prison?

Once again, Salmi and her colleagues were confused about why I was so surprised. But of course women had to be given a break from being incarcerated, they explained. Assuming that the women hadn't committed any major infractions—and if they were not generally perceived as a serious threat to the community—they would be allowed to go home to spend a predetermined amount of time with their families. An offender who would be denied leave would have to be deemed likely to pose a threat to the community. That bar is intentionally set very high, and is not based solely on the primary offense for which a woman is incarcerated. Fully one-third of the women doing time in Hämeenlinna are in for some kind of violent offense, usually committed under the influence of alcohol, but just because a woman had committed such a crime in the past did not mean that she was automatically denied the opportunity to leave for a family visit. As the staff admitted, some of the women came back a few hours or a day later than they were supposed to—and some came in with alcohol on their breath—but everyone returned.

A *vacation* from prison. No, not a prison furlough, buried in layers of paperwork and years waiting for official clearance to be able to sit with one's own children at home for a few days. Pigs would have to learn to swim and fly, I thought, for American prisons to even begin to entertain this kind of an idea. A vacation from doing time, just to reconnect a person with what exists on the other side of the wall.

ALOUETTE CORRECTIONAL CENTRE FOR WOMEN (British Columbia, Canada)

It's just about a three-and-a-half hour drive from Seattle, Washington, to the town of Maple Ridge in British Columbia, if you include the likelihood of being questioned by the U.S. Department of Homeland Security—that's right, as you're headed into Canada—about why you're headed north.

Spotting the uniformed personnel even before my father and I hit the checkpoint on our scenic jaunt up to British Columbia was strange in itself;

I realized that I hadn't tried to cross that particular border since 9/11. Even stranger was the hostile intensity of their line of questioning, seemingly after taking a critical look at my father's green card—clearly indicating his permanent residency in the United States—and then my U.S. passport, indicating a birthplace of foreign origin.

"Where are you headed?" the agent barked.

"To the Alouette Correctional Centre for Women," I answered honestly.

The answer didn't go over well; the agent came closer and peered in to take a closer look: "Why are you going there?"

I explained that the visit was part of my research for a book about women in prison, and that I was expected up in Maple Ridge early the next day.

"Now, *why* would you want to write a book about women in prison?" he demanded. My answer seemed to at least quell his suspicion about our countries of origin, but the gruff confusion on his face was still evident as he waved us through to the next checkpoint.

Why a book about women in prison, indeed? A few feet up, and the Canadian border guard greeted the answer with a whole different kind of attitude—even a noticeable tinge of interest. "Enjoy your time up there," he said, and waved us through.

Of all of the English-speaking countries, Canada's approach toward incarceration is, arguably, heading faster toward American-style lockups than any other country's. But it's not there yet, and clear evidence still exists of just how differently our neighbors to the north think about women and criminality.

Like Hämeenlinna, the Alouette Correctional Centre for Women (hereafter referred to as Alouette) is also located in an idyllic, forested area. Because the prison is so removed from urban life, however, no public transportation runs to this part of Maple Ridge, and this certainly isn't the kind of spot you'd accidentally wander into. But once you're there, there's no question that you've found the prison.

Much more so than the other two international prisons, the full-perimeter, barbed-wire fence was a very strong reminder of the kinds of facilities I had already seen back in the United States. Alouette is technically designed as a medium-security prison, although most of the women doing time there are minimum-security inmates. (In order to be sent to a provincial prison, and not into Canada's federal prison system, a person's sentence has to be two years or less.)

An intercom and two remote-operated fences let me onto the grounds; a jaunt to the left revealed the indoor reception area, where I checked in my belongings and my passport. Here, as in the other countries, I noticed that the guards wandered around amiably, chatting with prisoners. Cigarette-smoking appeared to be the primary activity, after women's walking or running laps around the prison grounds with their headphones on. After an introductory chat with Deputy Warden Matt Lang, we headed off for a tour of the prison grounds. Female prisoners wore drab, baggy clothes, and the prison guards had standard uniforms on, but no weapons, batons, or pepper spray on their person. I took note of the unusual presence of gazebos, totem poles, a beautifully decorated native spiritual hut, a meditative rock garden, and well-groomed pathways throughout the grassy compound. All of that *did* look different from what I was accustomed to, but something else was different in a way that I absolutely couldn't put my finger on. It took me a full ten minutes to realize what was throwing me off: Other than the deputy warden, there were no men anywhere.

As it turned out, Lang was one of only three men employed at this prison containing roughly two hundred women, something that is apparently standard practice at most provincial prisons in Canada. (Male guards are employed in greater numbers in the federal prison system, with the attendant problem of occasional reports of sexual abuse.) I couldn't help but wonder if the absence of men at the facility made Lang feel awkward, or if he felt as though men were being discriminated against in terms of their eligibility for employment. (This is the crux of the issue in the United States, where the logical end to race and gender discrimination in employment has been extended to women's and men's jails and prisons, with very mixed results.)

Lang, a tall, soft-spoken man with a relaxed demeanor, took the time to really ponder my question. No, he answered in all seriousness, he had never felt that being one of very few men at the prison was awkward. In fact, as he put it, "I feel honored to be able to work here."

Warden Brenda Tole had been called out to a meeting of provincial wardens earlier that morning, and Lang was apologetic that I did not get the chance to meet her. But the opportunity to spend time with one of the few male correctional employees at Alouette was actually more eye opening than if I had been shown around by a woman.

More specifically, anytime we headed toward a housing unit, it had to be established that a female guard was actually present in the unit. If so, she had to call out and let the prisoners know that a man was entering the premises—the kind of logical heads-up in an all-female environment, to alert women to cover themselves up or close their doors for privacy, that most U.S. women's prisons and jails do not extend to their inmates. If a female guard was not present, then Lang simply couldn't go inside. (Unaccompanied, neither could I.)

Like the other two international women's prisons that I had already visited, Alouette also had a mother–baby unit, although of the three, this was the least impressive. The changing room had been colorfully painted, but it was dark and very cramped. The mothers were enjoying their time with their infants and toddlers, and talking animatedly with one another, which was a good thing to see. In light of the less appealing aspects of the unit, I was surprised to find out that some of the women in the unit were not mothers of newborns, but female prisoners who had been approved to live there because they enjoyed taking care of children.

I stepped into one of the cells after asking permission from one of the women in the mother–baby unit. As at Holloway, the rooms were bare and rather depressing, with the very flat, uncomfortable mattresses common in American prisons. I asked the woman if she had back problems as a result. "Everyone does," was her honest answer.

As all other prisons do, Alouette obviously has its issues, including a very serious shortage of medical and psychological counseling staff, something that is of particular concern because of the poor shape in which many women arrive at the prison. By one nurse's estimate, at least one-half of the women already had hepatitis C. Two percent of the women have HIV. The situation was even more alarming once I found out that no medical treatment whatsoever was made available to the women with hepatitis C, although HIV medicines are readily available. In lieu of medication for HCV, the medical staff members educate prisoners on the warning signs of advancing illness and provide advice about healthy nutrition. The prison seems to walk the walk of its dietary talk: The kitchen there bakes its own bread and muffins, provides fresh fruit and vegetables, and does not load women up with unnecessary starches and sugars.

Deputy Warden Lang and I spent a bit of time outside Alouette's sweat lodge, maintained by First Nations women—which has an open invitation for nonindigenous women to participate, so long as they respect and honor the accompanying traditions and ritual observances. ("First Nations," "aboriginal," or "indigenous" are more commonly used terms in Canada than "native" or "Indian.") The sweat lodge is never subject to inspection and is considered an entirely sacred space for the women, who cannot enter except for ceremonial purposes. The Eagle Hut, on the other hand, was a place that Lang and I were allowed to enter, with the permission of the women who were in the process of cleaning it for the next meeting. Again, although the hut was clearly decorated and furnished with First Nations artwork, drums, and feathers, nonnative women were allowed to participate in all of the meetings and drum circles held inside.

Lang told me that many women who end up at Alouette actually consider it a "healing" space, something echoed by several women entering the Eagle Hut. The prison, despite its constraints and restrictions, is a place where women can finally be free of the abuse—externally and/or internally inflicted—that has followed them for most of their lives.

The loss of children in the process, however, is not something that any imprisoned woman I have ever spoken with feels is acceptable, although some women will readily admit that they were not fit to be good parents when they were arrested. But many of these women also feel as though they were not given a real chance at drug rehabilitation, or enough access to social services that would have provided them with quality prenatal care or basic parenting skills. Most of the women who have talked openly to me about this feel as though their class, and especially their ethnicity, played a huge role in the severity of the sentence that they were given.

Herein lies the most common thread between all of the women's prisons and jails I have ever visited: the grossly disproportionate number of poor women and ethnic minorities held in captivity. Natives and Latinas in New Mexico and Arizona; Latinas and African Americans in California, Florida, and Texas; African Americans and natives in Washington; Asian and black women in the United Kingdom; Roma in Finnish prisons; aboriginal women in Canadian prisons—the colors and cultures differ, but minority and marginalized class and social status do not.

In Canada's case, the rate of imprisonment of First Nations women even exceeds that of their male counterparts, in both the provincial and the federal prison systems. The provincial numbers were based on estimates, but Lang estimated that the First Nations female population at Alouette stood at about 30 percent. To offer an indication of just how serious the problem is, while aboriginal women represent just 3 percent of all women in Canada, they made up 29 percent of female inmates in the federal system as of July 2003. From 1996 to 2002, the number of federally sentenced aboriginal women increased by nearly 37 percent, compared with 5.5 percent for aboriginal men.[20]

No one at Alouette seems to be in denial about any of this; there isn't any talk, for instance, of how these prisoners brought everything "on themselves."

"We see that many of these women are very sick," says Jette Gilbert, a psychiatric nurse at the prison. "There are so many mentally ill women here . . . and we can't even provide real treatment as such. We're just trying to maintain their well-being so they can get on with their lives."

Gilbert speaks openly of the fact that Canada, like the United States, is sending far too many mentally ill people into the prison system, which is ill equipped to handle them. She wishes there were more halfway houses and other middle steps to help a woman reacclimate to society. "We throw them right out of prison and they're back on the streets," she tells me.

In this sense, things did not seem that different on two sides of the northern American border, until I considered the ease and comfort of the prisoners around each other and the correctional officers. Not one woman was being held in solitary confinement, and by all accounts, self-harming behavior was very rare.

Alouette's approach to its female prison population was notably different from that of most state prisons in the United States (with some significant exceptions, including the Washington Corrections Center for Women and the Central California Women's Facility), in that women were being trained in numerous nontraditional occupations, including forestry and fishery management. Alouette allows women to sell their pottery and beadwork to the outside world, and, unlike in most other prisons, the women get to keep all of the profits. With that money, prisoners can buy items from the commissary, weight equipment, and their own clothing. Contact with the outside world is not verboten, and visits from family members and friends are encouraged, to the extent that women can apply for "hardship" to be closer to their loved ones.

Because of the influence of the harm-reduction approach in nearby Vancouver, B.C. (which has decriminalized injected-heroin and cocaine use at supervised sites, in order to bring down HIV and hepatitis C rates and prevent overdoses in general), Alouette does not take a judgmental approach toward women incarcerated on drug offenses, nor does it mandate attendance at twelve-step meetings as a condition of regaining custody of children or early release. Everything along those lines is voluntary and is heavily reliant on a comprehensive outside volunteer base that comes into the prison to lead every kind of support and therapy group imaginable.

One of the women whom I met toward the end of my day at Alouette was precisely the kind of prisoner who would have rejected an attempt to force her to conform to a recovery program. Left to follow her own path, and with the support of some of these volunteer groups, Renee Chan, thirty-six, told me that she finally felt like there was some hope for her, after all.

Chan's story was one of the most harrowing I heard throughout my international prison travels; her narrative came out in hesitant bits and pieces, finally flowing as she built up the steam to get it all out.

Her sentence at Alouette, for forgery and breaking and entering, had been just the latest of a string of arrests and convictions over a nine-year period of addiction and abuse. All six of her children were wards of the court, and she had met them only twice in the decade since the last one was taken away. Chan's exposure to alcohol and drugs didn't hit in her teens or twenties; it was there from the time she was born. Her entire family, she explained, was addicted to one substance or another, and until she left her family home and neighborhood as a teenager, she had no idea that this wasn't the way the rest of the world operated.

"I had never met someone who didn't do drugs or drink," she told me. "I couldn't figure it out. I thought, *What planet do you people live on?*"

Chan could not kick the habits that she had acquired as a child and gravitated toward heroin, methamphetamine, and then crack cocaine. The time before this most recent sentence, Chan had entered prison weighing ninety pounds, with a court order for a medical detox to save her life. "I didn't even know what detox was," she recalled.

Her constant drug use came with a predictable toll: Chan tested positive for HIV and hepatitis B and C. The father of her children, her common-law husband, deserted her after finding out.

"I was going on a real uneducated understanding of what these diseases were. I thought I was going to die. The social workers wouldn't let me near my kids."

Chan grew more despondent, trying to survive by taking drugs and committing small crimes to support her habits. All of it led to the day when she decided none of it was worth living for. She jumped off a three-story building, but walked away with only a scratched knee.

The experience, she said, left her with the sense that there was nothing left for her to be scared of, and no one to keep pushing her down, except for her own self. Chan didn't clean up right away; it took a series of crimes to land her back in prison, where she was finally put on HIV medications. Like so many women prisoners that I have met over the years, Chan went from being an angry woman, convinced of her inevitable demise, to being the kind of person who takes it upon herself to do everything possible to better the lives of the people around her. Once a month, Chan is allowed to head out to the University of British Columbia with half a dozen other women to explain the nature of women's criminality and incarceration to sociology students. Although Chan knew that she would be out of prison soon, she still poured all of her energy into heading the Alouette Inmate Committee, and participated twice a month in a talking circle: an aboriginal-run HIV/HCV support group called Healing Our Spirits.

And with that, Chan asked if she could excuse herself, because she had pressing matters to attend to. With a hearty shake, a determined expression, and a large binder in hand, the petite, curly-haired woman disappeared down a path to her next meeting. It appeared that at Alouette, Chan's life of abject misery, strife, and struggle had evolved into something much, much more beautiful.

Prison was the place where she found it, but, thankfully, it doesn't seem as though it will be the last place where she'll express it.

Chapter 12: Hope and Healing

"I walk the Red Road with the Native American sisterhood. We live our
cultural way: [we go to the] sweat lodge, [we] sing and drum, and we have our
yearly powwow. I bead for my spirit. This is a plea for help. . . . Without proper
education, what type of ground can I stand on when I get out? I desire to walk out
of here as a grown woman, better mother, sister, friend, and human being."
—Maxina Rabang, thirty-seven, serving a ten-year sentence for armed robbery
at the Washington Correctional Center for Women

"The women in prison, they want their words to be heard.
They want people to know they still exist,"
—former prisoner Sheryl Jefferson, thirty-nine, who did time in the
Los Angeles County Jail and California state women's prisons for
check fraud and parole violations

Yraida Guanipa and Amy Ralston know all too well what it feels like to be a
woman facing drug charges dragged into the modern-day American criminal

justice system, only to find that an overriding presumption of guilt, not innocence, informs how she is treated and how her case is adjudicated.

Guanipa and Ralston have never met; in fact, they had not even heard of each other when I wrote this chapter. I chose to pair their stories because of the callous treatment that both of them had to endure from law enforcement agents and federal prosecutors, who tried to force the women to be pawns in their hunt for "big fish." When they failed to play the roles that were demanded of them, Guanipa and Ralston were sent down the river like discarded refuse.

I chose to highlight these two cases in part because Guanipa and Ralston were middle-class women without criminal records, who truly weren't involved in the drug trafficking conspiracies for which they were sentenced, and who had never even contemplated the possibility that they might one day be spending years on end within the confines of prison walls.

This trend toward sentencing women on so-called drug conspiracy charges is colloquially known as the "girlfriend problem," in reference to the fact that so many of these convicted women were not involved in the drug manufacturing, dealing, or trafficking operations that their boyfriends or husbands were participating in—not unlike the situation in which Catherine Zeta-Jones's character finds herself in *Traffic*. (One of the best movies at the turn of the twenty-first century to portray the hypocrisy and brutality of the American drug war.)

Usually, women like Guanipa and Ralston have no actual information to share with prosecutors. Anecdotally speaking, women are also far less likely to snitch on their loved ones, family members, friends, or casual acquaintances, often at great cost to themselves. In contrast, many of the so-called drug kingpins will roll on anyone and everyone in sight in order to escape a lengthy prison sentence.

Before her imprisonment, Guanipa enjoyed her life in Miami, the city that she had fallen in love with as a legal immigrant from Venezuela. She worked as the general manager of an office supply and mail service business, and reveled in her role as the mother of two young boys. All of this happiness came crashing to a halt in March 1996, when Guanipa made the mistake of agreeing to drive a friend of a friend to the airport in Miami.

According to Guanipa, she called ahead, at the man's behest, to verify that his "luggage" had arrived at the airport. Both during the phone call and at the airport counter, Guanipa clearly explained that the luggage was not for her, but for her friend, who was supposed to provide his airplane ticket to retrieve what turned out to be two large boxes. As it turned out, this man was on his way to pick up a substantial stash of smuggled cocaine. When they got to the counter, he may have suspected something when he saw Avensa Airlines "employees" who had never worked the counter before. They were actually agents with the United States Customs Service (USCS).

Whatever the deciding factor may have been, the Venezuelan national told Guanipa that he was going to get the two of them cups of coffee. He never returned.

As it turned out, the stash of cocaine was discovered, and Guanipa was detained on the spot. According to her account, she was baffled by what was happening, particularly when she couldn't find the person whom she had driven to the airport. When she was allowed by the agents to look for the man she had arrived with, Guanipa says that she panicked and jumped into her car to drive away, an act that certainly only added to the appearance of her guilt.

When Guanipa was arrested later that day, she insisted on her innocence. Although a guilty plea would have reduced her sentence by several years, she wouldn't buckle. It does appear that the USCS and the federal prosecutors knew that she wasn't involved in the cocaine trafficking. They wanted her to identify other members of the trafficking ring—information that she could not provide. But, as seems to happen with most of these federal drug stings, *somebody* needs to go down. Prosecutors resorted to getting a grand jury to indict her on a very rare and highly dubious charge that skirts the need to prove that an actual crime has been committed: "attempted possession with intent to distribute" a Schedule II drug. (Note the words "attempted" and "intent" in the same charge, something that shouldn't have passed legal muster.)

It worked. Despite her lack of a criminal record and the fact that she had recently given birth to a son, the judge sentenced her to nearly thirteen years in federal prison. Guanipa spent most of this time at FCI Tallahassee and FCC Coleman, the women's portion of the largest federal prison complex in the nation, located in central Florida.

"I cannot describe with words the feelings of terror that I suffered," Guanipa explained. "I could not think. I was not functioning. I only wanted to close my eyes and die."

Seven years before Guanipa was sentenced to prison, Ralston's unwitting journey toward incarceration began in 1989, when her husband, Sandy Pofahl, was arrested by German federal agents on charges of smuggling the popular rave drug ecstasy. Sandy was a wealthy Dallas businessman whose ownership of numerous successful computer, real estate, and mortgage lending companies covered for his most profitable venture—a major international ecstasy manufacturing and distribution ring. Sandy's arrest came as an enormous shock to Ralston, who said from the beginning that she knew absolutely nothing about his operation. Her lack of involvement in Sandy's drug smuggling ring was something that federal agents appear to have known about too: They asked her to wear a wire to try to entice him to finally disclose what he had been hiding from her all that time.

As the joint German–U.S. Drug Enforcement Administration bust of the ecstasy ring unfolded, and Sandy's actual business partners began to be rounded up, Ralston was initially left alone. But she went on to make a fateful mistake after Sandy pleaded with her, in coded language, to assist him in recovering some of his drug profits so that he could post bail.

Although she had already separated from her husband because of his serious alcoholism, Ralston agreed to help. No matter what her personal struggles with him had been, his seeming desperation about the prospect of staying incarcerated convinced her to help him in a manner that would eventually result in her incarceration.

"Anyone who knows me knows that I can't turn away a person in need," she told me.

The feds were quickly onto her, doing their damnedest to get her to crack, ostensibly to catch as many of the "bad guys" as possible. In addition to in-person and phone interrogations, agents conducted house raids that left all of her belongings strewn about, and even went so far as to harass her family.

Eventually arrested for recovering and spending some of the drug money, Ralston still refused to roll over and incriminate the man whom she had fallen in love with. Snitching might have won her freedom, but she wasn't going to let Sandy go to prison. And, in truth, there was no one else for her to tattle on.

As was true in Guanipa's case, Ralston didn't play by the rules, and she got hit hard: She was sentenced to a staggering twenty-four-year term in federal prison, as if she had masterminded the entire ecstasy operation. Her punishment became all the more outrageous when Ralston learned that her husband had ended up with only a few years of incarceration in Germany and a three-year probation term in the United States.

Guanipa and Ralston were sent to penitentiaries in Florida and California, respectively—prisons with large female populations, in locations far removed from their families and loved ones.

Initially, the two women were baffled by seemingly endless lists of rules and regulations that governed every aspect of their lives. They found themselves having to obey commands relating to when and how fast they could eat, how they could dress, how they made their beds, even what kind of tone they could use to respond to correctional officers and other prison employees. Even more disturbing was what they witnessed—and sometimes had to personally endure—regarding the attitudes of and outright abuse by correctional employees. To hear the two women tell it, these employees were usually male guards who took the inherent power differential to mean that that they could exercise all manner of sadistic impulses on a captive female population.

Neither of the women were interested in serving their time without consideration for the plight of the women they were surrounded by, most of whom were also doing time for drug-related charges. Guanipa and Ralston both earned the confidence of other prisoners, sharing their compassion and advice to support heartbroken women through difficult times, as well as advocating for their civil and human rights.

The resilience of so many current or formerly imprisoned women whom I have met over the years continues to amaze me. Not only are women's experiences in prison traumatic to begin with, but they also have to reckon with serious attendant consequences of their imprisonment—including the custodial loss of their children and spousal and familial abandonment—that their male counterparts don't experience to nearly the same degree.

Guanipa didn't lose custody of her children or the love of her family, but she did nearly die when she went on a hunger strike after years of pleading to be moved to a prison closer to where her sons lived. The experience so educated and politicized her that she became a jailhouse lawyer, a woman known for her willingness to rise up against the establishment for the sake of her fellow prisoners.

Released to a halfway house in December 2006 after serving more than a decade behind bars, Guanipa is now employed as a paralegal at a Miami law firm. She continues to advocate for the rights of women at FCC Coleman and FCI Tallahassee, the two primary prisons where she did her time. Guanipa is also in the process of suing the federal government over the trauma of what she has termed unlawful sentencing and incarceration.

After a brief period of hibernation following the presidential clemency she received in 2000, Ralston soon joined forces with drug sentencing reform organizations across the country, making presentations everywhere she could to try to bring attention to the pervasive injustices surrounding the war on drugs. Ralston also started the CAN-DO Foundation, to spread awareness about the thousands of women serving lengthy drug-related sentences—particularly on conspiracy charges.[1]

In decades past, women who had been incarcerated tended to go out of their way to make sure no one would know about what they had been through. Things aren't much different now; incarceration still carries an enormous social stigma. Like Guanipa and Ralston, however, some exprisoners are willing to speak to the lives and experiences of the half-million men and women currently imprisoned for drug-related offenses.

Although the actual wording of our nation's Bill of Rights certainly hasn't changed, many civil rights activists observe that the interpretations and implementations of its key provisions have changed dramatically—and for the worse—particularly regarding the right to privacy, the right to be free of unwarranted search and seizure, and the right of the accused to receive a fair trial, all of which signify a major deterioration of the function of our law enforcement agencies and our legal system as a whole.

One of the most obvious examples of this shift can be seen in the way women accused of nonviolent, low-level, drug-related crimes are treated.

In the likely scenario that a woman or her family cannot afford bail, women are left to sit in packed or beyond-capacity jails, often reminded by a public defender (or a hired defense attorney) that insisting on her right to a fair trial will most certainly ensure a lengthy jail stay before the case can be tried. The prospect of spending many weeks, months, or even years in jail is not appealing on any level, particularly because these institutions tend to be loud, chaotic, and filled with people suffering from a plethora of mental illnesses and diseases. Jails also tend to be more dilapidated than state or federal prisons, although there are some notable exceptions, including the gleaming, high-tech downtown jail in Phoenix, where the notorious sheriff, Joe Arpaio, still forces female inmates to work on chain gangs.

From Phoenix to Newark, girls and women are being arrested, sentenced, and incarcerated in far greater numbers than ever before, although the 1.3 million American females currently under some form of correctional supervision are still largely invisible to the public eye.

In this context, stories of hope and healing in the lives of incarcerated or formerly imprisoned girls and women are often overlooked by the few people who focus on female incarceration to begin with. It's not hard to understand why. Egregious violations of the civil and human rights of prisoners are so pervasive and entrenched as to constitute a serious domestic crisis, albeit a largely unrecognized one. In the context of this country's pathologically punitive approach toward "criminality"—as it has always been subjectively defined by people with the power to do so—it is difficult for many of us who write about prison and criminal justice issues to remain optimistic in any regard, or even to celebrate the genuine triumphs of imprisoned women when they do occur.

Sadly, positive stories like these are hard to come by.

I am personally gratified to know that some of the women I spoke with will have been released by the time this book is published. Most of them seem ready to face the challenges of the "free world," having worked hard during their incarceration to better themselves, improve their educational and vocational skills, and understand the roots of the situations that landed them in prison. They have hope for their respective futures, because they were able to use their periods of incarceration to work through and begin to comprehend the complexity of their histories, life experiences, and dysfunctions, despite their bleak surroundings. Even more remarkably, many of the women I encountered were able to do so even in the face of nonexistent or limited programs geared toward helping women transition back into society successfully.

I met one such woman, Debra Armstrong, at the New Mexico Central Women's Facility when I walked into a small but inviting creative art workshop. This cluttered, colorful environment was one of very few programs at the prison that struck me as having a true rehabilitative purpose and power. Armstrong found her strength there, through artistic expression and the solitude she craved.

In August 2007, Armstrong became a free woman, something she anticipated with bittersweet emotion because her husband passed away from cancer while she was locked up. Armstrong was not allowed to attend his funeral, and she mourned the loss by cutting off all her long hair, in accordance with her Cherokee heritage and spiritual tradition.

"I am really looking forward to being released," she wrote to me in early 2007. "I am tired of being in a cage."

Armstrong's mature demeanor and high level of educational attainment are very likely to give her a leg up once she leaves prison. Unfortunately, she does not typify most females coming out of detention centers, jails, or prisons. Once girls and women have been incarcerated, it is very likely that they will be imprisoned again. Nationally, almost 60 percent of adult women who have done prison time are rearrested within three years of their release. Forty percent are reconvicted, and 39 percent return to prison because of a parole violation. When both genders are taken into account, fully two-thirds of prisoners are rearrested within one year of their release.[2]

Recidivism rates for women are consistently high in states with massive prison systems. In California, for instance, only one-third of women in prison are able to participate in some kind of vocational or educational training,[3] and more than half of the population in every one of the state's women's prisons reads below a ninth-grade level.[4]

Although the federal government yanked funding for college-level classes in prisons in 1994, in-prison and long-distance learning programs still exist in some facilities. Female inmates who are able to access college classes are four times more likely to stay out of prison after their release.[5] Without heightening their literacy skills and education levels, and without any vocational training, women coming out of prison tend to not fare well at all.

In conjunction with the "collateral effects" of incarceration, ex-offenders with drug felonies on their records are usually prohibited from accessing public housing, food stamps, Temporary Assistance for Needy Families, and federal college grants. It doesn't matter one bit what a former prisoner does to prove their rehabilitation, sobriety, or their value to the community. It doesn't matter that the majority of formerly incarcerated women are trying to take care of not only themselves, but their children and sometimes their parents as well. In addition to the 100:1

sentencing disparity between crack and powder cocaine (a person caught with five grams of crack cocaine receives a five-year minimum sentence, while an offender must possess five hundred grams in powder form to receive the same punishment), it's fair to say that the federal ban on most forms of public assistance for former drug felons is one of the most idiotic and offensive results of the drug war, not only in terms of callous disregard for the struggles of people trying to reintegrate into society, but also because of the long-term economic impact. It doesn't take rocket science to figure out that people struggling to make ends meet are more likely to turn to illicit activities—and therefore to end up back in prison, costing taxpayers tens of thousands of dollars per individual per year.

Instead of the $36,000 spent annually per prisoner in California, taxpayers could be cut a break if the state funneled more money into programs like A New Way of Life, in Watts, California. There, for $12,000 per year per person, a remarkable woman named Susan Burton gives exprisoners a real, meaningful chance at putting their lives back together.

Watching Burton in action, energetically rounding up the residents of two adjacent houses for a group meeting, it's hard to believe that she was once a crack addict and homeless prostitute. Weighing just ninety pounds, Burton was at death's door in 1997. Her hair was falling out in clumps, she shook uncontrollably, and her attention span had diminished to the point that she couldn't even read more than a couple of sentences at a time. Whereas other programs might have considered her beyond rehabilitation, the Claire Foundation in Santa Monica took her in.

Within a year, Burton hadn't just recovered and regained control over her life; she had embraced it in a way she hadn't ever imagined was possible. But with drug felonies on her record, Burton could barely find work anywhere, except in home healthcare for seniors. (Even then, when Burton went to get her home-health-worker certification, she was told that her criminal history prohibited her from obtaining licensure.)

Burton turned her frustration into something amazing: She opened A New Way of Life, an unique clean-and-sober residence for women who have found themselves in bad places in their lives but who don't want to go back to jail or prison. The program's adjacent houses are modest, but impeccably organized and spotless. Children aren't just accepted, they are welcomed at A New Way of Life—unlike most drug recovery houses, which allow adults only.

A New Way of Life operates on the principle that no set formula or recovery process works for everyone. Women's individual needs and personal histories have to shape the course of their healing, and this is an area that Burton excels in. She's endlessly compassionate but dishes out strong words and tough love when necessary—which appears to be much of the time. Burton plays the role of guidance counselor, mother, and grandmother, something that the residents from broken homes are initially mystified by because no one has ever put this much energy into their lives before.

"This is a special-needs population," Burton explained to me during my visit in February 2007. "The tenderness and hardness have to blend together to give the women the kind of support and consideration they need. Most clean-living programs are cookie cutter, which doesn't work because everybody is unique."

I talked a bit with one of the residents, Delilah Hurtado, a former meth addict born in East Los Angeles. Hurtado is a wise-talking thirty-one-year-old with a fierce demeanor but an infectious laugh that clearly stems from a gentle place inside her. Burton found this in her, too, after Hurtado arrived at A New Way of Life with no money, no clothes, and a life full of trauma and dejection. Within a few months of arriving, Hurtado had already begun to blossom under Burton's care.

"When I leave, I want to leave on my own two feet," Hurtado told me.

I asked her how she felt about Burton, and I saw a hint of tears welling up in her eyes. "There's nothing I wouldn't do for her," she said earnestly. "She's gonna be a part of my life forever."

Unfortunately, only 20 percent of parolees in California are provided with programs and services like these that help them stabilize their lives and stay out of prison.[6] The fears surrounding release are thus very real for many of the women whom I've interviewed. Currently incarcerated at the Central California Women's Facility (CCWF), Audrey Rayford is a thirty-six-year-old woman who spent most of her teenage and young adult life on the streets and cycling through the criminal justice system. Rayford will be released soon—a fact that should be cause for relief, even celebration. Instead, she is consumed by trepidation about the world outside CCWF's prison gates.

I'm an ex–drug user and prostitute. I've given the California Department of Corrections fourteen long years of my life, in and out. Now I discharge 10/14/07, and that should be the highlight of my life, but it's not! I'm scared to death; no more security, or free room and board. After fourteen years the CDC is telling me to fend for myself.

That means responsibilities! Something I haven't had in a long time. . . . I've worked so hard learning to read and write on my own. I only have a sixth-grade education. But now, through the grace of God, I can read, write, and spell.

Other women won't be released for several years or decades from now. Most disturbing to me is the fact that a significant number of these women won't ever get the chance to experience life outside prison again, most commonly because their first and only crime has been murdering a male partner.

In my experience interviewing both prisoners and correctional employees, unless a woman has demonstrated consistent behaviors that would indicate her inability to be rehabilitated, most women do deserve another chance at reentering society and moving forward with their lives. In the event that a woman is deemed too dangerous to walk freely in society, a decision of such enormous gravity should not be made by members of a parole board or correctional administrators, but by true professionals in the field of prison psychiatry and rehabilitation.

Barring such a circumstance, imprisoned girls and women deserve a chance to heal from past abuse, and to learn from their life experiences and the nature of their crimes. Before women are released, they must be given the tools to ensure that their reintegration into society is not fraught with immediate economic and social struggle, and to help increase the odds that they will be released into families or communities that will actually support their reintegration. Former prisoners must be given the tools to become productive members of society; that is, if they weren't productive already, and if they even needed to be locked up in the first place. In general, women in prison aren't given one iota of the emotional, social, and vocational skills they need to overcome the vast hurdles awaiting them beyond the gates that have confined them for years or decades on end.

I want to close this chapter by sharing a story that has haunted me since the day I picked up the phone to call a woman by the name of Grace Ortega, who had written me an impassioned email asking if I would talk to her about the life of her daughter, Gina Muniz.

In our first conversation, Grace and I talked for two hours—or, to be more precise, I listened for those two hours. It actually didn't click until a few days after that conversation that something sounded very familiar about what Grace had been telling me in great detail. Sure enough, I had once actually written about Gina, albeit briefly, in an article about the allegations and emerging evidence surrounding shoddy, abusive, and sometimes life-threatening medical "care" in two adjacent women's prisons: Valley State Prison for Women (VSPW) and the Central California Women's Facility (CCWF) in Chowchilla.

Grace and I stayed in touch, and I made it known that I would be interested in researching the details of her case for *Women Behind Bars*. I asked her to send me court documents, medical records, prison memos, grievances, or anything else she might have that would enable me to grasp the chronology of events in Gina's life, and to look more deeply into her situation. A few weeks later, a cardboard box the size of an orange crate arrived at my home. Grace had taken my request seriously and literally; from what I could tell, she had sent me absolutely everything she possessed pertaining to her daughter's case.

I didn't actually examine the contents of the box closely until I was already well into a few chapters of this book. When I did finally start to sort through the material, I saw that Grace had included four 8" x 11" color photos of her daughter. I set them down on my kitchen table and just stood there, staring at them. I don't know how much time passed, but I know it was long enough that the images were actually seared into my mind.

When I mentioned earlier that I was haunted by Gina's story, I meant that I have also been haunted by these images. For a time, I actually buried the photos under piles of paper in a strange attempt to block out my emotional reaction to them. It didn't matter; my mind couldn't erase any of it.

As I write this, these pictures are out of hiding, because I can finally give Gina's story a voice. The photograph that I have placed next to me is of her emaciated body, shackled to a bed in a community hospital near CCWF. Another of Gina's photos, which was taken just two months before her arrest on August 8, 1998, is on top of my desk. This is a snapshot of a naturally, strikingly beautiful woman with thick, dark curls framing her wide smile. Gina's warmth and kindness radiate from that picture, just as the one taken just a few weeks before her death conveys the agony of living in a body taken over by cervical cancer, which had started out as an entirely treatable, early-stage illness.

Gina's face in the hospital picture is that of a much, much older woman. The only parts of her that still look young are her hands and long fingers, which resemble a pianist's. Her left arm is shackled to the bed, per the requirement of the California Department of Corrections and Rehabilitation that even terminally ill prisoners be shackled to their beds and guarded twenty-four hours a day, seven days a week. Her right arm tenderly cups the head of her then-eight-year-old daughter, Amanda.

Her eyes give away the intensity of her suffering, which started out as horribly as it ended. When she was first taken to the LA County Jail, Gina began to bleed so profusely that she would go through many sanitary pads in the space of a few minutes; most of the time, she was just left to bleed all over herself and her cell. When her cries got loud enough, jail guards would typically come over and look at her with disgust, and then throw toilet paper rolls into her cell.

All of this went on until Gina passed out while talking to her mother on the phone after nearly eight months of nonstop bleeding in jail. Gina's collapse was apparently what it took for her pleas for medical assistance to be heard. Even then, it would be months before she was examined properly and diagnosed with Stage IIB cervical cancer, which has a high success rate of being treated and stopped in its tracks if it is treated aggressively and consistently.

Gina's pleas for justice, however, were not heeded. She received a life sentence in state prison, with an additional seven years tacked on. A life sentence would seem to indicate that she had committed a heinous crime, and most certainly a crime of violence. But Gina had actually committed a nonviolent act, although even she thought she should be punished for stealing $200 from a fifty-one-year-old Vietnamese American woman. Gina did not have a gun, knife, or any other weapon with her, but she admitted that she "strong-armed" the woman into going to a nearby ATM and giving her the money. Even the victim herself, when the police arrived on the scene, stated that Gina had not hurt her in any manner.

Gina hadn't been a career criminal by any stretch of the imagination. Her only violations were for car-related misdemeanors, including a June 30, 1998 charge for driving without a permit. (Gina did not do jail time, although the incident did go on her record.) What happened that pushed this twenty-seven-year-old, with no history of criminal behavior, to the point of robbing someone?

Grace explained to me that Gina's father's death on April 22, 1998, triggered a serious, debilitating spiral of depression in her daughter's life. Although Gina's father had periodically been a heavy cocaine and heroin user, and Grace had left him when Gina was just a child, Gina still adored him and tried to see him as much as possible.

By all accounts, cocaine hadn't even been a part of Gina's life until after her father died. Although she had gotten involved with men who hadn't exactly done right by her, Gina had set her sights on becoming a nurse and paving the way for a good life for Amanda.

Seeing her grief, a much older, married male family member offered his "support" to Gina, and then gave her a taste of a drug that he promised would help her get through the pain. His encouragement of her cocaine use was obviously far from being in Gina's best interest. When her use turned into dependency, he started demanding sexual favors, which she provided to him for a time in exchange for money to buy more drugs.

The "exchange" went on for a few months, until a day when she asked for $200 and this relative demanded another sexual favor. As Gina later admitted to her mother, she was suddenly consumed by hatred and disgust—toward him and toward herself. She refused his advances, and he in turn refused the money. But Gina's desire for more cocaine overtook her ability to think clearly. As her mom put it, "Gina did something that she would have considered unthinkable" in the not-so-distant past.

A mere surface examination reveals that Gina's poor attempt at a crime was obviously a fumbling act of desperation by a woman addicted to drugs. But that's not how the court saw it. Gina's own defense attorney took Grace's hard-earned money (which he was eventually forced to return when Grace filed a complaint with the California Bar Association), did nothing to argue her case, and then urged Gina to plead guilty in exchange for a short sentence. While the judge was announcing the terms of her sentence, Gina heard the words "life" and "seven years," and anxiously asked her lawyer what was happening.

As a bailiff would later testify, Gina's lawyer had lied to her, telling her that entering a guilty plea would get her only a seven-year sentence, not life in prison.

Gina did not find out until she was sent to CCWF that she was going to spend the rest of her life in prison. Medical "decisions" made at some level in the process ensured that she was denied the necessary hysterectomy, radiation, and chemotherapy that would have saved her life. In essence, her already cruel and unwarranted life sentence was hastened into a death sentence over just a few horrible months of pain and suffering, during which she and her mother pleaded constantly for medical intervention and urgent treatment.

It took many months of letter writing, and the volunteer assistance of the San Francisco–based advocacy group Legal Services for Prisoners with Children, for Grace to get her daughter out of a depressing community hospital room under the constant watch of prison guards. Gina wanted to die at home, and so she did. On September 29, 2000, Gina Muniz slipped away in silence, surrounded by her immediate family, just two days after her mother took her home.

Where is the healing or hope in a story like this? Gina was certainly not given the chance to experience either.

Instead, they have manifested themselves in Grace's ability to turn her own grief into advocacy on the part of other women in prison. Grace has traveled across California, testifying before legislators and advocating for compassionate release for terminally ill women in prison so that they do not have to endure anything akin to the needless and slow death that Gina suffered.

Grace still looks at the pictures of her daughter every day, and she worries that her daughter's life will be forgotten entirely or, worse yet, dismissed as the plight of a criminal whose life and death were of no particular significance.

"Please," she asked me again at the end of our last conversation, "Please make sure that Gina isn't forgotten."

Afterword: Chasing the Beam, Chasing Dignity

"Unfortunately, that's what prison does to us: It takes the human feelings out of our body and we just try to survive. . . . Prison life changes us; it is a fact of life. The hardships we endure here will be part of our lives when we are released."

—Yraida Guanipa, free after nearly eleven years in federal custody for her first, nonviolent offense

I t's a blazing 108 degrees in July 2006, and I'm sweating my way through the yards of the Central California Women's Facility (CCWF) in Chowchilla, California. It's been almost six years since I visited the other side of this sprawling prison complex, the Valley State Prison for Women (VSPW).

With a population of over 4,000 women, CCWF holds roughly half of all the female prisoners incarcerated in what is now the world's largest women's prison complex. Across the street, VSPW houses another 4,000 plus women in nearly identical conditions. Both prisons house eight women to a cell in their "general population," and these cells all contain women of various ages (from juveniles to senior citizens), religions, ethnicities, disabilities, medical conditions, drug histories, sexual orientations, classifications (from minimum to maximum security), and criminal histories (from drug possession to murder). Together, the two prisons hold the majority of the women locked up by the California Department of Corrections and Rehabilitation, a figure that came in at just under 11,500 in March 2007.

After just two hours of walking through CCWF's various yards, my clothes are drenched, and I'm finding it difficult to keep up with my chaperone for the day, Lieutenant Bart Fortner, a no-nonsense prison guard of the self-described "old-school." Lieutenant Fortner, the public information officer for CCWF, chuckles a bit every time I stop to wipe my brow on the sleeve of my suit jacket or grab a drink of water; even in this heat, he's not breaking a sweat. After all, this is the climate to which he is accustomed. Extreme summer heat and extreme winter cold are part of daily reality for everybody who lives and works here—most of all for the prisoners, for whom air conditioning is a distant memory, and who face the elements with the least variety of clothes at their disposal.

Fortner and I keep walking over sun-weathered concrete paths and roads, and I can't help but take note of the prominent display of even more weather-acclimated, tanned, muscular male and female guards, set atop oversize adult tricycles. This is how the guards are able to monitor the hundreds of "movements" that prisoners make daily between various locations: education classes, workshops, laundry, commissary, pill dispensary, and work assignments.

Watching them blaze on through the heat—even to the point of racing one another in impromptu displays of competitive heat-resistance—I decide to just suffer through it. It's then that I notice that handfuls of female prisoners have gathered under overhead sprinkler systems that let out a fine, barely perceptible mist that dries on skin the moment it hits. For half a minute, I seriously consider joining them there. I realize that doing so would probably mean losing face in the eyes of the surrounding correctional officers, to say nothing of the fact that it would probably set the whole yard off laughing about the sight of the reporter in the black suit, soaking herself for a bit of relief from the heat.

No prison mist for me.

Fortner is the kind of man who wants to make sure that I understand everything I'm seeing, and that all of my questions get answered. He seems relieved that I actually take the time to greet guards and inmates alike with respect, and to ask open questions about their feelings and experiences. He notes that it's nice to talk with an outsider who knows more than her fair share of prison terminology, including the swirl of endless acronyms that make a prison tick. I also know more than a little about California's bizarre trajectory toward becoming one of the biggest prison states in the world. As such, I know better than to assume that men like Fortner himself have been actual, active proponents of the enormous, rapid-fire expansion of the state prison system.

It's already been a long road for Fortner; he's going on his twentieth year at CCWF, having gotten there by way of Folsom State Prison and setting up the Security Housing Unit (SHU) for male inmates at California State Prison—Corcoran, where he even had occasion to act as the gunner who supervised the notorious Charles Manson during his brief "exercise" outings.

Why a women's prison, then? Wouldn't it be infinitely more fascinating for an "old-school" guard to be watching over "celebrity" male captives and feeling the daily adrenaline/terror rush when a male-on-male prisoner fight breaks out, as it inevitably does in one of the many dozens of CDCR prisons?

"Women are more interesting to work with," he explains, noting that it's also a relief to not have to watch his back constantly, since rates of violence in women's prisons are lower overall. "They are more willing to talk about their histories, their struggles, and they really respond to respect by showing back respect."

Women are also always asking "why," something that Fortner and many other prison employees seem to be alternately irritated and impressed by. "Just giving a woman a command doesn't work well," he says. "They need to understand why that command is being given, and that's kind of a good thing. It's usually a sign of their own level of respect for themselves."

Fortner has chosen to stay at CCWF because he finds working with women to be rewarding. Women who turn their seriously damaged lives around, he says, are "inspiring," and he has learned to appreciate the survival and resilience of many of the women he's come across over the years. But sometimes, Fortner shrugs, there are people in this profession who have ended up in the wrong job, getting paid too much money for not caring enough about doing their jobs right.

"Nut jobs, sadistic power trippers, sexist pigs?" I offer, only half-jokingly.

Fortner is taken aback for a second. He lets out an approving half-cough, half-laugh, and then tells me he likes the way that I just say what I want to say, that I don't just bullshit around the issues.

No, he doesn't disagree. Like every other workplace, he says, there's a little bit of every kind of character in the mix— maybe even more than a few "nutters" when it comes to jobs that give men and women the permission and power to restrain, pummel, spray, or beat someone into submission.

Fortner admits that he finds some of the younger correctional officers too quick to use force, far too ready to try to prove themselves in inappropriate ways. I offer my impression that some prison guards actually do seem to be in this job for all the wrong reasons—especially when it comes to the much more intensive and sensitive issue of guarding women who must undress, use the toilet, and be left in close quarters with the people hired to watch over them, most of whom are men. I do not try to hide my conclusion that there are simply far too many women in prison for enough people to be drawn to the difficult job of guarding and rehabilitating them, and addressing their needs. I question whether there could possibly be enough men and women who are adequately trained and educated in handling the stressors and complexities associated with this population of women.

"This isn't a job that everyone is going to be good at," Fortner replies with equal forthrightness, but without naming any names.

With that, Fortner pardons himself briefly when a woman on her way to a drug rehabilitation program waves him down to ask him a question about her housing situation and some underlying mental health issues.

He's polite, she's polite, and the exchange goes smoothly, as do most conversations between Fortner and the female prisoners. Fortner promises to get back to her, and the woman seems to walk away with confidence that this will likely be the case. (The same certainly can't be said for every other exchange I witnessed, whether in this prison or many others.)

There's a brief pause as we stroll and wait for the momentum of the conversation to propel us into the next topic.

After a relatively docile tour of yet another crammed housing unit, where relatively bare, dingy cells are maintained by the women with military-style precision and order, Fortner and I cross the yard again. We get to our next talking point: the issue of what happens to women when they get out of a prison where they've been for several years or decades. But we never finish that conversation, because that topic comes to an awkward halt. When I get an immediate look, taste, and feel of how punishment can take shape in a women's prison.

The building we have just walked into is thick with OC pepper spray that immediately hits my eyes and lungs. This, apparently, is the other kind of prison mist. Although a huge fan has already done its job of dissipating most of it, the smell and feel of the spray, in tandem with the overwhelming heat and humidity, leaves me somewhat disoriented.

I am not so disoriented, however, as to not notice the two women locked in adjacent cages, their faces bright red and tear streaked, their eyes nearly swollen shut, their white shirts and tan pants soaked with water from being hosed off. They moan and fan themselves frantically, begging loudly for relief from the pain and discomfort.

The two women had apparently gotten into a physical fight on the yard, but the severity of the fight was impossible to deduce. Was this level of action on the part of the guards truly necessary? The fight couldn't have actually gotten very far, as neither of the women looks particularly injured, outside of the suffering evident on their faces from having been sprayed with the chemical agent that prisoners and guards alike refer to as "orange crush."

The women in their adjacent cages, the desperate fanning and pleading for more water, their shamed expressions when they realized that a female civilian had entered the room—all of this was hard enough to witness. But more disturbing was the initial sight of the two beefy male guards who had apparently broken up the fight, and then sprayed and hosed the women. When I first rounded that corner, I noticed them before they had a chance to see me. What I saw were two men sitting just a few feet from the cages, chowing down on sandwiches, laughing at the women, and providing them with no relief or medical attention whatsoever.

The expressions and demeanor of these two guards changed, of course, once they realized that they were in mixed company, but the incongruous visual remained: a bit of sadistic pleasure and sandwich-eating amidst the smell of chemicals, as well as the sight and sound of suffering, pleading women. These were precisely the kind of guards that represent the other end of the prison employee spectrum—the opposite of the engaged, firm but compassionate women and men I had met in the field from time to time. These men—cruel, unforgiving, and ill equipped to work with women—represent the kind of prison employees that should quickly be identified and relieved of their frontline duties, but they rarely are when prison unions, overcrowding, and understaffing are the weighty factors that they are.

True dignity is a hard thing to come by in prison for anyone immersed in that world, particularly for prisoners. It is the struggle for this dignity that resonates most deeply for me when I think about my travels and the conversations and letters I exchanged with imprisoned females.

"This morning, I was chasing the beam," forty-eight-year-old Delicia Hammock wrote me from a Memphis, Tennessee, women's prison. "I was in [an outdoor] cage . . . with a two-foot beam of sunshine coming over the roof into the cage. It was shining in the back, so I sat there for a few, then kept following it up the cage 'til my hour was up. We [prisoners] may be a lot of things, but we're still looking for a little warmth, just like the rest of the human race."

Like Hammock, nearly everyone I've communicated with behind bars wants to still feel like they are worth something to someone, that they might actually be loved or embraced by someone, and, most important, that they haven't been forgotten altogether. Hammock committed her first felony when she killed her abusive husband. Now serving a thirty-two-year sentence, she has developed chronic health problems during her incarceration. Although she has "trustee" status as someone with an impeccable record in prison, she, like most inmates, does not want her crimes to define the totality of her existence, or the public to stop believing in the power of rehabilitation. (It is true, in my experience, that most female prisoners will not brag about the crimes they have committed under any circumstance, while men's tendencies toward braggadocio about toughness—including real or exaggerated descriptions of criminal acts—seem far more common.)

Prisoners like Hammock also believe that the people overseeing them should treat them like human beings deserving of basic human rights, including medical care, mental healthcare, simple but nutritious food, and the right to not be physically or sexually coerced or abused. Most female prisoners are also desperately in need of just a few precious comforts that you and I might take for granted: visits with their children and family members; a mattress that doesn't feel like cement; regular access to sanitary pads and showers; the ability to wear something other than baggy men's clothes; and even the ability to express even the slightest bit of femininity by doing their hair, or wearing a bit of lipstick and mascara. (If you think the latter is laughable, consider that nearly every woman I interviewed brought this up as a crucial way in which she felt like she could feel a bit better about herself, particularly given the drab clothes and surroundings, and the poor, starchy diets that typically lead to acne and weight gain.)

The public mindset in America still seems to be that prison, even for women, should not be an even remotely comfortable or even healing place for the people sent there to do time. For those of you who feel that detention facilities, jails, and prisons should be as uncomfortable as possible, you can rest assured that they most certainly are not pleasant places to be.

Back at CCWF, I am acutely aware that the level of repression and deprivation in many other remotely located women's jails and prisons nationwide—particularly those run by private prison companies (New Mexico, Arizona, Colorado), or those that house women in crumbling prisons (Alabama), horse barns (Texas), or outdoor tents (Arizona)—is actually far worse than what I saw in California.

But the extensive overcrowding in this state lends itself to a concentration of medical and mental health problems that the prison system was never designed to handle. As a part of my CCWF tour, Fortner and I also visit the Skilled Nursing Facility (SNF), which is itself an outcome of lawsuits about poor medical care for chronically ill women, where many women go to die in very monitored but entirely bleak surroundings. Adjacent to the SNF is a small, intensive pseudo-psych ward where women are apparently sent with some regularity from

Ad Seg or VSPW's Security Housing Unit when they are no longer manageable in those places.

Here, the women are under twenty-four-hour watch, but it is unclear what, if any, psychiatric services they are really receiving.

There's a bit of unease all the way around as I'm led through this area, especially once I take the initiative of peeking into the cells. One woman has torn off her clothes and is screaming nonstop about something of coherence to no one but her. The only things I can decipher from her speech are the generously laced expletives that pepper her otherwise imperceptible slur of furious outpourings. (The general consensus among the staff is that she is not really insane but puts on an attention-seeking show that they seem to find amusing, a common prison response to women who behave in this manner.)

One of the other women, on the other hand, isn't doing anything at all.

She isn't speaking. In fact, she's not even moving.

This woman is huddled as far away from the cell window as possible. Every part of her little body is covered by a drab blanket, although she must, apparently, let her face peek out for count.

I can't tell how old she is. I don't know anything about her, except her name, which I can't ask her personal permission to use.

Her thin mattress is pressed to the concrete floor. A sliver of shaded light filters into the room. A tray of uneaten food still sits in the corner.

In that chilling moment, that woman somehow comes to represent every other huddled mass of a broken human being I've ever seen in a juvenile detention center, jail, or prison.

Fortner sees the look that crosses my face. "She's not there anymore," he says softly, pointing to his temple.

"Does she ever move?" I ask.

Fortner shakes his head. There is no more conversation to be had right now. He and I leave the building and walk in silence for a few minutes. I know a carefully groomed public relations act when I see one, but this man's body language isn't doing anything along those lines. His brow furrows with worry lines. We walk away from the facility quickly. Even the merciless sunshine fails to reach my consciousness for another ten minutes.

What it was, precisely, among the myriad possibilities of psychiatric complications, that caused this one woman to end up motionless and detached from the world, on the floor of a bleak crisis cell, is now probably impossible for anyone to discern.

I still wake up, from time to time, to the image of her body buried under that blanket, and contemplate her fate. I wonder if she still huddles on some concrete floor of the prison, or if some kind of miracle has finally intervened to lift her from the darkness and despair that enveloped her.

And I wonder, most of all, if she'll ever make it out into the free world, or if she will spend the rest of her life in captivity, in her spirit, her body, and her mind.

All quotes and interviews not cited in these endnotes consist of original, in-person, telephone, or written interviews and correspondence.

INTRODUCTION: THE INVISIBLE STRUGGLE

1. Bureau of Justice Statistics, "One in 32 Adults Was in Prison, Jail, on Probation or Parole at the End of 2005," press release, 30 November 2006.

2. Editors, "U.S. Inmate Populations on the Rise: U.S. Leads World in Number of Incarcerated," *Correctional News*, July/August 2006.

3. "Public Safety, Public Spending: Forecasting America's Prison Population: 2007-2011," Pew Charitable Trusts, February 2007. (This figure only represents people projected to be in state and federal prisons in 2011. It does not include projections on juvenile detention, immigration detention, jail populations, or the numbers of people on parole or probation.)

4. Paige M. Harrison and Allen J. Beck, "Prisoners in 2005," Bureau of Justice Statistics, November 2006; Nell Bernstein, "We Are All Prisoners Now," New American Media, 23 May 2006.

5. Ibid; Harrison and Beck, "Prison and Jail Inmates at Midyear 2005," Bureau of Justice Statistics, May 2006; Lauren E. Glaze and Seri Palla, "Probation and Parole in the United States, 2004," Bureau of Justice Statistics, November 2005.

6. Natasha A. Frost, Judith Greene, and Kevin Pranis, "Hard Hit: The Growth in the Imprisonment of Women, 1977-2004," December 2006, 9.

7. Ibid., Harrison and Beck, "Prisoners in 2005."

8. "Custody and Control: Conditions of Confinement in New York's Juvenile Prisons for Girls," Human Rights Watch, September 2006. (According to HRW, 70 percent of delinquency cases involving Euro-American girls are dismissed, compared to 30 percent of cases involving African-American girls.)

9. Ibid.

10. Ibid., Pew Charitable Trusts.

CHAPTER 1: HERE'S YOUR ONE-WAY TICKET TO PRISON

1. Jessica Mitford, *Kind & Usual Punishment: The Prison Business* (New York: Alfred A. Knopf, 1971), 16–17. (Out of print.)

2. Natasha A. Frost, PhD, Judith Greene, and Kevin Pranis, "Hard Hit: The Growth in the Imprisonment of Women, 1977–2004," Institute on Women & Criminal Justice, May 2006; William J. Sabol, Ph.D, Todd D. Minton, and Paige M. Harrison, "Prison and Jail Inmates at Midyear 2006," Bureau of Justics Statistics, June 2007.

3. Ibid.; Sabol, Minton, Harrison.

4. Paige M. Harrison and Allen J. Beck, PhD, "Prisoners in 2005," Bureau of Justice Statistics, November 2006.

5. E.g., Silja J. A. Talvi, "The New Plantation," *Gadflyer* (reprinted by AlterNet), 9 July 2004.

6. Silja J. A. Talvi, "Until the End of Their Days," ColorsNW magazine, November 2003.

7. Marc Mauer and Meda Chesney-Lind, editors. *Invisible Punishment: The Collateral Consequences of Mass Imprisonment* (New York: The New Press, 2002), 79.

8. Ibid., Frost, Greene, and Pranis; Christopher J. Mumola, "Incarcerated Parents and Their Children," Bureau of Justice Statistics, August 2000.

9. Ibid., Harrison and Beck.

10. John J. Gibbons and Nicholas de B. Katzenbach, "Confronting Confinement: A Report of The Commission on Safety and Abuse in America's Prisons" (June 2006): 19.

11. Ibid., Harrison and Beck.

12. Ibid.; "Prison and Jail Inmates at Midyear 2005," Bureau of Justice Statistics, May 2006; Lauren E. Glaze and Seri Palla, "Probation and Parole in the United States, 2004;" Sabol, Minton, and Harrison. (Ibid.)

13. Federal Bureau of Investigation, "Crime in the United States 2005," Uniform Crime Report, Table 33.

14. Ibid., Harrison and Beck and Ibid., Sabol, Minton, Harrison. (The Bureau of Justice Statistics does not report numbers for incarcerated Native Americans, Asian/Pacific Islanders, or people of other ethnicities (including people of mixed ethnicity), because there is no standardized reporting process from state to state. Furthermore, collected racial demographics are often based subjectively on a correctional employee's assessment of a person's ethnic background. In many cases, people with

light complexions are assumed to be "white," and people with darker complexions are designated as "black," even though they may self-describe as Latin or South American indigenous or Hispanic. In many states, Native Americans are simply lumped in with Euro-Americans.)

15. Earl Ofari Hutchinson, "Why So Many Black Women Are Behind Bars," AlterNet, 5 December 2006.

16. E.g., Eileen Poe-Yamagata, MS, and Jeffrey A. Butts, PhD, "Female Offenders in the Juvenile Justice System," Office of Juvenile Justice and Delinquency Prevention, June 1996; Joyce Burrell, "Juvenile Justice & Mental Health," American Institutes for Research, 2005; Cindy Liderman, Gayle Dakof, Maria Larrea, and Hua Li, "Characteristics of adolescent females in juvenile detention," *International Journal of Law and Psychiatry,* 27 (2004): 321–337.

17. Silja J. A. Talvi and Blak Washington, *Living Diary,* Powerful Voices, 2005.

18. Francie Latour, "Report says legal system fails girls in trouble," *The Boston Globe,* 27 May 2003.

19. Campaign for Youth Justice, "The Consequences Aren't Minor: The Impact of Trying Youth as Adults and Strategies for Reform," 21 March 2007; "Juvenile Injustice," *The New York Times,* 11 May 2007.

20. Ibid., Campaign for Youth Justice; National Council on Crime and Delinquency, press release, 5 January 2007.

21. Ibid., *The New York Times;* Dr. Robert Johnson, "Effects on Violence of Laws and Policies Facilitating the Transfer of Juveniles from the Juvenile Justice System," Centers for Disease Control and Prevention's Task Force on Community Preventive Services, *American Journal of Preventive Medicine,* April 2007.

22. E.g., Torsten Ove, "It only looks like the girls have gone wild," *Pittsburgh Post-Gazette*, 28 January 2007.

23. Brian A. Reaves, "Violent Felons in Large Urban Counties," Bureau of Justice Statistics, July 2006.

24. Ibid., Frost, Greene, and Pranis.

25. Mark E. Kann, *Punishment, Prisons and Patriarchy: Liberty and Power in the Early American Republic* (New York: New York University Press, 2005), 82.

26. CNN, *Showbiz Tonight*, 19 May 2007.

27. Sarah Stillman, "A Far Cry from Camp Cupcake," *The Huffington Post*, 30 January 2007.

28. "Judith Miller Talks about Her Jail Conditions," TalkLeft.com, 13 November 2005. (Miller spent eighty-five days in jail after she refused to disclose the federal government sources that had leaked the identity of CIA operative Valerie Plame.)

29. Karen Voyles, "Change in air at women's prison," *South Florida Sun-Sentinel*, 23 October 2006.

30. The Associated Press, "California Report Criticizes Prisons as 'Dysfunctional,'" 4 July 2004.

31. Little Hoover Corrections Crisis, "Time Is Running Out," February 2007.

32. M. L. Lyke, "Number of female inmates soars," *Seattle Post-Intelligencer*, 5 March 2003.

33. Kathryn Watterson, *Women in Prison: Inside the Concrete Womb* (Boston: Northeastern University Press, 1973), 290.

34. Ibid., 79.

35. ASPC—Perryville, "Perryville Staff Adapts to Female Inmates," internal newsletter, 2001.

CHAPTER 2: WOMEN IN WARTIME

1. Natasha A. Frost, Judith Greene, and Kevin Pranis, "Hard Hit: The Growth in the Imprisonment of Women, 1977–2004," Institute on Women & Criminal Justice, 2006.

2. Marc Mauer, *Race to Incarcerate* (New York: The New Press, 2006), 159; Federal Bureau of Investigation, "Crime in the United States, 2005," Uniform Crime Report, table 29, 2006 (Exact number totaled 1,846,351.)

3. U.S. Drug Enforcement Administration, "Drug Scheduling." Found online at: www.usdoj.gov/dea/pubs/scheduling/html.

4. Federal Bureau of Investigation, "Arrests for Drug Abuse Violations," Uniform Crime Report.

5. "The Good, the Bad, and the Ugly—2008 U.S. Federal Drug Control Budget," *Drug War Chronicle,* 9 February 2007.

6. Mike Stobbe, "Drug overdose deaths surging, CDC reports," The Associated Press, 9 February 2007.

7. "The Good, the Bad, and the Ugly," *Drug War Chronicle.*

8. "ONCDP Media Campaign: Drug Czar's Anti-Drug Ads a Flop, GAO Says," *Drug War Chronicle,* 1 September 2006.

9. National Institute on Drug Abuse, "Women and Drug Abuse," 2007. Found online at: www.nida.nih.gov/WomenDrugs/Women-Drugabuse.html.

10. Break the Chains, and the Brennan Center at NYU School of Law, "Caught in the Net: The Impact of Drug Policies on Women and Families," 2005; Darlene Superville, "Few of 22 million drug users receive treatment," The Associated Press, 16 September 2003; U.S. Department of Health and Human Services, "22 Million in the U.S. Suffer From Substance Dependence or Abuse," press release, 5 September 2003; Rita Rubin, "1 in 5 adults have a close relative who is or was addicted to drugs or alcohol," cover story, USA Today, 20 July 2006. (One in five adults in the United States has a close relative who is/was addicted to alcohol or drugs, or both. Far more women say that a loved one's addiction has hurt them emotionally and physically (35 percent of females, versus 22 percent of men); hurt their personal finances (19 percent versus 12 percent); and hurt their marriages (21 percent versus 11 percent).

11. The National Center on Addiction and Substance Abuse at Columbia University, "Wasting the Best and the Brightest: Substance Abuse at America's Colleges and Universities," 15 March 2007.

12. National Institute on Drug Abuse, "Women and Drug Abuse."

13. Bureau of Justice Statistics, "Drug Use and Dependence, State and Federal Prisoners, 2004," October 2006.

14. Bureau of Justice Statistics fact sheet. Found online at: www.ojp.usdoj.gov/bjs/crimoff.htm.

15. Jesselyn McCurdy and Deborah J. Vagins, "Cracks in the System: Twenty Years of the Unjust Federal Crack Cocaine Law," American Civil Liberties Union, October 2006.

16. Bureau of Justice Statistics, "Prisoners in 2005," 8.

17. Mauer, 163.

18. Columbia University, "Wasting the Best and the Brightest."

19. Susan Boyd, *From Witches to Crack Moms: Women, Drug Law, and Policy* (Durham, North Carolina: Carolina Academic Press, 2004), 40.

20. Ibid., 38–44.

21. Ibid.; Silja J. A. Talvi, "Big, Bad, Black Dealers and Junkie White Girls," AlterNet, 13 March 2001.

22. U.S. General Accounting Office, "Women in Prison: Issues and Challenges Confronting U.S. Correctional Systems," 1999.

23. Angeli Rasbury, "Out of Jail, Mothers Struggle to Reclaim Children," Women's eNews, 17 September 2006.

24. "Cracks in the System," 1.

25. Ibid., i.

26. "Caught in the Net," 25.

27. "Despite Supreme Court Ruling Throwing Out Federal Sentencing Guidelines, Federal Drug Sentences Get Longer," *Drug War Chronicle*, 24 March 2006.

28. National Institute on Drug Abuse, "Women and Drug Abuse."

29. *Turning a Corner*, Beyondmedia Education, 2006.

30. Stamper, Norm. *Breaking Rank: A Top Cop's Exposé of the Dark Side of American Policing.* (New York: Nation Books, 2005), 39–52.

31. Ibid., 47.

32. Ibid.

33. Silja J. A. Talvi, "The Truth About the Green River Killer," AlterNet, 12 November 2003.

34. Ibid.

35. Ibid.

36. Ibid.

37. Katherine Beckett, "Race and Drug Law Enforcement in Seattle," University of Washington Department of Sociology, 3 May 2004.

38. U.S. Census Bureau, "American Community Survey: Seattle Fact Sheet," 2005.

39. Stamper, 100.

40. Ibid., 101.

41. "Caught in the Net," 17–18.

42. Silja J. A. Talvi, "Dog: The Bounty Hunter," WIMN's Voices, a Group Blog on Women, Media and Criminal Justice/Prisons, 22 August 2006. Found online at: www.wimnonline.org/WIMNsVoicesBlog/?p=233).

43. Arianna Huffington, "The War on Drugs Is Really a War on Minorities," *Los Angeles Times,* 28 March 2007.

44. Fox Butterfield, "Women Find a New Arena for Equality: Prison," *The New York Times*, 29 December 2003.

45. Silja J. A. Talvi, "Finally, Justice in Tulia," AlterNet, 3 April 2003.

46. Ibid.

47. Ibid.

CHAPTER 3: ABUSE BEHIND THE WALL

1. Tamara Lush, "Behind bars, sex charges the air," *St. Petersburg Times*, 24 September 2006, 7A. (Price received a two-year probationary period.)

2. Ibid. (Bolton later sued the BOP in civil court, eventually receiving a $35,000 settlement.)

3. Ibid. (The officer's names, respectively, were Mark Knight and Derrick Jackson.)

4. Office of the Inspector General and the Department of Justice, "Deterring Staff Sexual Abuse of Federal Inmates," April 2005.

5. E.g., Principle 6 of the United Nations Body of Principles for the Protection of All Persons Under Any Form of Detention or Imprisonment; the International Covenant on Civil and Political Rights; The Declaration on the Elimination of Violence Against Women, which recognizes that women in detention are particularly vulnerable to physical and sexual violence; and the International Covenant on Economic, Social, and Cultural Rights, which the United States has signed but not yet ratified. In a 1994 decision in *Farmer v. Brennan,* the U.S. Supreme Court also recognized that the rape of a prisoner constituted a violation of the Eight Amendment of the U.S. Constitution, prohibiting "cruel and unusual punishment."

6. Rule 53 of the Standard Minimum Rules for the Treatment of Prisoners, which provides that "women prisoners shall be attended and supervised only by women officers," with allowances made for male guards accompanied by women on staff.

7. Dana M. Britton, *At Work in the Iron Cage: The Prison as Gendered Organization* (New York: New York University Press, 2003), 9–10.

8. "Female Offenders: As Their Numbers Grow, So Does the Need for Gender-Specific Programming," *Corrections Compendium,* March 1998.

9. CCWF gender breakdown of correctional employees, obtained 20 July 2006, on-site. California Prison Focus, "Dignity for Women Prisoners Campaign," press release, 12 May 2007. (The nationwide percentage of all female correctional officers is 13%.)

10. Stop Prisoner Rape, "Stories from the Inside: Prisoner Rape and the War on Drugs" (2007): 8.

11. Allen J. Beck and Paige M. Harrison, "Sexual Violence Reported by Correctional Authorities 2005," Bureau of Justice Statistics, 2006.

12. E.g., Human Rights Watch (HRW) and the American Civil Liberties Union (ACLU), "Custody and Control: Conditions of Confinement in New York's Juvenile Prisons for Girls," September 2006; Governor's Juvenile Justice Committee, "Minority Youth in the Juvenile Justice System," Washington State Juvenile Justice Report, 2005; Child Trends Databank, "Juvenile Detention: Adolescents in Residential Placement," 2005; Meda Chesney-Lind, "What about the girls? Delinquency programming as if gender mattered," *Corrections Today* (February 2001): 38–45; Gayle A. Dakof, Maria A. Larrea, Cindy S. Lederman, and Hua Li, "Characteristics of Adolescent Females in Juvenile Detention," *International Journal of Law and Psychiatry* 27 (2004): 321–37.

13. Ibid., HRW and ACLU.

14. Michael Rigby, "Colorado Teenagers Raped by Guards Settle for $165,000 Each," *Prison Legal News* (August 2005): 35; Editors, "Girls Sue Alabama Juvenile Prison for Abuse," *Prison Legal News* (September 2002): 15.

15. United States General Accounting Office, "Women in Prison: Issues and Challenges Confronting U.S. Correctional Systems," Report to the Honorable Eleanor Holmes Norton, House of Representatives, December 1999.

16. Caroline Wolf Harlow, PhD, Bureau of Justice Statistics, "Prior Abuse Reported by Inmates and Probationers," April 1999.

17. The names of jail inmates, most of whom were in pretrial detention, are withheld here at the request of the sheriff's department. I have assigned pseudonyms instead.

18. Allen J. Beck and Laura M. Maruschak, Bureau of Justice Statistics, "Mental Health Treatment in State Prisons, 2000," 2001.

19. American Psychiatric Association, "Psychiatric Services in Jails and Prisons: A Task Force Report of the American Psychiatric Association," 2000.

20. National Geographic Channel, *Lockdown: Women Behind Bars*, DVD, 2007; aggregate in-person and written interviews with prisoners in these facilities.

21. E.g., *Drug Sense Weekly* 237, 8 February 2002.

22. Amnesty International USA, "Abuse of Women in Custody: Sexual Misconduct and Shackling of Pregnant Women," 6 March 2001; Stop Prisoner Rape, "In The Shadows: Sexual Violence in U.S. Detention Facilities," Alternative NGO Report to the 36th Session of the U.N. Committee Against Torture, 2006. (The states that allow the "consent" defense include Colorado, New Hampshire, and Wyoming.)

23. Michael Rigby, "Michigan's Dirty Little Secret: Sexual Abuse of Female Prisoners Pervasive, Ongoing," *Prison Legal News* (January 2006): 12–15.

24. Human Rights Watch, "All Too Familiar: Sexual Abuse of Women in U.S. State Prisons," 1996.

25. Human Rights Watch, "Nowhere to Hide: Retaliation Against Women in Michigan State Prisons," 1998; Human Rights Watch, "Human Rights Watch Challenges Michigan's Subpoena to Reveal Confidential Information," press release, 15 October 1998.

26. Michael Rigby, "Ban on Male Guards in Michigan Women's Prisons Upheld," *Prison Legal News* (December 2005): 34.

27. Ava Azizi, "New York Department of Corrections Sued Over Systematic Rape of Women Prisoners," *Prison Legal News* (December 2003): 17.

28. Editors, "New Mexico Jail Prisoners Raped by Judge and Guards Settle for $890,000," *Prison Legal News* (March 2006): 19.

29. Holly Ross Hughes, "Suit claims jailers ignored inmate sex," *Houston Chronicle* (Austin bureau), 16 February 2006.

30. Hector Castro, "Sexualized Atmosphere in county jail, study says," *Seattle Post-Intelligencer,* 14 November 2006; Natalie Singer, "County Jail officer to become an inmate," *Seattle Times,* 2 December 2006; Mike Carter, "Inquiry into jail begins," *Seattle Times,* 5 December 2006; Natalie Singer, "Former jail guard sentenced in sexual-misconduct case," *Seattle Times,* 6 December 2007; Editors, "Justice Department review," *Seattle Post-Intelligencer,* 6 March 2007.

31. Sarah Etter, "Legal Roundup," Corrections.com, 21 November 2006; Stop Prisoner Rape, "Stories from Inside: Prison Rape and the War on Drugs," 10.

32. Etter; John J. Gibbons, and Nicholas de B. Katzenbach, co-chairs, the Commission on Safety and Abuse in America's Prisons, "Confronting Confinement" (June 2006): 34.

33. Brent Kallestad, "2 People killed in Fla. prison shooting," The Associated Press, 21 June 2006.

34. Indictment in U.S. District Court for the Northern District of Florida Tallahassee Division, *United States of America v. Alfred Barnes, Gregory Dixon, Ralph Hill, Vincent Johnson, Alan Moore, and E. Lavon Spence,* 20 June 2006.

35. When I spoke with Peggy's parents in March 2007, they confirmed that the entire prison environment has remained restrictive, and that there is more surveillance of the women than ever before, including enhanced listening devices to catch hushed conversations. For many weeks after the shooting, female prisoners were denied all visitation; family members who made the long journey to visit their loved ones were notified only when they arrived that they had to go home.

CHAPTER 4: DANGEROUS MEDICINE

1. For more on Southerland's claims of innocence, see www.deniedjustice.com.

2. Texas inmates are always put to work, often in labor-intensive blue-collar jobs, but do not earn any money, sick time, or vacation time, regardless of the quality of their work or their seniority.

3. Southerland believes that some male prisoners rigged the machine when they were informed that their jobs were being given over to female prisoners.

4. Heavy-labor "hoe squads" and chain gangs have made a comeback in states like Arizona, Louisiana, Alabama, and Texas. Hoe squads and chain gangs are notorious for making prisoners endure hard labor and humiliation. Guards are known to count

how many times a prisoner's dulled hoe hits the ground, and if they do not work fast enough, if they fail to obey an order immediately, or if they fall back because of heat exhaustion, Southerland told me that a prisoner can be placed in a real dog cage in the work area as punishment, and/or can be written up for a disciplinary violation, which can result in one to two months of segregation. Prisoners who pass out from heat exhaustion often end up very ill and dehydrated.

5. It is typical for prisoners to have to pack up all of their belongings for any kind of transfer, even if they are expected to have a short stay at a hospital, because subsequent transfers to other prisons are not unusual, and the officers at the originating facility do not want to be responsible for the extra work of shipping clothing and purchased items (such as televisions, radios, books, and so forth).

6. E.g., Silja J. A. Talvi, "Prison as Laboratory," *In These Times*, 10 January 2002.

7. Christopher J. Mumola, "Medical Causes of Death in State Prisons, 2001–2004," Bureau of Justice Statistics, January 2007.

8. Ingrid Binswanger, MD, Marc Stern, MD, Richard Deyo, MD, Patrick Heagerty, PhD, Allen Cheadle, PhD, Joann Elmore, MD, and Thomas Koepsell, MD, "Release from Prison: A High Risk of Death for Former Inmates," *New England Journal of Medicine* 356 (2007): 157–65. (The study followed released prisoners in any of the facilities operated by the Washington Department of Corrections from July 1999 through December 2003.)

9. E.g., Alan Elsner, *Gates of Injustice: The Crisis in America's Prisons*, (Prentice Hall: New Jersey, 2004), 122–125; Tammy Anderson, PhD, "Issues in the Availability of Health Care for Women Prisoners." In *The Incarcerated Woman: Rehabilitative Programming in Women's Prisons*, edited by Susan F. Sharp (New Jersey: Prentice Hall, 2003), 49–60.

10. Ibid., Anderson, 50.

11. Leah Thayer, "Hidden Hell," *Amnesty* magazine, fall 2004.

12. Maeve Reston, "Study Faults Women's Prison Healthcare," *Los Angeles Times,* 7 October 2006.

13. ACLU of Wisconsin, "Judge Rejects State Government Attempts to Evade ACLU's Claims of Deficient Medical Care in Wisconsin's Largest Women's Prison," 15 March 2007.

14. Ibid., Anderson, 50–51.

15. One example of the lack of fresh produce in prisoner diets is exemplified by the Texas prison system, in which ketchup is considered a vegetable for inmate meals, something that harkens back to former president Ronald Reagan's infamous proclamation about the content of school lunches.

16. Ellen M. Barry, "Bad Medicine: Health Care Inadequacies in Women's Prisons," American Bar Association, *Criminal Justice Magazine* 16, no. 1 (spring 2001).

17. Cassie Pierson, "LSPC Mourns the Loss of Sherrie Chapman," Legal Services for Prisoners with Children press release, December 2002.

18. Silja J. A. Talvi, "Criminal Procedure," MotherJones.com, 19 August 1999; Talvi, "Public Interest Law: An interview with Ellen Barry," *Z Magazine,* July 2000; A. Clay Thompson, "Cancer in the cells," *San Francisco Bay Guardian*, 24 February 1999.

19. Ibid., Talvi, "Criminal Procedure."

20. Ibid., Thayer. (Prisoners often poke fun at the ridiculous prevalence of over-the-counter palliatives for serious medical conditions, mimicking the question posed by correctional employees when women ask for pain relief: "Tylenol or Maalox?")

21. Ibid., Talvi, "Criminal Procedure."

22. Talvi, "Female inmates allege deficient medical care," *San Francisco Examiner,* 12 October 2000.

23. Talvi, "Critical Condition," *In These Times,* 2 April 2001. (Precedent-setting health-care-related court decisions in the United States have included: *Estelle v. Gamble* (1976), which ruled that prisons had to provide adequately for the medical needs of inmates; and *Brown v. Beck* (1980), which ruled that medical care to prisoners needed to be "reasonable," but that there was no requirement past that point regarding the excellence of care. Lawsuits that take on medical and/or mental health-care in prisons often cite violations of the Eighth and Fourteenth Amendments to the U.S. Constitution. Respectively, the amendments prohibit cruel and unusual punishment and mandate that federal and state governments guarantee equal protection to women and ethnic minorities.)

24. Ibid., Talvi, "Criminal Procedure."

25. Ibid., "Critical Condition."

26. Ibid., Pierson.

27. Alexa K. Apallas, "The Five Faces of America's Looming Correctional Health Crisis," *Correctional News,* September–October 2005; Silja J. A. Talvi, "Hepatitis C: A 'Silent Epidemic' Strikes U.S. Prisons." In *Prison Nation: The Warehousing of America's Poor,* edited by Tara Herivel and Paul Wright (Routledge: New York, 2003), 181–86.

28. Ibid., Talvi, "Hepatitis C"; Laura M. Maruschak, "HIV in Prisons, 2004" and "Medical Problems of Jail Inmates," Bureau of Justice Statistics, 19 November 2006. (AIDS-related deaths decreased from 2001 to 2004, in large part because of the newer generation of protease inhibitors and combination antiretroviral medicines. However, there has been an *increase* in prisoners with AIDS, at three times the rate within the general U.S. population.)

29. Ibid., Talvi, "Hepatitis C"; The Associated Press, "Prison's deadliest inmate, hepatitis C, escaping," 14 March 2007. (The latter article puts the percentage of HCV infections at 40 percent.)

30. Ibid., Talvi, "Hepatitis C."

31. Ibid.; Joe Mandak, "Epidemic of hepatitis C in nation's prisons," The Associated Press, 5 September 2001; David Rohde, "A Health Danger from a Needle Becomes a Scourge Behind Bars," *The New York Times*, 6 August 2001.

32. Ibid., Rohde; National Commission on Correctional Health Care, "Health Status of Soon-to-Be-Released Inmates: A Report to Congress," 2002.

33. John J. Gibbons and Nicholas de B. Katzenbach, "Conditions of Confinement," the Commission on Safety on Abuse in America's Prisons (June 2006): 50.

34. Ibid., 40.

35. Interviews with San Francisco's Department of Public Health and the San Francisco Sheriff's Department.

36. Michael Rigby, "Staph Infections Kill Women Prisoners in Pennsylvania, Coroner's Office Raided," *Prison Legal News*, December 2003.

37. Shelbi Harris, "The health care system in prison has failed us," the California Coalition for Women Prisoners, *The Fire Inside* 34, fall 2006–winter 2007.

38. Brent Staples, "Treat the Epidemic Behind Bars Before It Hits the Streets," *The New York Times,* 22 June 2004.

39. Matthew T. Clarke, "Deadly Drug Resistant Staph in Prisons Throughout USA," *Prison Legal News,* December 2003.

40. National Commission on Correctional Health Care, "Health Status of Soon-to-Be-Released Inmates: A Report to Congress," 2002; Marc Mauer, *Race to Incarcerate* (New York: The New Press, 2006), 200.

41. CBSNews.com, "Cost Cutters Slash Prison Food Budgets," 14 May 2003; Fox Butterfield, "States Putting Inmates on Diets to Trim Budgets," *The New York Times,* 30 September 2003.

42. The November Coalition, "RazorWire" newsletter, 26 November 2006.

43. "Fake Meat, Real Scandal," *The Daily Texan,* 14 August 2001.

44. Alexa K. Apallas, "The Five Faces of America's Looming Correctional Health Crisis," *Correctional News,* September-October 2005.

45. Ibid.

CHAPTER 5: TRYING TO STAY SANE

1. Silja J. A. Talvi, "Female inmates allege deficient medical care," *San Francisco Examiner,* 12 October 2000, sec. A-6.

2. As it turned out, there was cause for this wariness about outsider presence in the SHU. Just two years prior to my visit, Amnesty International USA had visited this facility, releasing their findings in 1999 in a report entitled, "Not Part of My Sentence: Violations of the Human Rights of Women in Custody." Included in that report was a strongly worded critique of the facility, which resulted in a temporary upswing of attention from the news media to the conditions at VSPW Ad Seg/ SHU, as well as in other such lockdown facilities around the country.

3. In 2007, federal Judge Lawrence Karlton ordered California Governor Arnold Schwarzenegger to spend more than $600 million to improve mental health services for prisoners (Pam Belluck, "Mentally Ill Inmates at Risk in Isolation, Lawsuit Says," *The New York Times,* 9 March 2007).

4. Mary Beth Pfeiffer, "A Death in the Box," *The New York Times,* 31 October 2004.

5. Silja J. A. Talvi, "What We Do to Women in Prison, " *Sojourner: The Women's Forum* (May 1999): 13, 16.

6. Jeffrey Kluger, "Are Prisons Driving Prisoners Mad?" *Time,* 26 January 2007.

7. Terry Kupers, MD, *Prison Madness: The Mental Health Crisis Behind Bars and What We Must Do About It* (San Francisco: Jossey-Bass Publishers, 1999), 57.

8. National Geographic Channel, *Lockdown: Women Behind Bars,* DVD, 2007.

9. Complaints about medical and mental health conditions at WCCW are less frequent than they once were, according to prisoners and staff members whom I interviewed, but it is of note that I was not allowed to see either the prison's control unit or the nearby mental health ward, allegedly because it would cause agitation among the prisoners housed there. (Silja J. A. Talvi, "Criminal Procedure," MotherJones.com, 17 August 1999.)

10. "Suicide-resistant" clothing, showers, bedding, mattresses, utensils, and toilet and sink combos form a burgeoning portion of the correctional-industry market, something that seems to reflect institutional concern over lawsuits more than over the actual comfort or safety of prisoners themselves. Products like the "suicide-resistant" toilet-sink combo are regularly advertised in the prison industry's trade publication, *Correctional News,* in which Willoughby Industries proclaims that they are "designed to reduce the risk of a fixture being used as a suicide device. . . . Suicide-resistant showers are also available!"

11. American Civil Liberties Union, "Judge Rejects Government Efforts to Block Details of Deficient Medical Care in Wisconsin's Largest Women's Prison," press release, 15 March 2007.

12. Michael Rigby, "Lawsuit Filed Over Healthcare at Wisconsin's Women's Prison, More Possible," *Prison Legal News* (January 2007): 20–21.

13. Center on Juvenile and Criminal Justice, "The Risks Juveniles Face When They Are Incarcerated with Adults," 2002.

14. Elise Castelli, "Mentally Ill Kids Incarcerated, Study Finds," *Los Angeles Times,* 25 January 2005; Nancy Holland, "The juvenile justice system and youngsters with mental illness," 21 March 2007. Found online at: www.khou.com.

15. Sasha Abramsky, *American Furies: Crime, Punishment, and Vengeance in the Age of Mass Imprisonment* (Boston: Beacon Press, 2007), 165.

16. Kupers, 233.

17. Ibid., 227–228.

18. Ibid.

19. Paula M. Ditton, "Mental Health and Treatment of Inmates and Probationers," special report, Bureau of Justice Statistics (1999): 8.

20. Sasha Abramsky and Jamie Fellner, "Ill-Equipped: U.S. Prisons and Offenders with Mental Illness," Human Rights Watch, 2002.

21. Sally Satel, "Out of the Asylum, Into The Cell," *The New York Times*, 1 November 2003.

22. The notable exception is the fact that men in jails and prisons can be locked down without having committed any infraction if they are presumed to be gang members.

23. Editors, "Prison Horrors for the Mentally Ill," *The New York Times*, 23 April 2007.

24. Mark Arax and Mark Gladston, "State Whitewashed Fatal Brutality and Mismanagement at Corcoran," *Los Angeles Times*, 5 July 1998.

25. Angela Davis and Cassandra Shaylor, "A Question of Control," *San Francisco Chronicle*, 9 April 2000.

26. Norman Johnston, *Forms of Constraint: A History of Prison Architecture* (Urbana, Illinois: University of Illinois Press, 2000), 72–82; Mark E. Kann, *Punishment, Prisons, and Patriarchy: Liberty and Power in the Early American Republic* (New York: New York University Press, 2005), 181–82; Norval Morris and David J. Rothman, editors, *The Oxford History of the Prison: The Practice of Punishment in Western Society* (New York: Oxford University Press, 1995), 104–14.

27. Kann, 181.

28. Ibid., 182.

29. Detective Joseph Petrocelli, "Are Supermax Prisons a Good Idea?" Officer.com, 12 October 2006.

30. National Campaign to Stop Control Unit Prisons, findings posted online, 1997.

31. Lorna Rhodes, Total Confinement: Madness and Reason in the Maximum Security Prison (California: University of California Press, 2004).

32. John J. Gibbons and Nicholas de B. Katzenbach, co-chairs, "Confronting Confinement: Report of The Commission on Safety and Abuse in America's Prisons" (New York: Vera Institute of Justice, 2006), 56.

33. "Treating Mental Illness in Prison," The New York Times, 2 November 2003.

34. "Suing for Sanity," ABCNews.com, 1 February 2001; David Fathi, telephone interview by author, 6 April 2006.

35. "Confronting Confinement," 57.

36. Ibid., 55.

37. Ibid. (The damage that can be inflicted by punitive isolation was brought to renewed public attention in early 2007, as defense attorneys and journalists took notice of the poor emotional state of terrorism defendant Jose Padilla, who had been locked away in supermax-style cells and subject to continued sensory deprivation.)

38. Lockdown: Women Behind Bars, 2007.

39. "Study: Women Inmates Have Higher Rate of Mental Health Problems," Correctional News (November–December 2006): 14.

40. Jennifer Warren, "Mental Ills Common in Prison, Jail," *Los Angeles Times,* 7 September 2006.

41. Bernard E. Harcourt, "The Mentally Ill, Behind Bars," *The New York Times,* 15 January 2007.

42. Ibid.

43. Alexa K. Apallas, "The Five Faces of America's Looming Correctional Health Crisis," *Correctional News* (September–October 2005): 37–38.

CHAPTER 6: CRIMINALIZING MOTHERHOOD

1. Phillip Caston, *The Charleston Post and Courier* (7 October 2003): 1–2.

2. Rick Bragg, "Defender of God, South and Unborn," *The New York Times,* 13 January 1998.

3. Ibid.

4. National Advocates for Pregnant Women, "What's wrong with making it a crime to be pregnant and have a drug problem?" fact sheet, 9 March 2006.

5. Andrew Racine et. al., "The Association Between Prenatal Care and Birth Weight Among Women Exposed to Cocaine in New York City," *JAMA* 270 (1993): 1581, 1585–86.

6. Cynthia L Cooper, "This woman was thrown in jail for being pregnant," *Marie Claire,* 77.

7. Cooper, 77.

8. Petition for Writ of Certiorari to the Supreme Court of South Carolina in *Regina D. McKnight v. State of South Carolina*, 2003.

9. "Free Regina McKnight," *Anderson Independent Mail*, 21 November 2002.

10. David Firestone, "Woman Is Convicted of Killing Her Fetus by Smoking Cocaine," *The New York Times*, 18 May 2001.

11. Sheigla Murphy and Marsha Rosenbaum, *Pregnant Women on Drugs: Combating Stereotypes and Stigma* (New Brunswick, New Jersey: Rutgers University Press, 1999), 140.

12. Ibid., 141.

13. E.g., Alan Mozes, "Poverty Has a Greater Impact than Cocaine on Young Brain," ReutersHealth.com, 6 December 1999.

14. The number of children living in poverty in the United States increased by more than 11 percent between 2000 and 2005, to exceed 13 million children, according to an analysis by the Children's Defense Fund and the National Center for Children in Poverty. Overall, Americans living in "low-income" families comprise at least thirty-nine million, reports the Working Poor Families Project.

15. Darshak Sanghavi, "Baby Gap: The Surprising Truth About America's Infant-Mortality Rate," 16 March 2007.

16. Murphy and Rosenbaum, 104.

17. Julie B. Erlich and Lynn Paltrow, "Jailing Pregnant Women Raises Health Risks," Women's eNews, 20 September 2006.

18. Katha Pollitt, "Pregnant and Dangerous," *The Nation* (26 April 2004): 9; National Advocates for Pregnant Women (NAPW) press release, 17 July 2006.

19. Ibid., NAPW.

20. Drug Policy Alliance, "Supreme Court Will Not Review Murder Conviction of Woman Who Suffered a Stillbirth," press release, 6 October 2003. South Carolina also has quite a reputation for strange punishment policies, as it is the only state to have come up with a plan to cut a period of incarceration for prisoners who donate their internal body parts, placing a specific value on such organs as kidneys, which would earn a prisoner 180 days off his or her sentence. (Seanna Adcox, "S.C. May Cut Jail Time for Organ Donors," The Associated Press, 9 March 2007.)

21. Stephanie Nelson, "Pregnant mom in jail," *The Andalusia Star-News*, 10 December 2006; Michele Gerlach, "New mom arrested," *The Andalusia Star-News*, 5 October 2006.

22. Editors, "Arkansas Law Criminalizing Mothers Whose Newborns Test Positive for Drugs Accomplishes Little, Study Finds," *Drug War Chronicle*, 9 February 2007.

23. Linda M. Worley, MD, and Curtis Lowery, MD, "Treat, don't incarcerate pregnant women with drug problems," *Arkansas Sentinel-Record* (25 June 2005): 8.

24. Andrew A. Green, "Jailing women who used drugs while pregnant sparks debate," *Baltimore Sun*, 18 August 2005.

25. Karen Blakeman, "Prosecution in 'ice' case pregnancy triggers debate," *The Honolulu Advertiser*, 20 October 2003, 1B.

26. Jessica Fargen and O'Ryan Johnson, "Fearful teen swallowed black market pills to kill fetus," *The Boston Herald*, 25 January 2007.

27. Cooper, 74.

28. Ibid., 74–78.

CHAPTER 7: WOMEN WHO KILL

1. Silja J. A. Talvi, "Cycle of Violence: Battered women who kill their abusers are being jailed," *In These Times,* 11 October 2002.

2. Martha Stout, PhD, *The Sociopath Next Door* (New York: Broadway Books, 2005). (Despite this book's overwhelming focus on male sociopaths, the publishers chose a cover with two sets of female eyes out of three.)

3. Sara Eckel, "The devil wore J.Crew," *Salon,* 22 March 2005.

4. Catherine Wilson, "Aileen Wuornos says prison guards abusing her," The Associated Press, 13 July 2002.

5. Sharon Krum, "Lady killer," *Guardian* (U.K.), 2 August 2001.

6. Kathleen J. Ferraro, *Neither Angels nor Demons: Women, Crime, and Victimization* (New Hampshire: Northeastern University Press, 2006), 44–45.

7. Academy Awards transcript. Found online at: www.oscars.org/76academyawards/winners/03_lead_actress.htm.

8. Katherine Ramsland, PhD, *The Human Predator: A Historical Chronicle of Serial Murder and Forensic Investigation* (New York: Berkley Books, 2005), 227.

9. Ibid., Eckel.

10. Ibid., Ramsland, 84–85.

11. Callie Marie Rennison and Sarah Welchans, "Intimate Partner Violence 1993–2001," U.S. Department of Justice, 2003.

12. The Commonwealth Fund, "Survey of Women's Health," 1999. (In addition, one million women are stalked each year, according to the Stalking Resource Center.)

13. Ibid. (According to this study, the number could be anywhere from one million to three million. There is no official measure of this number, however—in large part because of the difficulty of obtaining this information from women who are experiencing domestic violence. This number is therefore derived from a variety of estimates, including Surgeon General Everett Koop's statement in 1989 that between three and four million American women are battered each year, and the American Psychological Association's estimate that 3.3 million children are exposed to violence from their mothers or caretakers.)

14. Ibid., Rennison. (Additionally, only one-quarter of incidents of rape or sexual assault were reported to police.)

15. Violence Policy Center, "When Men Murder Women," September 2004.

16. Federal Bureau of Investigation, "Uniform Crime Report, 2005," 2006.

17. U.S. Conference of Mayors, 2005.

18. Marcia Helme, "Domestic violence victims find no room left at shelters," *Seattle Post-Intelligencer*, 6 April 2007. (The cities with 0 percent domestic violence turn-away rates are: Arlington (TX), Cincinnati, El Paso, Fort Worth, Fresno, Honolulu, Indianapolis, Las Vegas, Miami, Tampa, and Tulsa.)

19. E.g., Elizabeth Dermody Leonard, "Stages of Gendered Disadvantaged in the Lives of Convicted Battered Women," in *Gendered Justice: Addressing Female Offenders* (Durham, North Carolina: Carolina Academic Press, 2003), 99–101; and *Neither Angels nor Demons: Women, Crime, and Victimization*, 33. (Many women even consider or commit suicide because they view it as their only logical way out of a domestic-violence situation.)

20. Violence Policy Center, "American Roulette: Murder-Suicide in the United States," April 2006.

21. Claire Renzetti, PhD, research conducted at the Department of Sociology, St, Joseph's University, 1991.

22. B. Giller and E. Goldsmith, "All in the Family: A Study of Intra-Familial Violence in the Los Angeles Jewish Community," Hebrew Union College, 1980.

23. Marie Tessier, "Black Women Seek Protection Closer to Home," Women's eNews, 10 January 2007. (Cited along with other facts about domestic violence in African American communities.)

24. National Center for Women and Policing, "Police Family Violence Fact Sheet." Found online at: www.womenandpolicing.org/violenceFS.asp.

25. Norm Stamper, *Breaking Rank: A Top Cop's Exposé of the Dark Side of American Policing* (New York: Nation Books, 2005), 1–16.

26. The Associated Press, "Woman killed in CNN headquarters complex," April 3, 2007; Christine Frey and Casey McNerthney, "Killer eluded police with fake names, frequent moves," *Seattle Post-Intelligencer,* April 4, 2007. (Less than two weeks later, on April 16, Cho Seung-Ho went on a shooting rampage at Virginia Tech, killing thirty-two students and teachers in the worst school shooting in U.S. history. The first person murdered was Emily Hilscher, whom Seung-Ho had stalked and grown obsessed with. She had never dated him, despite initial reports that she had broken up with, cheated on, or led on Seung-Ho. For more on the ways in which mainstream media and the university initially spun and dismissed the first Virginia Tech shooting as a "domestic dispute," see James Ridgway, "Mass Murderers and Women," MotherJones .com, 20 April 2007.)

27. The Associated Press, "Man who ran ring of brothels receives prison sentence," 14 April 2007.

28. My correspondence and interviews with women across the country who have been sentenced to life terms for their first nonviolent or violent offenses are indicative of the prevalence of unnecessarily punitive sentencing, especially for drug "conspiracy," crack cocaine possession or sales, and homicide related to an abusive partner. There is a clear need for quantitative research on the subject.

29. Paige Hall Smith, Kathryn E. Moracco, and John D. Butts, "Partner Homicide in Context: A Population-Based Perspective," *Homicide Studies* 2, no. 4 (1998): 410.

30. Ibid., Ferraro, 171.

31. Meda Chesney-Lind, Lisa Pasko, *The Female Offender: Girls, Women, and Crime* (Thousand Oaks: Sage Publications, 2004), 98.

32. Elizabeth Dermody Leonard, "Stages of Gendered Disadvantage in the Lives of Convicted Battered Women." In *Gendered Justice,* edited by Barbara Bloom (Durham, North Carolina: Carolina Academic Press, 2003).

33. Jeffrey N. Epstein, Benjamin E. Saunders, and Dean G. Kilpatrick, "Predicting PTSD in Women with a History of Childhood Rape," *Journal of Traumatic Stress* 10, no. 4 (1997); Maura O'Keefe, "Posttraumatic Stress Disorder Among Incarcerated Battered Women," *Journal of Traumatic Stress* 11, no. 1 (1998).

34. Ibid., Ferraro, 188.

35. Stephen H. Pollak, "Prosecutor Challenges Sentence Reviews," *Fulton County Daily Report,* 7 May 2004; Karen Collier, "Moseley lawsuit thrown out," WALB News Channel 10 website, 15 June 2004.

36. "A prisoner of politics," *San Francisco Chronicle,* 9 April 2007.

37. Jenifer Warren, "Davis' Parole Decisions Protested," *Los Angeles Times,* 21 August 2002.

38. Jill Stewart, "Maria Suarez, The Counselor," *LA Weekly,* 9 May 2007.

CHAPTER 8: WOMEN LOVING WOMEN

1. Allmovie.com, "Women in Prison."

2. S. Halleck and M. Herski, "Homosexual Behavior in a Correctional Institution for Adolescent Girls." *American Journal of Orthopsychiatry* 32: 911–17.

3. Joycelyn M. Pollock, *Women, Prison & Crime,* 2d ed. (Belmont, California: Wadsworth Group, 2002), 133.

4. Anthony Cuesta, "Lesbian Inmates Tie Knot: First Women to Marry in Canadian Prison," GayWired.com, 8 January 2007.

5. "Women Loving Women in Prison," *Sinister Wisdom* 61, winter 2003–2004.

6. Alan Mozes, "Inmates Fuel Sexual Assaults in Women's Prisons," Reuters, 28 November 2002.

7. Cassie Pierson, "'Illegal Sex': CDC's Biased Definition," California Coalition for Women Prisoners, *The Fire Inside* 18, summer 2001.

8. Kansas state legislation, 2003.

9. Correspondence with Washington Department of Corrections spokesperson, 8 January 2004.

10. M. L. Lyke, "The state has never executed a woman," *Seattle Post-Intelligencer,* 5 March 2003.

11. "Gay Prisoners Not Entitled to Double-Occupancy Cell," *Prison Legal News* (November 2003): 25.

CHAPTER 9: LIVING IN THE GOD POD

1. Freedom From Religion Foundation, "'Single Faith' Federal Prison Programs Canceled After FFRF Filed Suit," news release, October 2006.

2. "Third faith-based prison opens in Florida," *Sun-Sentinel,* 23 November 2005.

3. White House Faith-Based and Community Initiatives, "WHOFBCI Accomplishments in 2006," 2007.

4. David Miles, "Group sues over prison's 'God Pod,'" *The Santa Fe New Mexican,* 9 November 2005.

5. Institute in Basic Life Principles, "What We Do: A brief overview of our ministry." Found online at: www.IBLP.org.

6. Silja J. A. Talvi, "Beyond the God Pod," *Santa Fe Reporter,* 15 November 2005.

7. Institute in Basic Life Principles, informational materials found online at: www .iblp.org.

CHAPTER 10: SHIPPING WOMEN'S BODIES

1. Kevin Dayton, "Women inmates may go to Kentucky," *The Honolulu Advertiser*, 19 August 2005; Kevin Dayton, "Years of Problems Yield Few Answers," *The Honolulu Advertiser*, 3 October 2005.

2. Ibid.; Kevin Dayton, "Female Hawai'i inmates leave Colo. for Ky. prison," *The Honolulu Advertiser*, 29 September 2005; ACLU of Hawai'i and Community Alliance on Prisons, "Joint Statement by Community Alliance on Prisons and the ACLU of Hawai'i Calls Upon Community to Press Governor and Department of Public Safety to Mount a Thorough and Independent Investigation of Growing Scandal at Brush Prison in Colorado," 24 March 2005.

3. Kevin Dayton, "State can penalize prison operator," *The Honolulu Advertiser*, 3 November 2005; Ibid.; Andrew Wolfson, "Doing time a long way from home," *The Courier-Journal* (Louisville, Kentucky), 19 February 2006.

4. Ibid.; author interview with Kat Brady, Community Alliance on Prisons, 5 April 2006; Joan Conrow, "Women prisoners in Hawaii must cope with overcrowding and few amenities in facilities that were devised primarily to incarcerate men," *Honolulu Star-Bulletin*, 3 October 1996. (Jails in Hawaii are known to house up to six women per cell.)

5. Jason Thomas, "Prison is 2nd chance for some," *The Indianapolis Star*, 29 October 2004; Corrections Corporation of America information sheet on Otter Creek Correctional Center.

6. Ibid., Wolfson.

7. Ibid., Dayton, 4 November 2005; Interview with Frank Smith, Private Corrections Institute, 4 April 2006.

8. Jenifer Warren, "State plan to house inmates out of state is called unconstitutional," *Los Angeles Times,* 27 October 2006; Don Thompson, "Judges OK transfer of prisoners out of state," The Associated Press, 6 November 2006.

9. E.g., author interview with Kat Brady; personal interviews with prisoners in states including California, Georgia, Virginia, Tennessee, Texas, etc.; "The Bankrupt-Your-Family Calling Plan," *The New York Times,* 22 December 2006; Center for Constitutional Rights telephone monopoly lawsuit, *Walton v. NYSDOCS,* in the New York State Court of Appeals, October 2006. (The correctional phone market rakes in over $1 billion annually, according to the Florida Prisoners Legal Aid Organization.)

10. Pat Omandam, "Relapses high for inmates from isles," *Honolulu Star-Bulletin,* 21 January 2003.

11. Carla Crowder, "Alabama women dislike newer, safer prison," *The Birmingham News,* 11 May 2003.

12. Ibid.

13. Ibid., Dayton, 4 November 2005; Silja J. A. Talvi, "No Room in Prison? Ship 'Em Off," *In These Times,* May 2006.

14. Andrew Wolfson, "Hawaii to study death of prisoner," *The Courier-Journal* (Louisville, Kentucky), 15 January 2007; Hawaii Department of Public Safety; U.S. Census Data, 2004. (The exact percentage of native Hawaiians is 22.14 percent of the total state population.)

15. *Olim v. Wakinekona,* 461 U.S. 238, 103 Supreme Court 1741, 1983; *Froelich v. State of Wisconsin DOC,* 196 F. 3d 800, Seventh Circuit, 1999.

16. Kat Brady and Peter Gellatly, "The Real Cost of Exporting Hawai'i's Inmates," *The Honolulu Advertiser,* 2006.

17. *Floyd County Times* (Prestonsburg, Kentucky), 12 April 2006.

18. (Must add to chapter): Ibid., Talvi; Community Alliance on Prisons, compiled report of confidential prisoner anecdotes from Otter Creek, 7 December 2005.

19. (Must add to chapter): Ibid., Talvi; Ibid., Wolfson, 15 January 2007.

CHAPTER 11: INTERNATIONAL LOCKUP

1. Amnesty International, "Not part of my sentence: Violations of the human rights of women in custody," 1999.

2. William J. Sabol, Ph.D, Todd D. Minton, and Paige M. Harrison, "Prison and Jail Inmates at Midyear 2006," Bureau of Justics Statistics, June 2007.

3. BBC News In Depth, "World Prison Populations," 2007. Found online at: http://news.bbc.co.uk/1/shared/spl/hi/uk/06/prisons/html/nn1page1.stm.

4. Paige M. Harrison and Allen J. Beck, PhD, "Prisoners in 2005," Bureau of Justice Statistics, November 2006; Lucy Ward, "Too many women jailed, says [wife of the British Prime Minister Cherie] Booth," *The Guardian* (UK), 1 October 2002; Prison Justice Canada. Found online at: www.prisonjustice.ca/politics/facts_stats.html; The Criminal Sanctions Agency (Finland). Found online at: www.rikosseuraamus.fi.

5. Ibid., Sabol, Minton and Harrison.

6. Ibid., BBC News In Depth.

7. Ibid.

8. Randall McGowen, "The Well-Ordered Prison, England 1780–1865," in *The Oxford History of The Prison: The Practice of Punishment in Western Society,* edited by Norval Morris and David J. Rothman (New York: Oxford University Press, 1998), 71–99.

9. Norman Johnston, *Forms of Constraint: A History of Prison Architecture* (Chicago: University of Illinois Press, 2000), 88–94.

10. Holloway Prison background information provided by prison officials, 2006.

11. Ibid. (It is interesting to note that the prison's own informational material includes this unflattering background.)

12. Raekha Prasad, "Jailing women 'is a waste of money,'" *The Guardian* (UK), 12 July 2001.

13. Elizabeth Vincentelli, "Where Sisterhood is Bleached, Glossed, Dolce-Clad, and Powerful," *The New York Times,* 23 October 2005.

14. Matt Roper, "Prison by Numbers," the *Mirror,* 26 January 2007.

15. Islington Gazette, "Woman Found Hanging in Holloway Prison Cell," 4 July 2007. (no author)

16. "Smart Justice: Unlocking Solutions to Crime." Found online at: www.smartjustice .org/presssjwlaunch.htm.

17. "Ethnic Minorities: Crime and Criminal Justice." Found online at: www.rouncefield .homestead.com/files/.

18. "Women in Prison" fact sheet. Found online at: www.womeninprison.org.uk.

19. Eric Allison, "Women must be freed from self-harm," *The Guardian* (United Kingdom), 21 March 2007.

20. Canadian Human Rights Commission. Found online at: www.chrc-ccdp.ca/legislation_policies/chapter1-en.asp.

CHAPTER 12: HOPE AND HEALING

A portion of this chapter first appeared in an April 24, 2001, article entitled "Caught in the Drug War" that I wrote for AlterNet.

1. CAN-DO stands for Clemency for All Non-violent Drug Offenders. The organization can be found online at: http://candoclemency.com.

2. Patricia O'Brien, PhD, MSW, "Reducing Barriers to Employment for Women Ex-Offenders: Mapping the Road to Reintegration," SAFER Foundation, June 2002.

3. Corey Weinstein, MD, CCHP, "Parole for Women in California: Promise or Pathos," *Prison Legal News,* November 2005.

4. California Department of Corrections and Rehabilitation, "Gender Responsive Educational Re-Design," handout provided to attendees at a meeting of the Gender Responsive Strategies Commission in Fresno, California, 18 July 2006.

5. The Graduate Center of the City University of New York, "Changing Minds: The Impact of College in a Maximum-Security Prison," November 2001.

6. One of the most nonsensical aspects of the "welfare reform" bill signed into law by President Bill Clinton in 1996.

Selected Bibliography

BOOKS

Abramsky, Sasha. *American Furies: Crime, Punishment, and Vengeance in the Age of Mass Imprisonment.* Boston: Beacon Press, 2007.

Abramsky, Sasha. *Hard Time Blues: How Politics Built a Prison Nation.* New York: Thomas Dunne Books/St. Martin's Press, 2002.

Atwood, Jane Evelyn. *Too Much Time: Women in Prison.* London: Phaidon Press, 2000.

Bernstein, Nell. *All Alone in the World: Children of the Incarcerated.* New York: The New Press, 2005.

Bogira, Steve. *Courtroom 302: A Year Behind the Scenes in an American Criminal Courthouse.* New York: Vintage Books, 2006.

Boyd, Susan C. *From Witches to Crack Moms: Women, Drug Law, and Policy.* Durham, North Carolina: Carolina Academic Press, 2004.

Britton, Dana M. *At Work in the Iron Cage: The Prison as Gendered Organization.* New York: New York University Press, 2003.

Chesney-Lind, Meda and Lisa Pasko. *The Female Offender: Girls, Women, and Crime,* 2d. ed. Thousand Oaks, California: Sage Publications, 2003.

Corriero, Michael A. *Judging Children as Children: A Proposal for a Juvenile Justice System.* Philadelphia: Temple University Press, 2006.

Coyle, Andrew, Allison Campbell and Rodney Neufeld. *Capitalist Punishment: Prison Privatization & Human Rights.* London: Zed Books, 2003.

Díaz-Cotto, Juanita. *Chicana Lives and Criminal Justice: Voices from El Barrio.* Austin: University of Texas Press, 2006.

Elsner, Alan. *Gates of Injustice: The Crisis in America's Prisons.* Upper Saddle Creek, New Jersey: Pearson Education, 2004.

Ferraro, Kathleen J. *Neither Angels nor Demons: Women, Crime, and Victimization.* Boston: Northeastern University Press, 2006.

Gilmore, Ruth Wilson. *Golden Gulag: Prisons, Surplus, Crisis, and the Opposition in Globalizing California.* Berkeley: University of California Press, 2007.

Golden, Renny. *War on the Family: Mothers in Prison and the Families They Leave Behind*. New York: Routledge, 2005.

Gonnerman, Jennifer. *Life on the Outside: The Prison Odyssey of Elaine Bartlett*. New York: Picador, 2004.

Gottschalk, Marie. *The Prison and the Gallows: The Politics of Mass Incarceration in America*. Cambridge, England: Cambridge University Press, 2006.

Hallinan, Joseph T. *Going Up the River: Travels in Prison Nation*. New York: Random House, 2001.

Harris, David A. *Profiles in Justice: Why Racial Profiling Cannot Work*. New York: The New Press, 2002.

Herivel, Tara and Paul Wright, eds. *Prison Nation: The Warehousing of America's Poor*. New York: Routledge, 2003.

Jacobson, Michael. *Downsizing Prisons: How to Reduce Crime and Mass Incarceration*. New York: New York University Press, 2005.

Johnson, Paula C. *Inner Lives: Voices of African American Women in Prisons*. New York: New York University Press, 2003.

Johnston, Norman. *Forms of Constraint: A History of Prison Architecture*. Urbana, Illinois: University of Illinois Press, 2000.

Kann, Mark E. *Punishment, Prisons, and Patriarchy: Liberty and Power in the Early American Republic*. New York: New York University Press, 2005.

Kraska, Peter. *Militarizing the American Criminal Justice System*. Boston: Northeastern University Press, 2001.

Kupers, Terry, MD. *Prison Madness: The Mental Health Crisis Behind Bars and What We Must Do About It*. San Francisco: Jossey-Bass Publishers, 1999.

LeBlanc, Adrian Nicole. *Random Family: Love, Drugs, Trouble, and Coming of Age in the Bronx*. New York: Scribner, 2003.

Maerz, Curtis. *Drug Wars: The Political Economy of Narcotics*. Minneapolis: University of Minnesota Press, 2004.

Mauer, Marc. *Race to Incarcerate,* revised and updated. New York: The New Press, 2006.

Mitford, Jessica. *Kind & Unusual Punishment: The Prison Business*. New York: Alfred A. Knopf, 1973.

Morash, Merry and Pamela J. Schram. *The Prison Experience: Special Issues of Women in Prison*. Prospect Heights, Illinois: Waveland Press, Inc., 2002.

Morris, Norval and David J. Rothman, eds. *The Oxford History of the Prison: The Practice of Punishment in Western Society*. New York: Oxford University Press, 1995.

Murphy, Sheigla and Marsha Rosenbaum. *Pregnant Women on Drugs: Combating Stereotypes and Stigma.* New Brunswick, New Jersey: Rutgers University Press, 1999.

O'Brian, Patricia. *Making It in the "Free World": Women in Transition from Prison.* Albany, New York: State University of New York Press, 2001.

Owen, Barbara. *"In the Mix": Struggle and Survival in a Women's Prison.* Albany, New York: State University of New York Press, 1998.

Pollock, Joycelyn M. *Women, Prison & Crime,* 2d. ed. Belmont, California: Wadsworth Group, 2002.

Rathbone, Cristina. *A World Apart: Women, Prison, and Life Behind Bars.* New York: Random House, 2005.

Rhodes, Lorna. *Total Confinement: Madness and Reason in the Maximum Security Prison.* Berkeley: University of California Press, 2004.

Sharp, Susan F., ed. *The Incarcerated Woman: Rehabilitative Programming in Women's Prisons.* Upper Saddle Creek, New Jersey: Pearson Education, 2003.

Sikes, Gini. *8 Ball Chicks: A Year in the Violent World of Girl Gangs.* New York: Anchor Books, 1997.

Stamper, Norm. *Breaking Rank: A Top Cop's Exposé of the Dark Side of American Policing.* New York: Nation Books, 2005.

Talvi, Silja and Blak Washington, eds. *Living Diary*. Seattle: Powerful Voices, 2005.

Van Wormer, Katherine. *Counseling Female Offenders and Victims: A Strengths-Restorative Approach*. New York: Springer Publishing Company, 2001.

Wright, C. D. *One Big Self*. Port Townsend, Washington: Copper Canyon Press, 2003, 2007.

MAGAZINES
COLORS 50: Prison (July 2002): 50.

JOURNALS
"Women Loving Women in Prison," *Sinister Wisdom* 61, winter 2003–2004).

Mustard, David B. "Racial, Ethnic, and Gender Disparities in Sentencing: Evidence from the U.S. Federal Courts." *Journal of Law and Economics* XLIV, 2001.

GOVERNMENT REPORTS
Federal Bureau of Investigation. "Crime in the United States." Washington, D.C.: U.S. Department of Justice/Uniform Crime Reporting Program, 2006.

Glaze, Lauren E. and Seri Palmer. "Probation and Parole in the United States, 2004." Washington, D.C.: Bureau of Justice Statistics, 2005.

Greenfield, Lawrence A. and Tracy L. Snell. "Women Offenders." Washington, D.C.: Bureau of Justice Statistics, 1999.

Grieco, Elizabeth M. and Rachel C. Cassidy. "Overview of Race and Hispanic Origin: Census 2000." Washington, D.C.: U.S. Census Bureau, March 2001.

Harrison, Paige M. and Allen J. Beck. "Prison and Jail Inmates at Midyear 2005." Washington, D.C.: Bureau of Justice Statistics, 2006.

Harrison, Paige M. and Allen J. Beck. "Prisoners in 2005." Washington, D.C.: Bureau of Justice Statistics, 2006.

Sabol, William J. Ph.D, Todd D. Minton, and Paige M. Harrison, "Prison and Jail Inmates at Midyear 2006," Bureau of Justics Statistics, June 2007.

U.S. General Accounting Office. "Drug Offenders: Various Factors May Limit the Impacts of Federal Law That Provide for Denial of Selected Benefits." Washington, D.C.: U.S. General Accounting Office, 2005.

U.S. General Accounting Office. "Women in Prison: Issues and Challenges Confronting U.S. Correctional Systems." Washington, D.C.: U.S. General Accounting Office, 1999.

REPORTS

Amnesty International USA. "Abuse of Women in Custody: Sexual Misconduct and Shackling of Pregnant Women." New York: Amnesty International USA, 2001.

Amnesty International USA. "Rights for All." New York: Amnesty International Publications, 1998.

Gibbons, John J. and Nicholas de B. Katzenbach, co-chairs. "Confronting Confinement: Report of The Commission on Safety and Abuse in America's Prisons." New York: Vera Institute of Justice, 2006.

Frost, Natasha A., Judith Greene, and Kevin Pranis. "Hard Hit: The Growth in the Imprisonment of Women, 1977–2004." New York: Institute on Women & Criminal Justice, 2006.

Hartney, Christopher. "The Nation's Most Punitive States for Women." California: National Council on Crime and Delinquency, July 2007.

Hirsch, Amy E., Sharon M. Dietrich, Rue Landau, Peter D. Schneider, Irv Ackelsburg, Judith Bernstein Baker, and Joseph Hohenstein. "Every Door Closed: Barriers Facing Parents with Criminal Records." Philadelphia: Community Legal Services, Inc. and the Center for Law and Social Policy, 2002.

Human Rights Watch/Women's Rights Project. "All Too Familiar: Sexual Abuse of Women in U.S. State Prisons." New York: Human Rights Watch, 1996.

Human Rights Watch, Amnesty International. "Custody and Control: Conditions of Confinement in New York's Juvenile Prisons for Girls." New York: Human Rights Watch, 2006.

Human Rights Watch. "Nowhere to Hide: Retaliation Against Women in Michigan State Prisons." New York: Human Rights Watch, 1998.

Human Rights Watch. "Punishment and Prejudice: Racial Disparities in the War on Drugs." New York: Human Rights Watch, 2000.

Lapidus, Lenora, Namita Luthra, Anjuli Verma, Deborah Small, Patricia Allard, and Kirsten Levingston. "Caught in the Net: The Impact of Drug Policies on Women and Families." New York: American Civil Liberties Union and Brennan Center for Justice, 2005.

O'Keefe, Maura. "Post-Traumatic Stress Disorder Among Incarcerated Battered Women: A Comparison of Battered Women Who Killed Their Abusers and Those Incarcerated for Other Offenses." *Journal of Traumatic Stress* 11, no. 1 (1998).

The Sentencing Project, "Women in the Criminal Justice System." Washington, D.C.: The Sentencing Project, May 2007.

Stemen, Don. "Reconsidering Incarceration: New Directions for Reducing Crime." New York: Vera Institute of Justice, 2007.

Stop Prisoner Rape. "In the Shadows: Sexual Violence in U.S. Detention Facilities, A Shadow Report to the U.N. Committee Against Torture." Los Angeles: Stop Prisoner Rape, 2006.

Stop Prisoner Rape. "Stories from the Inside: Prisoner Rape and the War on Drugs." Los Angeles: Stop Prisoner Rape, 2007.

Strupp, Heidi and Donna Willmott. "Dignity Denied: The Price of Imprisoning Older Women in California." San Francisco: Legal Services for Prisoners with Children, 2005.

Vagins, Deborah J. and Jesselyn McCurdy. "Cracks in the System: Twenty Years of the Unjust Federal Crack Cocaine Law." New York: American Civil Liberties Union, 2006.

VIDEOS

Abused. 38 min. DVD. Braverman Productions, 2005. DVD.

Crime and Punishment. 21 min. *Nightline* with Ted Koppel, 21 April 2000.

Daughters Left Behind: Who Cares About Girls? 60 min. Oxygen, 25 March 2007. *Lockdown: Women Behind Bars*. 60 min. DVD. National Geographic Channel, 2007.

Our Voices Within: Out of the Shadows. 34 min. DVD. Free Battered Women, 2005.

Turning a Corner. 58 min. DVD. Beyondmedia Education, 2006.

Acknowledgments

The honesty and participation of incarcerated girls and women made this book possible. Without asking anything in return, these girls and women were grateful to be heard, and to not be dismissed or disrespected as human beings because they had been sentenced to do time. I am indebted to them for their honesty, vulnerability, and willingness to refer other women who had stories to share. None were paid for their participation.

I am also grateful to the prison administrators and correctional officers who granted me the time and space I needed to understand the specific cultures of each jail or prison, and to conduct private or semiprivate interviews. On many occasions, these jail and prison employees spoke to me with surprising disclosure about what they saw as the genuine weaknesses and problems within their facilities; about their support for sentencing reform and the elimination of mandatory minimums. Of particular note is that most correctional employees I talked with expressed a belief that mentally ill and drug-addicted offenders would be better served by treatment facilities than by prison terms.

I am particularly grateful to the staff of the following institutions and programs for their time and insights: Lieutenant Bart Fortner at the Central California Women's Facility (CCWF) in Chowchilla; Jane Silva and Montaigne White of the Phoenix House at CCWF; the staff of the Washington Corrections Center for Women in Gig Harbor; Sheriff Michael Hennessey and the staff of the San Francisco County Jail, including the women of the SISTER program; Holloway Governor Tony Hassall and Zara Gill in London; Warden Brenda Tole and Deputy Warden Matt Lang at the Alouette Correctional Centre for Women in British Columbia, Canada; Anne Salmi at the Hämeenlinna Women's Prison in Finland; Powerful Voices in Seattle, Washington; and Susan Burton of A New Way of Life in Los Angeles.

I also want to thank national and regional organizations engaged in meaningful criminal justice reform work. Among those on which I have relied regularly for resources, reports, and story leads: Legal Services for Prisoners with Children; Drug Policy Alliance; ACLU National Prison Project; Human Rights Watch; Drug Reform Coalition; Law Enforcement Against Prohibition; CANDO; California Coalition for Women Prisoners; Private Corrections Institute; Drug Reform Coalition; Justice Works! and Real Change in Seattle; Partnership for Safety and Justice; November Coalition; The Center on Juvenile and Criminal Justice; Marijuana Policy Project; Vera Institute of Justice; Justice Now; The Commission on Safety and Abuse in America's Prisons; The Drug Reform Coordination Network; Families Against Mandatory Minimums; Women's Prison Association; Barrios Unidos; Stop Prisoner Rape; The Brennan Center at NYU School of Law; NAACP Legal Defense Fund; The Sentencing Project; and the National Council on Crime and Delinquency.

Personal thanks go to the Hedgebrook Foundation's Whidbey Island women's writing retreat for giving me the peace and solitude I needed to put together my book proposal; the staff and publishers at *In These Times* magazine; my family in Finland (RIP Irja Talvi); my father, Ilkka Talvi, and his family; my mother, Judith Aller; Sonja and Clarissa; David McCumber of the *Seattle Post-Intelligencer;* Steve Morris; Julia Goldberg of the *Santa Fe Reporter;* The Nation Institute's Investigative Fund; Britt Madsen, my dedicated women's studies intern from the University of Washington; New American Media; the Lott family; Jessica Clark; Steven Wishnia; Paul Wright of *Prison Legal News;* G. Roane; the Gustafson family; Sasha Abramsky; and Seattle's Twilight Exit, for giving me the space to write in my seat at the end of the bar.

My deepest gratitude is extended to my agent, Timothy Wager, of the Davis Wager Literary Agency; my Seal Press editors, Jill Rothenberg, Brooke Warner, and Laura Mazer, as well as my wonderfully eccentric cat, Mange, for putting up with my late hours and prison trips.

Index

A

abolition, prison: 229–230

abortion: false accusations of 70; persecution for attempted 160; in showers 70

abuse: case studies of murder and 169–170, 180–190; and children's well being 156; of girls 8–9; in Jewish homes 174–175; legal issues 304; mental illness and 144; as precedent to prostitution 41; and prison reform 17; and sentencing 164–165; statistics 64, 173–174, 321; sympathy for 171; traits of battered women 174–175; verbal 71; violence and 172; violent reactions to 177–178; walking away from 178–179

addiction: case studies of 38–39, 283–285; in jail 68; nicotine 26; during pregnancy 153; prescription drug 27; rock and roll 217; sex 24; statistics 299–300; threat-based treatment for 157; as U.S. historical problem 23–24

ACLU Drug Law Reform Project: 49

ACLU National Prison Project: 98, 225

Administrative Segregation (Ad Seg): 67, 119–122, 226

African Americans: drug arrests of 28; harassment of 46; imprisonment rates of xv; in incarceration statistics 7; unconsenting drug tests for pregnant 153–154

Ah Mau, Sarah: 218–219, 227

aid, denial of federal: 276, 277

alcohol abuse: by guards 71; and health of babies 155–156

Alouette Correctional Centre for Women (British Columbia): 257–266

A New Way of Life: 277

Anti-Drug Abuse Act: 34

Arizona State Prison Complex: 20

Armstrong, Debra: 275–276

arrests: of African Americans 28; drug-related 24; of prostitutes 40; racial profiling in 45; Tulia's community-wide 50–53

authority, blind submission to: 217

Silja J. A. Talvi is an investigative journalist and essayist. She is a senior editor at *In These Times* and has credits in more than seventy-five publications nationwide, including *The Nation,* AlterNet, the *Santa Fe Reporter,* and *The Christian Science Monitor.* Her articles on social issues—with a particular emphasis on criminal justice, ethnicity, and gender—have garnered twelve Society of Professional Journalists awards in the Pacific Northwest. Talvi received four consecutive PASS awards from the National Council on Crime and Delinquency for excellence in magazine journalism in 2004, 2005, and 2006, as well as a 2006 national New America Media award on immigration-related reporting. Her work appears in several book anthologies, including *Body Outlaws* (Seal Press, third edition, 2004); *It's So You* (Seal Press, 2007); *The W Effect: Bush's War on Women* (The Feminist Press, 2004); *Prison Nation: The Warehousing of America's Poor* (Routledge, 2003); and *Prison Profiteers: Who Makes Money from Mass Incarceration* (The New Press, 2008). Born in Helsinki, Finland, Talvi was raised in Hollywood, California. She earned her BA in ethnic studies (Mills College) and her MA in women studies (San Francisco State University). She lives in Seattle, Washington.

Selected Titles From Seal Press

FOR MORE THAN THIRTY YEARS, SEAL PRESS HAS PUBLISHED GROUNDBREAKING BOOKS. BY WOMEN. FOR WOMEN.

WWW.SEALPRESS.COM

One of the Guys: Women as Aggressors and Torturers edited by Tara McKelvey, foreword by Barbara Ehrenreich, afterword by Cynthia Enloe. $15.95, 1-58005-196-0. In this bold anthology, McKelvey and her contributors tackle complex issues of women and their involvement in torture and the abuse of power.

Women In the Line of Fire: What You Should Know About Women in the Military by Erin Solaro. $15.95, 1-58005-174-X. A wake up call on the damage and repercussions of government neglect, Rightist fervor, and feminist ambivalence about women in the military.

Intimate Politics: How I Grew Up Red, Fought for Free Speech, and Became a Feminist Rebel by Bettina F. Aptheker. $16.95, 1-58005-160-X. A courageous and uncompromising account of one woman's personal and political transformation, and a fascinating portrayal of a key chapter in our nation's history.

Abortion Under Attack: Women on the Challenges Facing Choice edited by Krista Jacob, foreword by Rebecca Walker, afterword by Gloria Feldt. $15.95, 1-58005-185-5. This book is a call to action, in this conservative time, for new and veteran pro-choice people alike.

Voices of Resistance: Muslim Women on War, Faith, and Sexuality edited by Sarah Husain. $16.95, 1-58005-181-2. A collection of essays and poetry on war, faith, suicide bombing, and sexuality, this book reveals the anger, pride, and pain of Muslim women.

Single State of the Union: Single Women Speak Out on Life, Love, and the Pursuit of Happiness edited by Diane Mapes. $14.95, 1-58005-202-9. Written by an impressive roster of single (and some formerly single) women, this collection portrays single women as individuals whose lives extend well beyond Match.com and Manolo Blahniks.

CPSIA information can be obtained at www.ICGtesting.com
Printed in the USA
LVOW08s0953290816

502281LV00003B/11/P